795

Ambitious Women

A NOVEL BY BARBARA WILSON

The Seal Press

The author gratefully acknowledges permission to reprint from the following: Susan Griffin's "I Like to Think of Harriet Tubman" in *Like the !ris of an Eye,* Harper & Row, 1976; Nadezhda Mandelstam, *Hope Against Hope,* translated by Max Hayward, Atheneum Publishers, 1970; Marge Piercy's *"In the men's room(s),"* in *Circles on the Water,* Alfred A. Knopf, Inc., 1982.

ISBN: 0-931188-36-9
Library of Congress Catalog Card Number: 85-22060

Cover design by Deborah Brown and Barbara Wilson

Seal Press edition, September, 1985 (previously published by Spinsters, Ink, 1982)

For Judith, and all our Seattle beginnings

CONTENTS

PART ONE:
TAKING CARE OF BUSINESS

Economy is the bone, politics is the flesh
watch who they beat and who they eat
watch who they relieve themselves on, watch who they own
The rest is decoration.
> Marge Piercy, "In the Men's Room(s)"

One: Monday

Allison is unlocking the door of the print shop at a quarter to eight on a fall morning. An old door, like the brick building itself, it is splintered along the bottom and opening side. The hinges creak as she patiently joggles the rusty lock in the doorknob; the larger bolt above the knob, the one that is attached to an alarm system, glides open easily.

The shop has never been broken into, but you can't be too careful in this part of Seattle.

Holly, Allison's partner, said, "An alarm, do you really think. . .?" but Allison's caution prevailed, in this as in so many things.

A wet morning, a ghostgray October morning. In a few weeks daylight savings time will end, marking the beginning of another dim northern winter. She'll have to bring a flashlight to help her key find the lock.

And Katey, eight now, will not want to get up in the morning.

"Mom, it's so dark." Huddling at the bottom of the bed as if the covers were a cave and her two pillows big boulders at the cave's entrance.

1

Ben, her ten-year-old son, is more like Allison, opening his eyes easily, unsurprised, on the new day. Translating the clock's configuration into a call for action. Racing Allison for the shower, outlining his plans for the day. Methodical.

Holly says Allison is too methodical. "But that's what we need," she hastens to add.

Allison is always the first at the shop. Holly gets there between eight-thirty and nine, when they open. Holly is like Katey in the morning, sullen, yawning continually, useless before two cups of coffee. When she has to work for a living, Katey will probably become a coffee addict too.

Allison flicks on one of the fluorescent lights and sets her thermos of tea down on the edge of a light table. She offered once to work by herself in the morning, let Holly work later—two shifts. But Holly laughed, "I'd *never* get up then. I'd read the *whole* night. And I'd feel *so* guilty."

Pouring herself a cup of lemon balm tea, Allison makes a list. They are working on small jobs now: a hundred business cards, a menu for the cafe at the corner, personal stationery. In spite of their printing equipment—the press, the platemaker, the camera, all bought on loan— right now the xerox machine, which also belongs to the bank, brings in at least a third of their income. Students from the community college run in and out asking for five-cent copies. The college library has two xerox machines but one of them is always out of order. Allison suspects, too, that people like to have their copies made for them. "You're not just selling a product, you're selling a *service*," her business teacher used to pontificate.

She usually does the copies; Holly does the designing and runs the press. Although they both took the same two-year printing class, Holly is much better than Allison at the job. She has an innate mechanical sense, she understands, instead of guessing like Allison, how to adjust the temperamental A.B. Dick press. Clockwise, counterclockwise, Allison can never remember. It used to gall her, she wanted to do everything. She took the printing class, after all, to learn a skill.

But even in those days she had depended on Holly. Probably that's when their partnership began: "Holly, I didn't really understand what he meant about how you raise or lower the plate. Could you show me?" And Holly, so obliging, would show Allison, would do the hardest parts of her work for her.

Most of the students in the small class had been women. The male teachers, three of them, were useless after the first month, preferring to let the students help each other. Which they did. Of course a few had dropped out, but one was now working as a typesetter, one had moved to San Francisco to work with a women's press collective, two more had jobs at Copy Center.

Only Allison had wanted to start her own business.

She turns on another light; it's a quarter after eight, time to look through the books and make out some checks.

"But how will you get the money?" Holly asked when Allison first mentioned the idea of a business.

"My ex-husband," she said bravely. "Or one of his banker friends."

They were at Allison's house; it was late, they were on a second bottle of wine. It was during the time when they were first becoming friends after having been classmates so long.

Allison brought out her wedding scrapbook. "Don't look at me," she warned, covering up a plump, frizzy-headed bride loaded with white lace, her eyes bright Kodak blue with reddish whites. "Look at the groom. Doesn't he look made for success?"

The young man was tall and so broadly built that his tuxedo strained at the shoulders. He was jut-jawed under a modified crewcut. Only his full lips gave a hint of sensuality to his handsomely rigid features. He was staring down, proud and vague, at the top of his bride's head.

"June bride," said Allison, mocking, singsong, more than a little drunk. "And he was a high school basketball star. Thomas High School, outside Spokane. Class of '63. I put him through college, working as a typist first for the minimum wage and then as a waitress after I had the kids. He always held it against me that he couldn't go out for basketball at the university and be in a fraternity. He didn't like the kids, he still doesn't much. He says they remind him of the times when he was trying to study for exams and they cried all night."

"What was he studying?"

"Business, of course. When it looked like my meager savings couldn't put him through graduate school, he divorced me and married someone else, conveniently the daughter of a Boeing VP. He's some kind of executive himself now."

"At first I didn't want anything to do with him after the divorce. I figured that if I'd supported the kids this long I could keep on supporting them. We were always renting, always having to move when the rent went up; we could never eat out, could hardly eat at home by the end of the month. It wasn't fair to them.

3

"One day I called him up at his office. Katey was just starting grade school and I was at the end of my rope, I mean it, at the end of that goddamn proverbial rope. I was going to ask him for a loan so Katey could get some new clothes. His secretary answered the phone and told me he was occupied and could he call me back? All of a sudden I got angry, really angry. No, I said, I won't wait, I can't wait, have him come to the phone. In the few minutes it took for the secretary to find him, I formulated what I really wanted. I wanted a house for my kids and I wanted him to give me the money for a down payment. He came to the phone and I told him that. It was funny, Holly, you know, he seemed relieved? I really hadn't counted on his guilt feelings. I suddenly thought, what a stuck-up jackass I've been—for five years of my life I supported him, I made it possible for him to get his job, and now I'd damn well better have something in return.

"And I'm going to get the money for a business in the same way," Allison said firmly, if drunkenly. "I'm a good risk; Tom knows it if the banks don't."

The door buzzes. Allison jumps, then carefully inserts the checks into envelopes and licks them. It's Holly.

"Hey, I'm early," she says. "Eight twenty-five! Have I ever been here this early?"

Four years younger than Allison, at twenty-six Holly is skinny, stoop-shouldered, golden blonde and strong as an ox. She has disproportionately large hands with ungainly knuckles and eyes the color of the wild iris. She comes in wearing jeans, boots that hike her up to five-eleven and a cobwebby scarf wrapped at least eight times around her thin neck. She's carrying two cups of coffee from MacDonald's.

"I suppose you had a Jack Omelette, too," Allison sighs.

"No, that's *Jack*-in-the-Box, Allison. I had an apple turnover if you're interested."

She pries off one of the plastic lids, gulps and shudders.

Allison wonders for the thousandth time what kind of jolting ride Holly's synapses take in the morning.

They are silent then; Allison continues to add and subtract on the pocket calculator, watching the red numbers sidle out like vaudeville dancers, while Holly wanders aimlessly back and forth across the shop, occasionally taking a gasp of coffee. When both cups are empty, she tosses them in a box and grabs an oil can. Humming, her body beginning to function, oiled by coffee, Holly attacks the movable parts of the press—a tiny squirt here, a quick drink for a hole there. Allison, locking up the calculator in the top drawer of the desk, watches her.

4

Holly knows the press inside and out. It never has problems when she's printing on it; the pages fly out like black and white birds and settle neatly into stacks to be collated. When Allison runs the press (which is less and less often now), there is a sense of sticking, of jamming. She over-inks, she under-waters. Crookedness spoils everything at the last minute.

"You just need more practice," Holly says helpfully.

It's true; in school she did much better. On the other hand, if Allison ran the press, who would do the books, the ordering, the xeroxing, the delivering? Not Holly.

Holly could not do a crooked layout if she tried, but she can hardly make sense on the telephone, talking to the binders, the typesetters, the paper suppliers. She knows how to order if she can read straight from a sheet in front of her, but she's at a loss if they ask her a question or tell her they don't have what she needs. Terminology fails her; it's this "thing" or that "you know, *thing.*" Instinctively she understands the machinery; her eye has a built-in ruler. She is invaluable, but limited.

Like Allison.

Allison thinks, we work well together, and is pleased.

But the thought nags at her irritably that she needs Holly more than Holly needs her. Holly would have been perfectly content to be an employee; she's not committed to the business like Allison is. The shop was Allison's idea, Allison's need. Holly was only reluctantly persuaded to borrow some money from her father and become a partner.

"No thanks," she told Allison when Allison first suggested a partnership. "I don't want the responsibility."

She seems perfectly happy now, Allison admits to herself, watching Holly prime the press with oil.

It is Allison who is dissatisfied. She wanted to be self-sufficient, wanted to be able to do everything herself. Holly doesn't seem to mind inequalities, divisions, will say easily, naturally, "Oh, you'll have to ask Allison about that."

But Allison, running the press, having to ask, "Why is it printing like this, what's wrong?" is unhappy and frustrated when Holly, mild-tempered Holly, says peremptorily, "Here, let me do it."

The door buzzes open with the first customer of the day and Allison goes to the counter.

It's a busy day. The phone rings, the door buzzes; the whole neighborhood wants something xeroxed; the cafe owner has a change in her menu; the typesetter they usually employ is on vacation and Allison has to call around for another. Everybody wants everything right away.

Holly prints and pastes-up, takes her scarf off about eleven, goes out and gets coffee and a sandwich for herself, milk for Allison who has brought leftover rice and eggplant casserole from last night's dinner. Holly also comes back with a newspaper, struck by the headlines.

"Hey, that group did another bombing last night. They bombed Safeway."

Allison is xeroxing poetry, purposely not reading it.

"Yeah, I heard about it on the radio this morning."

"It's disgusting, I think," says the customer, a woman in her late thirties, with a feminist symbol heavy around her neck. "Who do they think they are, do they really think they're speaking for the rest of us?"

" 'The store was closed. No customers or personnel were in the store,' " Holly reads.

"What does that have to do with it?" says the woman. "What's the point of blowing things up, what does that prove?"

Holly shrugs, reads on silently, unwrapping her sandwich, a slab of something pink between two off-color, well-margarined slices of white bread. Spam? Allison wonders. Ugh. She finishes the copies.

"Sometimes," she says cheerfully to the poet, taking her dollar and making change with one hand while pushing the copies over the counter with the other, "there's nothing like a good bomb-throwing to get it all out of your system, don't you think?"

"She'll never come back," predicts Holly with her mouth full.

"I hate those damn feminist symbols hanging around their necks. They're like the cowbells of liberalism."

"Still, you don't really think—."

"Oh, I'd never go around setting off bombs or anything like that. . . but to be honest, when I think about Safeway," Allison makes a quick, joking, revolutionary fist and laughs, "one less is. . . one less."

"It just destroyed the refrigeration system, it says here," Holly refers to the paper.

"Well, one refrigeration system less, then."

At four Allison runs the new menu down to the corner cafe and accepts a piece of freshly baked apple pie as a kind of tip. In spite of her commitment to health foods, she can't resist Mrs. Silver's baked goods when offered. "Just a little piece of pie, Allison, you girls work so hard, I know. And take one back to Holly, heaven knows she needs it, skinny as she is, it's unhealthy."

Heaven knows I don't need more sugar, Allison thinks ruefully. You'd think that long hours and business anxieties would be enough to take away her appetite. Instead, she is heavier than she has ever been, her belly rounding out the straight-cut overalls.

"No, just one piece, Mrs. Silver. But it's delicious, really."

It's raining hard by the time Allison returns to Last Minute Printing (Holly's suggestion, as opening day approached without a name to paint on the windows or list in the phone book). She runs for it with Holly's piece of pie, slipping on the wet trash which has dispersed itself all over the sidewalk from a paper bag in one of the dark, deserted doorways. She finds Holly at the counter, talking to a man with a bundle of damp newspapers in the crook of his arm. He's tall and dark and bearded like a circus strongman. He has a big thwacked-out-of-shape nose and a steep forehead.

Holly looks relieved to see Allison and reaches eagerly for the soggy piece of pie.

"This is Paul. He wants us to take out an ad in *this*," she blurts out. "I said I'd have to talk to you."

Allison takes off her jacket and glances at the familiar logo of the paper. The *Seattle News*, the local radical rag.

"Do *you* ever read it?" Paul wants to know.

"Sure, all the time."

Holly looks surprised. She touches a corner of the paper with one knobby finger. "I haven't seen it on the stands for ages," she claims. "I thought it had folded."

"We've had to cut back some," Paul says morosely. "But we're still around."

He is a real contrast to most of the salespeople who come into the shop, bouncy, all smiles, dexterous as magicians with their sample books. Allison studies the advertising rate sheet. "We haven't been advertising much," she says. "We don't really have the money for it."

"Advertising *creates* money," Paul says, rather woodenly, and then plays his trump card. "You know, we don't pay salaries. We depend on support from the community to keep the paper going."

Allison smiles, knowing herself an easy touch when community support comes up. "What do you think, Holly?"

Holly, for some reason, looks offended. "Sure, fine," she mutters as if they were one word and retires to the press.

"Okay, I guess," Allison gives in. "We'll bring in the ad copy. I think I know where the office is. I used to know Magda pretty well, she was my neighbor for a couple of years. She's still part of the collective, isn't she? I haven't seen her for a long time."

"She holds it together." Paul shifts the papers uncomfortably and looks as if he would say more. Is Allison interested? To be trusted? He apparently decides it's not worth it, mumbles something about "burnout" and "no money," then recovers his voice enough to explain that he's leaving town tomorrow for central Washington and wanted to get a few ads before... "drove by your shop"... and ...

Allison nods to all this, feeling Holly's displeasure hum like a beehive behind the press. What's wrong with her? The guy is not that strange, the salespitch perfectly legitimate. Why not advertise a little, at least one time? Can't understand her.

"We'll bring the ad copy over to the office," Allison repeats. "Will Magda be there?"

"She's always there." Paul's bearish head lifts as he realizes he's made a sale. He hastens to leave. "Good-bye, Holly," he calls.

Holly says nothing.

"What's with you?" Allison demands, after he's gone in a rush of cold, wet air.

"Nothing." Shortly. Holly hooks her golden hair behind her ears and bends over the light table. Her face is lit up, shadowless and distinct.

"You don't want to advertise?" Allison comes over to her.

"Not with them. But oh, I don't care, if you think it's a good idea. Really, I don't."

Allison doesn't want to let the subject drop. It's so hard to get a grip on the differences between them that she suddenly almost wants an argument.

"Not with them? Why not? It's not a bad paper; in fact, it's usually pretty good. Lots of people read it, not just leftists. I used to read it myself more, when I had time."

"It's too . . . rhetorical." Holly takes the plunge and is openly scornful.

"Read the editorial page of the *Times* sometime and see what's rhetorical. What do you call rhetorical, anyway?" Allison is aware that the discussion isn't focused, but she keeps on. "What?"

"I mean words like, like 'petit bourgeois' in a movie review."

"Maybe it was appropriate there."

"I don't like that kind of reviewing, writing—reducing everything to economics."

"Reducing, what reducing? That's what everything is based on."

"Allison the Marxist." Holly's voice is softer, she is trying to get out of the argument.

"I'm not, but what's the use? You don't have any idea about money, who has it, who doesn't, what difference that makes."

Holly flicks off the switch to the light table and walks to the cupboard on the other side of the room. Allison notices her bad posture with irritation, motherlike.

"I do think money's important," Holly says finally, back turned. "I just don't think it's the most important thing in life." Hearing herself, she laughs and turns to Allison vulnerably. "Don't let me start on my stock of cliches."

Impossible to be angry at Holly. But she's so goddamn naive. Loving poetry and novels and thinking about her dreams all day long.

The door buzzes and Allison moves automatically to the counter.

Later, as they're cleaning up, making ready to leave, Allison says, not in a conciliatory, but in a thoughtful way, as if the coversation were only continuing, "Anyway, I think you'd like Magda, the woman I asked Paul about, the writer."

"Why?" Holly is cleaning the press and has a streak of blue ink on her forehead.

"Because you like novels and she's like a character from a novel—a very eccentric, striking-looking woman, a real terror about getting what she wants. She used to live next door to us, two or three years ago. Wild hair, the color of a beer bottle. Dressed like a gypsy—big boots, scarves, very Salvation Army, but also posh—she was into shoplifting from the best stores. Now, don't get that disapproving look on your face, Holly. I know you're not as straight-laced as you make out."

"That was *food*. I stole so James and I could have enough to *eat*." There is real anguish on her fair, clean-boned, blue-streaked face. She hates thinking about the past, Allison knows, especially about her ex-husband.

"And I took food home from the restaurant when I was a waitress and didn't report all my tips. If you're a woman, you're almost driven to steal sometimes."

"But clothes. . ."

"You're right, I guess. Don't look so upset. Maybe she doesn't do it anymore." Allison laughs. "If you could see your face. You look positively outraged. And you've got blue on it. Still, I think you'd probably like Magda. She's very colorful. And she's a good writer; there's an article she wrote in this issue of the *News* if you want to read it."

Allison points to the paper still on the counter and goes out with a trash can.

It's still raining and the late afternoon looks more like evening. Only October; the shortest day of the year is still more than two months away. Another damn winter. Allison heaves the waste paper into the dumpster. Shouldn't tease Holly about a thing like that—her tortured confession of stealing hamburger once. Poor puritan. What a life she's had. Only daughter of an Army surgeon, her childhood spent in Guam and Germany. Lonely, reading, always reading and taking walks, she said. Left out of her older brothers' games, she made no friends on the bases for fear of losing them. Returning to Monterey for her senior year in high school, she was a misfit—gawky, tall, an Army brat with a superficial, Old World view of America. No wonder she married to get away from home. Her father sounds like a martinet, a general rather than a surgeon, though Holly says he's softened since her mother died.

James. Allison met him once earlier this year, wondered at the kind of terror he inspired in Holly. Like her he was tall, Nordic; he had a full blonde beard, well-cut hair. In spite of the cool spring day his shirt was open to show off a hairy chest and a religious medallion.

"Hi, Hol," he greeted her in a friendly, unsurprised way.

Allison felt Holly shrink beside her. He stopped, they stopped. Holly introduced them reluctantly. She did not mention that Allison was her new business partner.

"Nice day," he said; the two women agreed. Allison noticed his low monotonous voice. He was handsome, though, handsomer than her ex-husband. But Allison was more interested in Holly's rigidity, her air of bracing herself silently, than she was in James' studied politeness.

"I'll come and see you some time," James said finally. "You still in school or you working now?"

"Working," Holly mumbled.

"We have a—" Allison began.

"We work together," Holly said, with a quick, pleading glance at Allison.

"Why didn't you want him to know about the shop?" Allison asked after they were a distance away.

Holly was almost running, she was walking so fast. "He'd find a way to use the shop, me—get money from me again. I don't ever want him to know what I'm doing. I wish he'd just move away again."

Her vehemence shocked Allison a little. She'd heard that tone at the shelter for battered women where she volunteered, that tone of suppressed terror. Women explaining stiffly, "I never knew when he would change, when he would lash out. . ." While their eyes remembered fists and belts and chairs crashing down. She'd never heard that tone in Holly's voice before.

She didn't ask any more questions.

Now Allison shoulders the trash can in the dim, wet afternoon and walks slowly back to the shop. She must be kinder to Holly, not so demanding. If it weren't for her . . . Anyway, shouldn't tease her like that.

Holly is reading the *News* as Allison enters, leaning up against the counter with the long broom handle in one hand.

"This review is kind of interesting," she says shyly. "I saw this movie, did you?"

Setting the can down, Allison sighs, "I haven't been to a film in ages. It's either 'can't leave the kids' or 'nothing I want to see' or the shelter or visiting somebody. No time is what it comes down to."

"I went to the movies twice a week all summer, and go at least once a week now."

"Really?" Allison is amazed and slightly disapproving.

Holly nods, folding up the paper again dreamily, and reels off a list of the films she has seen. "I love going in the summer, coming out of the theater when it's still light, walking around the streets."

For a moment Allison is envious of that freedom—walking around the streets, that is—not going to the movies alone. She would feel too conspicuous by herself in a theater.

"Want to go out for a beer?" Allison asks impulsively, ignoring the fact of her children's dinner.

Holly looks at her watch nervously. "No, can't. Told. . . somebody. . . I'd be home at five-thirty and it's getting on five now."

"I'll close up, don't worry. You go ahead. I don't know what I was thinking of anyway. I've still got to go to the co-op and get some food for dinner."

Holly gets her coat and wraps up her long neck, dividing the fall of bright hair. At the counter she pauses and picks up the *News*.

"Mind if I take this?"

"Not at all. In fact, I'd like you to read it."

"Allison," Holly says suddenly. "Does it bother you that I'm not political?"

Surprised, Allison turns from the desk where she has been straightening papers. A dozen responses rise to her lips: Yes; no; I don't know;

nobody's apolitical; you are a little naive; all women are political. "What makes you ask?"

"Oh, just stuff today. The bombing and what you told that woman. And then this paper." Holly shakes her head. "And I've been thinking of all the things you're involved in—the shelter and the co-op and everything. And I don't do anything really, just work and go to movies and read. I guess I hate thinking about how screwed-up the world is. I might have to think about changing it then. Ooh, more clichés. . ." She laughs, a little uncertainly.

Allison holds bills, receipts, invoices, checks down with her hand. "Some radical I am. Small business is the bastion of capitalism. 'As small business goes, so goes the nation,' that's what someone from the SBA told me. Oh, I don't know, Holly, don't worry about it. We're feminists, anyway, if we're not revolutionaries. Besides, being a feminist *is* revolutionary. We're proving we can do something with our lives."

"Well, I will read Magda's article," Holly promises and goes out the door.

Allison locks it after her, straightens the "Closed" sign. They bombed Safeway, did they? She goes back to the desk. In spite of herself, she feels almost glad. There is a core of anger in her that has hardly been tapped, that all her work with volunteer alternative groups doesn't do enough to alleviate. That longs for violence, destruction, the end of established order.

She separates the invoices and the receipts, puts everything away except a scratchpad. Mechanically she begins to make a grocery list: eggs, carrots, navy beans, soap, Swiss cheese. . .

When the bomb went off did the groceries blow sky-high? She pictures eggs bursting out of their shells ready-fried, cans of cut-rate vegetables shooting up like rockets, tomatoes popping like grenades above the startled neighborhood. Everybody rushing forward afterward to gather up cigarettes and Oreo cookies.

. . . No, just the refrigeration unit. A bunch of pipes.

It's almost six when Allison carefully locks the door to the shop and walks to her car. The street lights are on now, her car waits for her in a pool of light.

If I didn't have the kids, would I be more radical?

Then she thinks: but the big difference between me and Holly, in everything—how we live, what we want and need from the shop, our ambitions—the difference is that I have kids and she doesn't. Isn't it?

Allison gets into her car and slams the door.

"Mom, mom, mom," Katey shrieks in that unnerving way she has recently developed, making Allison imagine disaster before she is even out of the car.

"Hi, sweetie." She lets Katey open the car door for her and take the sack of groceries. "Everything all right? How long have you been here?"

"Mrs. Thomas just dropped us off." Katey is staggering importantly under the weight of the groceries. "Guess what?"

"What?"

"Oh mom, no, *guess.*"

"You found a dollar on the way home."

"*Guess.*"

"Katey, I can't. I'm too tired."

"Oh. . . well, dad called. He's coming over tonight."

"How nice," Allison says neutrally. "What do you want for dinner?"

"Spaghetti. Spaghetti with clam sauce."

"Clam sauce. . . aren't *you* getting to be the gourmet."

"What's a gourmet?"

"Gourmets like to eat good food, baby. They eat and get fat."

"Like you, mom." A little resentfully. Allison has forgotten that she doesn't like to be called "baby" anymore.

"Yes and like you, if we don't watch out. I'm sorry to say you were born with my fat cells. Maybe we should have vegetables and fish tonight. That's what I bought." Because she had been thinking of her own indulgence in apple pie.

Ben opens the door for them. "Dad called."

"Yeah, Katey told me. Did he say what he wanted?" She gives her son a hug which he half accepts. Like Katey he is small for his age, but wiry where she is plump. His blonde hair needs combing. . . and cutting. When will she find the time to take him to the barbershop?

"No, he just said he's coming over later." Ben drifts back to the television before she can remind him to brush his hair.

Are they excited about seeing their father tonight, Allison wonders, or is it just ordinary childish interest in anything out of the routine? How much do they remember of the fights that went on between her and Tom when they were small? Surprisingly, during the years when they didn't see Tom, they asked little about him. It's only been in the past two years, since the money transactions began, that they've begun to call him "dad" again. He comes over once or twice a month, bringing them presents. The mysterious man with the money, is that how they think of him? More money than mom has, for sure. The man with the money, that's how Allison thinks of him, too; the man who takes a proprietary interest now in her finances.

Katey is already unpacking the groceries in the kitchen. She is in one of her housewifely moods. Some days she can hardly be persuaded to straighten her own room, other days she spends hours cozily rearranging everything in the house. "Milk," Katey sings to herself. "Bread in the drawer. Onions, onions, onions. Parsley and more pars-ley."

Allison moves around the kitchen with her daughter, pulling the curtains on the dark, wet back yard, wiping the counter, beginning to get out pans and pots for cooking. The kitchen is small, like all the rooms of the old wooden house, and painted a light gold. A carpenter friend put in new cabinets for them not long ago in partial exchange for some printing. Allison stops and stands for a moment, watching Katey clatter and sing. She runs her hand along the surface of one of the polished cedar cupboards and a feeling of warmth and love comes over her. No words for it. People doing things for each other. Exchanging or, simply, giving.

From the living room, gunfire ricochets wildly. Ben groans, "Got 'em."

"I don't want you watching that stuff, those cop shows, goddamn-it." Allison is angrier than she should be. She charges into the living room, just as Ben changes the channel to the evening news.

"Calm down, mom. It's just good ole everyday violence."

"Precocious creep, what do you know about real violence?" She sits behind him on the slipcovered sofa and regards his skinny ten-year-old shoulders, his corduroy legs staking out a compass claim on the worn rug.

"Hey, that's the Safeway they bombed," he says excitedly.

A Safeway official and the television reporter stand in front of the refrigeration unit. "Damage of upwards of twenty thousand dollars," the official intones righteously. Cut to a checker, a smocked, middle-aged woman behind a kingsize box of detergent, her limber fingers on the cash register. "I just don't understand why they did it. . ."

The TV reporter again. "The so-called Cutting Edge Brigade, a locally based terrorist group, has so far issued no statement regarding the bombing of a Safeway store in the Wallingford area. This is the fourth in a series of bombings which so far have destroyed thousands of dollars worth of property." As he enumerates the bombings, a small photograph fills each quarter of the screen: a power station; the home of a telephone company executive; the drive-up window of a bank; finally the Safeway store. "The group, which calls itself Marxist-Leninist, has eluded the FBI since it made its appearance two months ago in Seattle—"

"You won't let me watch cops and robbers, but you let me watch the evening news. What's the difference, mom?"

Mother, the moral leader, who doesn't know what she thinks about violence herself. Allison leans back on the sofa with a pillow behind her head. What should she tell him? That his favorite cop show glorifies violence, presents it out of context? So does the evening news. He can probably identify with the cops better than he can with the "so-called" Cutting Edge.

The cops stand for law and order, the right of the State to protect its citizens from violence by violence. And the villains on the show are never presented as anything less than totally deranged and evil.

"This group, these people they call terrorists," she begins slowly, "think that a lot of things are wrong with this country, that it's not right that some people have more money than other people, that some people run things and other people don't. . ."

Katey comes into the room and curls up on the sofa next to Allison. A little nervously, Allison fingers her daughter's hair, light brown and curly like her own. She is hesitant to disillusion her children, to spread a doctrine of discontent, her own discontent. When she was their age, and for years afterwards, she believed completely in what her parents and teachers taught her: that she lived in a democracy, the best of all possible forms of government; that everyone was equal; that communism made people like sheep; that poverty was just a temporary condition that anyone could climb out of, if they would stop being lazy.

"Well, anyway, in this country, there are certain ways to change things. We can vote for a new president, for instance, and hope that he, or she, will change things. But most presidents don't really know what it's like to be poor. . ."

"Lincoln was poor," Katey says suddenly. "He had to walk miles to go to school."

Allison is half amazed that Katey is following her. Unconsciously, she has been directing her remarks to Ben, who is quiet, staring at the ceiling. Hugging Katey, Allison says, "Yes, I think Lincoln was probably a good man, but he lived in a different time. It takes a lot of money to be president now, and in order to get the money they need, these guys have to promise things to people. Sometimes they promise that they'll make things easy for some people if those people give them money. . . So anyway, we have elections, and if we want things to change, we're

15

supposed to elect people to change them. But a lot of people think that way doesn't work very well."

"So they bomb things," says Ben.

"Yeah, some do, not very many. Other people try and change things in small or large groups just by trying to live their lives differently—like starting a food co-op or a free school or something."

"Why do some people bomb things, then, when they could start a co-op?" Ben wants to know.

"I guess because change happens so slowly, and it's never certain, and some people aren't satisfied with that. They want things to happen faster. . . and more completely."

She strokes Katey's hair rhythmically. Neither of them ask any more questions. Are they satisfied, how much can they understand? They understand the word "unfair" perhaps, but how can they understand the rage, abstract or otherwise, that builds up after years, a whole lifetime, of seeing and living injustice? How can they understand the anathema of "reformism" to radicals, the weighted charges of "liberalism" leveled against merely alternative groups?

She wishes she could capture the feeling she had just before this conversation, standing in the kitchen, touching the grain of the clear bright cedar, feeling a wholeness, a generosity. Now, again, everything seems tainted with bitterness and frustration.

But she doesn't want her children to feel that. . . . How to protect them?

"Turn off the TV, Ben," she says. "We can all help with dinner."

Ordinarily Allison loves the house they live in; she has stripped and revarnished the wood floors, has gradually furnished it with secondhand comfortable chairs and a sofa, has made the drapes herself from a heavy blue and green material. The only time she feels the least uncomfortable, the least conscious of the general smallness and shabbiness is when her ex-husband drops by. Not that she and Tom ever had anything much better; when he left her, they were living in a two bedroom duplex with peeling paint on the outside, splotchy wallpaper on the inside and a toilet that overflowed in spite of their continual attempts to fix it. Compared to that place this house is a mansion. Nevertheless, whenever Tom walks through the front door, tall, broad-shouldered and impeccably dressed, everything in the house seems to shrink, and grow either dingy or garish or both.

"Hello, Allison, hi, kids," he says and sits down in the largest chair, which doesn't seem large enough suddenly and whose bright, slipcovered colors contrast vulgarly with his worsted gray suit.

Allison is wearing overalls, clean but marked with ink; the children look grubby in spite of their just washed hands and faces. He gives her warning, he always calls first; she could have dressed herself and the kids up for him. But she wouldn't, and now, as a result, and as usual, she feels frumpy and poor beside him. And as usual, her discomfort and feeling of inferiority come across as peevishness.

"Hi. You're so late, we'd almost given up on you."

"Sorry. I had a Kiwanis meeting that went later than usual."

Katey is on his lap, greedily attacking a big bag of mints; Ben hovers over his shoulder. Of course Allison wants her children to know their father, to love their father, but sometimes it makes her feel like crying, this shy awe they feel for him, the way they try to get close, but not too close. They don't roughhouse with their father; Katey eats his candy and Ben hovers.

"Oh, Kiwanis now. Aren't you the responsible social member. Helped any retarded children lately, or is it cerebral palsy this year?"

Tom doesn't bother to answer. He only argues when he feels like it, about something important, like the national debt or the Environmental Protection Agency. This side of him has almost always infuriated Allison, though in the beginning she considered it a mark of his superiority not to want to engage in mundane quarrels. "You work it out for yourself, Allison, I'm satisfied doing what I'm doing," he would say. And he is satisfied. He goes right ahead with his plans, never questioning, never expressing any doubt about his ultimate destination: big business, big house, big car and big head.

"Hard day, Alli?" he asks suddenly, catching her off-guard with an almost tender look.

"Yeah," she sighs and laughs. No, she doesn't hate him. That's all over. And he's helped her a lot lately. "Can I get you a drink?"

"Sure. Make it something light, though, white wine maybe. I'm watching my weight."

A magazine she read in the check-out line yesterday said the trend was toward light alcoholic beverages. . ." Even the businessman is cutting his three-Martini lunch to a glass of Perrier with a twist of lime". . . blah, blah, blah. Right in step, Tom, right in step.

"Sorry, all I have is rum."

"Rum?"

"Left over from summer, you know. Daiquiris out on the lawn and all?"

"How about some coffee instead?"

"Sure."

He follows her into the kitchen. "Go on back to the TV, kids." So much for fatherly affection.

"So, how's it going, Allison the businesswoman?" He leans against the counter watching her search the cedar cupboards for an old bottle of Folger's Crystals. He's still so fucking handsome, she thinks, his fair cheeks sweetly pink from the razor (must have shaved again before the Kiwanis meeting), his blonde hair longer now than when she was married to him; fashionable sideburns now, no crewcut. No gray. Blue eyes, no bags under them. A surprisingly thick and sensual pair of lips, pouting down at the corners. How could any other businessman trust him with a mouth like that?

Beside him she feels dumpy and old. She feels her forbidden piece of apple pie like a little fat kangaroo in the pouch of her belly. She hasn't slept with a man since before the shop got started. Instead she's gained twenty unnecessary pounds and her hair has begun to gray. She knows she looks years older than she is; who would ever look at her anyway? The thing is, she hardly ever thinks about sex except when Tom is around. She's just too busy to entertain many erotic fantasies; even her masturbation is routine, more to ease a bodily tenseness than anything else. Allison remembers the last time she and Tom slept together, just before the divorce papers came through, with startling clarity, though it was years ago. Do you ever learn to hate someone's body, to even feel indifferent to it, after knowing it so well? "We always did have a good sex life, Alli," he said a few months ago. As for her, she has never met a better lover than this slab-mouthed bastard.

"Can't complain. Of course, things aren't easy, we still have the loans to pay off, but there's plenty of business and we work pretty hard."

"Jeff says you should be able to start paying off the second loan by the beginning of next month."

Allison spoons crusty brown crystals into an earthenware mug. "Well, it might be the month after."

"I thought you said things were going well."

"They are going well, but Jesus Christ, I mean, we're still paying on that first loan."

"Maybe you shouldn't have taken out that second loan then."

The water is boiling. Allison lifts the teakettle from the stove and pours too much water into the cup. It spills over. Don't get angry. Don't get defensive. You've talked about this before. Tom's just worried because Jeff Miller got you the second loan and Jeff's putting pressure on him. He knows you won't default. You just need more time. She stirs up the crystals in the cup and silently hands him the sugar bowl. But no, he's watching his weight; he refuses.

"Allison, I'd be glad to go over the books with you." His tone is firm and measured.

"I don't need your help. I can go over the books myself. Who do you think balanced the checkbook while we were married? It sure wasn't you with all your business classes."

"We have accountants to do that kind of thing; I'll find you a good man if you'd rather."

"Tom, please. You know the reason we had to get the second loan. We didn't figure in the cost of a xerox machine, and then we found out that it would be a big help to us if we had one. And it *is* a big help and it *is* bringing in money. But first we have to pay off the first loan and. . ."

"Look, Allison, if you're in trouble, it's better to come out with it. We have a better chance to figure out and stop a problem in the beginning than we do later on."

"What is this 'we' shit?" She is trying to keep her voice low, but it goes up sharply on the word 'we.' "It's my fucking business, mine and Holly's, not yours. If it fails, it's our responsibility, not yours. And we're not in any trouble, either, we're doing fine."

"That's another thing," he says, his big lips sipping slowly at his coffee as if Allison were not shaking with rage two feet from him. "Holly. I just don't get the feeling she knows what's going on."

"I don't want to discuss this, I won't discuss this. You just have to trust us for a while." She plunks the teakettle more firmly on the stove and turns to the living room again.

"Suit yourself." Allison almost doesn't hear his next words; she wishes later, as she tries to get to sleep that night, that she hadn't. "All I came to tell you was, that Jeff said if you don't start paying on that second loan by next month, they may have to repossess the xerox."

The eleven o'clock news is on. She should have put Ben and Katey to bed two hours ago, but they were all waiting for Tom.

"Look, mom. It's Safeway again. The tear-wrists," Katey says enthusiastically.

"That's enough, Katey. Time for bed."

"They bombed the house of a phone executive last week. It's incredible that the FBI hasn't caught them yet. They must leave clues everywhere." Tom crosses his well-upholstered arms sternly.

"Mom says they do it because they think things are unfair," Ben says.

"Those kind of people always think things are unfair. They won't be satisfied until we're living in a communist country."

"What's a communist?" Katey wants to know.

"It's a word they used to use a lot in the Fifties, before you were born," Allison breaks in before Tom can answer. "It's not used too much any more except by Republicans like your father and *Time* magazine."

"Oh," says Katey and runs upstairs.

Tom looks annoyed for the first time this evening. "Allison, I wish—"

"Off to bed with you too, Benjamin," says Allison, taking refuge in motherliness. "You'll be sleepy tomorrow."

"Okay. Nite, dad."

"Good night, Ben. Where's Katey?"

Katey reappears in a small flannel nightgown and charges over to be kissed. "How old is Krissy?" she wants to hear again. Krissy is her half sister.

"Two."

"Do you kiss her good night, too?" A little wistfully.

"Yes, I do."

"Well, mom kisses me every night before I go to bed."

Allison hugs her. "I'll be up in a minute to tuck you in, sweetie. Scoot."

Tom moves to the front door. "Do you really think she doesn't know what a communist is? Aren't they teaching these kids anything in school?"

Allison shrugs irritably. "Times change. The Red Menace isn't taken as seriously as it used to be, except, as I said already, by. . ."

"Allison, sometimes I wonder how you're bringing up these kids."

"Wonder all you want. You could have had the pleasure."

"Yes, I know."

At the door he purses his thick, sensual lips for a quick peck on the cheek. "I'm only trying to help."

"Yes, I know. Good night." She thinks he means the kids; after she closes the door on him, tired and relieved that they've gotten through another visit, she remembers the loan and the xerox machine.

I'd blow up the bank before I'd let them take it, she thinks, crossing the room to turn off the television.

Two: Tuesday

An ad for an alternative paper should be different from one for a regular paper. Or should it? Hypocrisy. Hypocrisy. Intermittently throughout the next day Allison struggles to make up a representative, slightly political ad for the *News*. Holly is busy printing. Besides, Allison doesn't want to ask her for help. In spite of their intimacy at closing the day before, they are distant and silent with each other today. Allison wanted to tell her about the bank's threat to take away the xerox machine, but then she considered both how little Holly understands the business side of things, and how upset she would be. There's nothing she can do about it anyway. Allison has lost her bravado; if it goes, it goes.

Struggling again with the ad, she thinks, this is silly; why not just say what we do and leave it at that? We're not a collective, not a cooperative, but a partnership in it for the money. The profit. Hah.

Finally, around three, Allison gives up the idea of making any kind of statement and tucks what she has into an envelope.

"I'm going to drop this off at the *News* office, Holly, after I've delivered those business cards. The ad, I mean."

Holly grunts from behind the press. All day she, too, has been preoccupied and moody, her blonde hair tightly braided and pinned back to give her fine-boned face a naked look. Naked, but not vulnerable; closed off, rather, stiff.

Then Holly says, "Wait, I'd like to go too." With an effort, as if throwing off something sluggish and heavy.

"How can you?" snaps Allison, exasperated. "It's not closing time yet and you're in the middle of a run. Unless you want to go yourself. I can stay here."

"No. Never mind."

"I'm not doing this for fun," Allison says in a quieter tone. "I'll just be gone a little while."

"It's okay." Holly is impassive now, bending over the press.

Allison bangs the door slightly on her way out, irritated at both herself and Holly. *Now I'll have to hurry.* Goddamn her. She can make me feel so guilty. Those moods. That longing. What happened to her last night that she's so down today? Should have asked her.

But I'm in a hurry.

The sun has come out briefly and Allison's old Volvo looks filthy as she gets into it. But otherwise the sun does handsome things for Warren Ave.; it's a warehouse and window street, the small-paned windows of the warehouses catching the sunlight and refracting it a hundred times above her head. So nice to be out of the frozenly lit print shop. No wonder Holly wanted. . . but she won't think about that. Holly has her opportunities, too.

The office of the *News* is on the third floor of an old wooden building sided with fake green brick, surrounded by parking lots in the seedier part of downtown. Allison hears raised voices and a door slam above her, then someone starting down at a furious pace. Instinctively she flattens herself against one of the walls. A tall woman, whose white-blonde braids swing back and forth across her face, stomps angrily past her. She's wearing clogs and each clog hits the step with a sound like firecrackers. She doesn't pay any attention to Allison, who, after a moment, continues up the stairs.

The office door is locked. She knocks and waits, knocks again. Muffled through several walls is the sound of a toilet flushing.

"I'm coming, I'm coming," a woman shouts. More clog sounds tromp across a wooden floor.

The door is flung open, almost off its hinges.

"Oh, Allison," says Magda, disconcerted and trying to look pleased. "It's been ages."

Magda looks the same, though older. Her ruddy brown hair is coarse and raggedly curly, as if a more fashionable haircut has been outgrown; it is bursting out of its pin-and-comb fortification to fall over her printed-silk collar. Her clothes are strange, but not unattractive. She has a bosomy, almost matronly figure, though she's only in her late twenties. She wears a thrift-store dress from the Forties, a rustly blue-flowered silk with a turquoise turtleneck sweater underneath. A pair of embroidered Alpine suspenders hold up a full, red cotton skirt with heart-shaped pockets over the silk dress. To complete her costume she has on thick, black-and-white striped, knee-high socks and black leather clogs. She has dressed this way, in numerous layers, ever since Allison has known her.

She is unusual looking and not only because of her dress. Her face is broad, slashed over the rather small brown eyes by heavy black brows; it is extraordinarily plain, dignified and, at the moment, overlaid with a fine sheen of anger.

"I hope I didn't interrupt anything," says Allison, following her into the first room of the cluttered little office. Here, among bales of newspapers, are a sofa, several badly stuffed chairs, and three desks, two piled with the current issue of the paper and one with a typewriter half-buried under correspondence, leaflets and typed copy. The peeling walls are plastered haphazardly with political posters in reds and yellow; the small-paned windows are encrusted with dirt and cobwebs. From this side of the building there is a view of the Sound; judging by the state of the windows, however, it's obvious no one is much inclined to look out. Through another door Allison glimpses a production room, where the light tables and work spaces stand up like islands in a sea of trash and boxes of empty beer bottles.

"I suppose you passed her on the stairs," Magda says.

"She passed me."

"That's Toni. She works here, too. Do you ever remember me telling you about her? The heiress who puts money into the paper every time it seems to be folding? We were having a fight. As you may have guessed." Magda throws herself into a battered armchair with a rustle of silk. "She's such a good writer—well, she's decent, anyway, but the things she wants to write about lately. It drives me crazy. She shouldn't be writing for us, she should be writing for, I don't know, a leftist *National Enquirer* or something. That's what I told her. Now it's terrorism, terrorism, terrorism. Who cares if some little group of radical crackpots bombed Safeway? . . . Well, Allison, how are you? Let me compose myself."

Allison hugs her and then settles into another chair. "Still the same, I see."

They burst out laughing.

"God, the last time I saw you I was in a twit, too, I remember," Magda says ruefully.

"The last time I saw you, you were moving out next door, and your friend with the U-Haul was backing up over your landlady's flower beds."

"God, remember that dump I used to live in? What a *dump*."

"I can't even remember his name, your friend with the U-Haul."

"Neither can I," Magda says wickedly, her plain face lit up. "But I was madly in love with him."

"Two years, can you believe it?"

Magda shakes her head. "No. What are you doing these days? You must be out of school?"

"Yeah. I'm in. . . business." She has promised herself she wouldn't be embarrassed. "That's why I'm here, actually. A guy named Paul got us to take out an ad."

"So he finally got one," says Magda, then sighs. "God, I'm in a rotten mood, don't mind me, tell me about your business. You? In business? What kind?"

"Printing. . . I didn't want to work for anybody. I have a partner, another woman." Magda looks interested, Allison thinks; she rushes on, gaining courage, finding explanations, justifications, triumphs.

Magda takes a weathered-looking cigarette out of one of her pockets and lights it.

"So you just went ahead and started your own business. How brash! How'd you get the money?"

"Pretty much through Tom, not directly, but. . . And Holly got a loan from her father."

"Nice of the boys to support our endeavors."

"They're the only ones who have it to loan."

"I say, rip 'em off for all they're worth."

Holly would be shocked at this. She fully intends to pay her father back, with interest; in fact, she's sending him fifty dollars a month out of her very small earnings. She showed Allison a letter her father sent her; he said he wasn't *loaning* the money to her; he was *investing* it in her.

"I'm not sure I like being invested in," Holly said miserably. "It makes failing that much worse."

She should have the bank payments hanging over her head. And Tom at the door with bad news every other week. They'll be up shit creek if they lose the xerox machine. But how can Allison tell her?

"So you're putting in an ad, that's great." Magda stubs out her cigarette on the scarred wooden arm of the chair and clogs over to one of the desks. She pries a notebook out of a stubbornly wedged drawer, crams back inside the papers that have fallen out with it. "Oh, he *did* write it down, what do you know?"

"It sounds like you don't like Paul very well."

"At this point, we can't really afford to lose anybody. All the same, he's done so little for the past six months that he might as well not have been here."

"You're still a collective, I take it?"

"Sure, we're a collective," says Magda sarcastically. "That's why I can do anything: advertising, editing, writing, layout, the works. No specialization here." She tosses the ad book back onto the desk. "I'll tell you, there are times when hierarchy starts looking pretty good to me."

A woman and a man come into the office.

"Did you get the pictures?" Magda demands.

"There's something wrong with the light meter," says the man. "But we got something. I hope they'll print."

Magda makes introductions. The man's name is Dennis. He is short, freckled, bearded and energetic. His running shoes give him an added springiness; somehow he looks larger than he really is. The woman is called Lisa. She has a pleasant round face and two inches of dark brown spiky hair. Chewing gum, she looks at first indifferent to, then increasingly impatient with the technical discussion between Dennis and Magda.

"Do you *have* to discuss all this now? I've got to get home. I'm expecting a phone call. Dennis said he'd drop me off."

"We don't have enough graphics for this issue," snaps Magda. "Don't you even care if the camera's broken?"

Lisa shrugs. "We'll have enough graphics. We always do. We can use someone else's camera. Stop making such a big deal out of it."

"Jesus Christ," Magda begins on a high note, but Dennis interjects hastily, "I'll borrow Sandy's camera. Don't worry."

Lisa is already halfway out the door. "Nice meeting you, Allison. Come and help us on production weekend."

"I hope you're planning to do layout this weekend," Magda calls after her.

"Sunday. I can't come Saturday. I'm busy. . ." Lisa shouts back up the stairs.

"Dennis, we don't have enough people to do production. . . ."

But Dennis, too, has disappeared.

Allison is expecting another storm of recriminations, but Magda merely sighs and links arms with her. "Hey, how about a beer?"

"Sure," says Allison, putting Holly out of her mind.

They settle into a booth at the tavern across the street and Magda pours them each a glass from the pitcher. Then she gets up and goes over to another table. She says something to one of the men and comes back with a cigarette.

"I'm trying to cut down," she explains. "I never buy them anymore."

The music here is loud and throbbing; the two women sit silently for a moment, adjusting to the noise level, finishing off their first glass. Their booth is near a window and the afternoon light splays through macramé curtains to make tiny, filigreed patterns on the thickly lacquered wooden table.

Relaxed by the beer, Allison thinks of confiding her troubles to Holly, thinks of beginning: It's hard to work with another person on a day-to-day basis without being sure that person wants what you want, and understands what you understand. It's hard to work with another person when that person has different tastes and experiences. It's hard when the other person. . .

But suddenly Magda says through the music, "The thing I didn't tell Toni and that I won't tell anyone on the collective is that I think I might know one of the Cutting Edge women. For one thing, the office may be bugged, and for another, Toni would expect me to be more sympathetic."

Magda drags deeply on her cigarette, her small eyes slit above the high cheekbones. Her voice is deep with suppressed excitement, and though she's trying to pretend this is an ordinary event, she's also watching for Allison's reaction. She's not disappointed.

"Good God. You know one of them?"

"Well, the Brigade's something new, though I should have expected it," Magda says self-importantly. "No, I knew her about three years ago, when I first came to Seattle. Remember I used to volunteer at the women's bookstore? So I was there one day reading *The First Sex*, and this baby-faced girl-woman came in, looking about fifteen, like some runaway, and said, "What are you reading?" . . . and then laughed. I said, I suppose you know all about it already? She said, Dream on, Amazon. Very funny. Then she ran out again. She'd put a notice up on the bulletin board about a new self-defense class that would also discuss the theory of armed struggle. I couldn't believe it."

Magda takes a long, reflective drink. "She'd come in from time to time; we weren't really friends. We'd have these little arguments while she was putting up another notice or poster. I found out from someone that she was really twenty-one, only a few years younger than me. And someone else told me that Deb spent all her time doing prison work. Later somebody else said she had a baby. I don't know about that, she never looked pregnant to me."

"How do you know she's part of the CEB?"

"I just put two and two together. She was a visible part of the far Left and now she's disappeared—at the same time as an underground group begins to bomb the hell out of Seattle. She's just the kind of person who'd be ready to do something like that."

And what kind of person is that? Allison thinks, immediately irritated, remembering now how Magda takes it for granted that everyone shares her opinions. But *I* don't know what kind of a person bombs Safeway. Yesterday I even felt good about it.

The music has shifted to a dancier beat, a song by the Average White Band:

"I'm taking care of business,
Woman, can't you see?
Gotta make it for you,
Gotta make it for me."

"You know, in some ways she fascinated me," confesses Magda. "I was a little in love with her. I get that way about people, especially when they make me feel inferior. . . not that I really respected what she was doing, but she was so convinced, even then, and I . . . ."

"Sometimes it might seem
That I've neglected you.
But I'd love to spend more time,
I've got so many things to do."

"Yeah, I know, some people can make you feel like that. There's this guy at the co-op—"

"And it wasn't that I ever knew her well enough to get disillusioned, either," Magda interrupts. "Of course, as I got more politicized myself, surer of where I stood, I began to think she was crazy. I wasn't working at the women's bookstore any longer, but I'd see her around. She dressed tough, in a leather jacket; she made speeches at rallies that were totally off the wall."

Magda suddenly jumps up and clogs over to bum another cigarette. She is charming to the man she "borrows" it from, making a deprecatory little face. . . . "Just quit. . . so hard. . . ."

"Ahhh, ahhh got work to do
Ah got work, baby
Ah got a gig
Ah got work to do,
So much work to do. . . yeah, yeah."

The pounding rhythm of the music barks out the word "work"

27

like a threat in double time. "Work, work. Work, work." Work to do, thinks Allison, watching Magda's hardly feminist performance. Christ. Holly will be furious at being left alone so long. And we sit around talking about revolutionaries.

"I've got to get back to the shop, Magda. It's late."

Magda pours herself a third glass and waves her hand. "But we've hardly talked at all. I wanted to ask you more about your business, your partner, everything."

"My partner's fine, but she's probably wondering where I am right now."

Magda nods, but her mind is on other things. She puffs vaguely at her cigarette and gulps her beer. "What do you think I should do about Toni? We can't go on like this. It seems like it's getting worse and worse. Every time she has to put more money into the paper she gets more convinced that she should be running it. We're the only two who work on it full-time, you know. She pays herself out of her dividends and she used to pay me too, before I wangled this CETA position. But it's ending in another couple of months. Christ, I don't want to be on her payroll again. And now this fight about the CEB. Do you think we should print something about them? I wish I knew if Deb was really involved. That *would* be a good angle. . . ."

"I've really got to get going, Magda."

"Okay, okay." Magda drains her glass and stubs out the cigarette. She waves cheerfully to the two men on their way out.

They walk over to Allison's car. The sun is slowly rusting the rain-filled western clouds; the sidewalks are faintly pink. Allison hopes it's not after five yet.

"You've changed a lot, Allison." This, too, Allison has forgotten until now, Magda's charm, her way of suddenly turning flattering and all attention, telling you her impressions of you.

"What, me? I'm the same. . . fatter, older. . ."

"No, really, I'm impressed. You seem much stronger and more sure of yourself. It's incredible what you've done. . . made a business go. It's damn hard, I know."

Allison stops, searches Magda's face, half opens her mouth to begin, I'm so afraid of losing it all. . .

But Magda has moved on, rapt as always, using words as a springboard into her own deep pool.

"I should be like you, trying something different, challenging, not a business, but something else. Christ, and I'm tired of being poor. . . I'm tired of scams, standing in lines, juggling forms. I tell myself I won't shoplift again, then I get mad about something. And as soon as I'm angry I go off to the department store. But all the same, I keep wondering, who else could I write for? Who else would give me this kind of power? No place—no place in this city."

"You wouldn't want to move?" Allison throws out, getting into her car. In spite of herself, she can't help being drawn into Magda's problems, though right now it's the last thing she wants.

"Would you believe it? I'm afraid to, afraid to get out of this little pool where I'm a big fish. I couldn't stand to start over, you know?"

"I started over. . ." She wishes she could be more encouraging but her impatience to be away is overwhelming her. Ahh got work to do, woman. . .

"I know, people do it all the time. . . and I've got to, got to, but. . ."

Allison turns on the ignition, drowning out the rest of Magda's sentence.

"Okay, okay," Magda laughs. She doesn't take it personally. "But let's get together soon!"

"I'll phone you some time," Allison calls out the window, gunning forward without looking behind her.

But on the way back to the shop she berates herself for her rudeness. Magda always brings it out in her. Why? Whenever she's away from Magda, all her good points stand out: her curiosity and intensity, her willingness to put everything on the line, her generosity, the sheer physical being of her. No doubt about it, Magda radiates a kind of aliveness most people only approximate. Why then, does her presence always end up irritating Allison. "Self-centered," "obsessive," are the words that come into Allison's mind. She goes over their conversation again. Monologue is more like it; Magda monologues. But Allison knows others who do the same; do they bother her as much? What gets her, she decides, is Magda's assumption that everybody is as interested in her life as she is. You can't just sit and listen to Magda, no, you have to become involved. She demands that of you. She keeps asking questions: What should I do? Do you think I did the right thing? No, you can't just listen to Magda; you have to be cross-examined about *her* life.

And she doesn't even want to know what you really think. If you'd told her that you could sympathize with the bombing. . . that you sometimes wonder if there's any other way to change things. . . .

Allison is half expecting the shop to be closed when she pulls up in front. It is, but Holly is still there, well after five-thirty. As she opens the door, Allison remembers how they parted. She can't stand for Holly to look at her reproachfully; to forestall any possibility of this, as soon as Allison sees her partner she launches into a dollars-and-cents attack having to do with the business cards she delivered earlier.

"The woman was really pleased with them; she says it was the fastest and cheapest job she's gotten in the city. And two friends of hers were there, and one of them was so impressed he wants to send all his work here. We should be getting a big order by the end of the week, and. . ."

She breaks off. Holly, far from looking reproachful, is wearily indifferent. She is stacking piles of paper in boxes, and the line of her shoulders is even more askew than usual.

"Oh hell," says Allison. "You're tired, I'm tired, we'll talk about it tomorrow. Maybe he won't even call us."

Holly seems hardly to have heard her. When she turns around Allison sees that her face is reddened and blotchy from crying.

"Holly, what *is* it? Is something wrong with the press?" she asks stupidly, coming over to her.

At this, Holly begins, shakily, to laugh. "No, the press is fine. . . it's me. I just don't think I'm cut out for this kind of work. It's too hard. I don't understand what I'm doing, what we're doing. We work so hard, and things don't get better, and. . ."

"What do you mean? I just told you we're probably going to get a big order, didn't I?" But Allison is not emphatic. This on top of everything else, she should have expected it. The moment when Holly would finally withdraw, would quit, would say aloud that it wasn't worth it. It isn't worth hell. They probably won't get the order, and even if they do, they'll need more orders, lots more before they're in the black. And meanwhile the bank will repossess the xerox and then the other equipment; no, better to quit now. If Holly quits, she'll quit. She can't make it without Holly and there's no one else.

". . . and now I have to move again."

"What?" Allison is startled out of her self-pity. "You just moved in there a few months ago."

"I have to move," Holly repeats, closing the box of paper up and looking half-heartedly around for the tape.

James of course. Suddenly Allison is furious. "Why should you move? You shouldn't have to move every time he turns up. You can get a restraining order, you don't have to put up with this shit, you can get legal recourse, for Christ sake."

"You don't know what he's like," Holly mutters, but she looks as if she feels a little better. She locates the tape canister and pulls out a big strip. "It's easier if I just move."

Allison, in her anger, feels somewhat better, too. A real, identifiable villain she can vent her anxiety on. If this is what Holly's upset about, then they can deal with it.

"You're not going to move," she says firmly. "I'm calling Legal Services tomorrow. Enough of this shit. What does he want, more money?"

"He wanted money," Holly says, taping the box. "I gave him money. Then, last night, he said he wanted to try again. He said he'd realized that I was the only woman he'd ever loved. . ."

"You didn't go for it, did you?"

"Of course not. . . he's said it so many times before. How could I believe him? I don't even feel sorry for him anymore; I used to, you know. I took him back over and over. I couldn't live with him again, I wanted to tell him that. But I was afraid of him getting angry, so I just said I'd think about it. . . he's coming back tonight. I have to move, right away."

"You're not moving, you're coming home with me. We'll call a lawyer tomorrow, we'll call the police, we'll. . ." Allison stops a moment to stare at Holly, bent over the box. "Did he rape you?"

Holly's voice is muffled, "It wasn't *rape*, Allison. . . I just didn't want him to get mad."

"Oh good God," Allison comes over and puts her arms around Holly, now crying silently. "Oh sweet Jesus, fucking Jesus."

"It wasn't rape, it wasn't. . ." Holly says over and over.

Allison rocks her and lets her cry. She sees this all the time at the shelter; why should she be so horrified that it's Holly? Not rape, how could it not be rape? Call it by its name and get good and angry enough to do something about it. But women never want to use that word, not even about a man they've come to hate. If they're married, even if they were married, then it's not rape, it's only a preventive measure that they've learned to protect themselves from that particular man. They refuse to see that they've been forced—it's not like being beaten, after all—it's love, even if they don't want it. Women prefer to feel they're giving something, however unwillingly, rather than having something taken from them.

But all Allison repeats now is, "It's all right, Holly, you're all right, you're coming home with me tonight. It's all right."

Katey and Ben are, as usual, pleased to see Holly, Katey especially.

"Oh, Holly's going to tell us stories," she shouts. Ben tries to look a little too old for such childish things, but as soon as dinner is over, he joins his sister on the couch with Holly. She hasn't been to see them in over two weeks, but they haven't forgotten the last installment of the rambling adventures of a little pair of twins called Cream Puff and Hot Dog.

"Cream Puff and Hot Dog," Allison screeched when she first made their acquaintance. "Not only is that the most incredibly sexist thing I've ever heard, but I'm trying to get them off junk foods."

But when it turned out that the girl was Hot Dog, because she was the best skateboarder on the block and the boy was Cream Puff because his tall tales were full of air and too sweet to be believed, Allison resigned herself. She'd never had a gift for storytelling and even read badly (an unforgivable sin in a mother), boring her children with her stumblings and dronings.

While Katey and Ben refesh Holly's memory about the amazing events that occurred in the last installment, Allison puts a load of wash in the machine. She washes up the dinner dishes and then decides it wouldn't be a bad idea to do a second load of laundry. These overalls she's wearing, for instance, are a little too dirty to go another day. Accordingly, she begins to empty her pockets. In the front bib pocket she is surprised to see the ad for the *News*, still in its envelope.

"Oh, shit." She thought she'd given it to Magda. This means another trip to the office tomorrow, another run-in with Magda, more monologues.

Maybe she could just drop it by tonight, push it under their door? Yes, that's a far better idea. It's only eight-thirty and Holly is the perfect babysitter.

Allison finishes changing her clothes and comes into the living room.

"So Hot Dog said, 'I'm not afraid of you. You're only an old rock.' And at that, the rock monster's little eyes got smaller and smaller until they turned back into little crevices, and his hands curled back up into ordinary roots, and he was as cold and hard again as. . ."

"A rock," Katey warbles happily.

"I'm going out for an hour," Allison mouths and Holly nods. Allison thinks she looks like a child herself, her thin straight blonde hair falling over her eyes, her dark blue eyes shining. The kids hardly notice her departure; Katey has her head in Holly's lap and Ben is stretched out on his stomach at the other end of the couch.

As Allison closes the door slowly on this happy picture, she hears again Holly's story, "I'm not afraid of you. . ." A good sign. Tomorrow they'll do something about James.

The door to the *News* office is, to Allison's surprise, wide open. She pokes her head in, unnoticed, to find Magda and a few others grouped around one of the desks, regarding a sheet of contact prints. They're all talking at once about what photograph to put on the front page of this issue.

"I'm sorry to interrupt." Allison advances hesitantly toward them. "I forgot to leave the ad this afternoon, Magda."

"Oh god, I forgot about it too. . . come in, come in. Why don't you stay a minute? We're just having a short editorial meeting." And Magda introduces the people Alllison hasn't met: Jill and Carl. Toni, too, though Allison recognizes the pale blonde braids. Toni has her arm around spiky-haired Lisa.

Allison perches on a chair, suddenly curious. How do others perceive Magda? What would it be like to work with her in a collective?

"Take a look at this shot, Magda," Dennis is saying. "I think it's the best we've got. I took it before the light meter went out."

"I'd rather use this one," the woman named Jill says. She is soft-spoken, has a southern accent and remarkable eyebrows that travel straight across her forehead, dividing the lower face abruptly from the upper.

They both look expectantly at Magda, who pulls out a cigarette from behind her ear.

"There's plenty of time for the photographs," Magda announces. "Let's decide first what's going in this issue."

While the others regroup themselves to face a blackboard covered with notes, Magda begins to tick off the articles they have, the articles they expect and the articles they still need to get. Allison notes that she has an excellent memory and a clear-cut, no-nonsense manner of speaking when she talks journalism. She seems to know exactly what she wants and to be conscious of herself as the controlling force in the room. She enumerates, only occasionally looking at the crowded blackboard:

"One. Features. An article on tenant rights and how to get them by a member of the tenant's union. Needs some rewriting, Carl said he'd do it. Then, Toni's piece on the politics of the public market renovation, fine as is. Then, that article about the effect of the Boldt decision on the fishing industry, that one needs a lot of work, but I've started on it. Okay. Lisa's piece on the women's coffeehouse, okay, fine. My one-pager on the clerical union. . . . Now, reviews. Here we're not in such good shape. A woman called up the other day and said she's majoring in film at the university and she wants to start reviewing for us. She said she'd review that new film at the Guild, but she hasn't managed to turn anything in yet. The other review we received is of some novels by a Canadian woman. It's not very well-written, but I thought somebody, maybe Toni, though she's already doing a lot. . ."

Allison sees Toni roll her eyes at Lisa. Magda catches it too and goes on irritably, "I guess I can. We really could use more reviews, though. We used to have lots, what happened? Everybody wanted to write them."

"Paul used to write a lot of them," Jill drawls.

"When's he coming back, did he ever say?" Dennis wants to know.

"Can we go *on*?" says Magda. "We can't count on him." She smiles at Dennis. "Why don't you do something on that photography show?"

"It's an idea, but I hate to write. . ."

"Well, am I supposed to write the whole fucking paper myself then?"

Everyone is silent. Allison sees Toni and Lisa exchange glances again. They are sitting very close; one of Toni's long blonde braids falls over Lisa's shoulder.

Magda is obviously making an effort not to notice their conspiracy.

"Well, anyway, that's it," she says. "It's Tuesday and we have just about enough for a sixteen-page issue, counting the editorial stuff, the letters, the calender and the news shorts."

"I think we should put the article on the public market on the front page," says Dennis, jumping up to retrieve the contact sheet. "The photos are great. I could see a split graphic, you know, with that old tavern on one side and then this shot of the new building with all the gourmet shops."

Now everyone crowds back around the table except Toni and Lisa.

The man named Carl says, "I think Magda's article on the clerical union should go on the front. Other papers are covering the market stuff. But clerical workers organizing, that's really news."

Allison surmises from this that he is a Magda-loyalist. There is something soft and silky and pleasant about him, like a cocker spaniel, with his goatee and long brown hair, long brown lashes, gold retriever eyes. Are they lovers, Allison wonders, and goes on to wonder about the others in the room. Collectives always have lovers; that's partly what holds them together and often what breaks them apart. Toni and Lisa, for instance, seem to form an anti-Magda faction, while Dennis appears, like Carl, at least partly on Magda's side. Jill is harder to pin down; of them all, she is the one Allison is most drawn to. She is both thoughtful and blunt.

Now she remarks scornfully, "Oh, Carl, those pictures are just a bunch of secretaries standing around talking. . . . And it's such a short article, just an update really."

"We could get more interesting photographs for the clerical union," Dennis interjects, though he clearly has his heart set on the market pictures.

Toni and Lisa say nothing. Toni runs her fingers through Lisa's hair, making it bristle. Lisa has high, freckled cheekbones and chocolate-colored eyes.

Magda squints down at the glossy sheet of tiny photos. Her coarse ruddy hair clumps out around her broad face like shrubbery. She is evidently thinking hard. The conflict, even in this small thing, is between her and Toni.

She looks up suddenly, smiling serenely at her rival. "I think we should feature the market story. The pictures are great and so's the article. I think it'll sell."

"Fantastic," says Dennis, much relieved.

Jill and Carl both nod their heads, though unasked. Allison is a little surprised at the lack of more collective input. Is it just because Magda is facilitating this meeting, or do her decisions always sound so final?

Toni nods, too, unappeased. Very deliberately she strokes Lisa's hair.

"There's something I think we should talk about," she says slowly, stroking. "I think we should include something on the CEB bombings. I've talked to Magda about this and she doesn't agree. She says we have to take a stand if we write about them, and that nobody here knows what they think about the Brigade. I haven't talked to other people. Is that true? Doesn't anyone have an opinion besides me and Lisa?"

Carl opens his mouth to speak and then coughs. He cracks his plump knuckles nervously and glances at Magda's narrowing eyes.

"I think they're fucked," Jill begins in her deceptively lazy way. "They say they're in solidarity with the working class and they set bombs in Safeway to prove it. Big deal, how does that help us, or anyone? I went into another Safeway tonight before the meeting, and there were guards all over the place. They looked through my purse before they let me come into their damn store. They were even pawing through the plastic purses of the ole women who just came in to buy some cat food for dinner. Who's more oppressed than them? Did anybody ever ask them what they thought?"

Jill's eyebrows are working furiously over her slow, blunt voice. Her outburst prompts Carl to join in.

"I'm in agreement with a lot of their aims, but I think Jill's right. It's just vanguardism—I mean, it would be different if they went into Safeway and started giving food away like they did in that Godard movie, *Tout Va Bien*. . ." His enthusiasm ends weakly; he looks more than ever to Allison like a shy golden retriever. "Of course, I know life's not a film. . . and . . ."

"We can't just sit here with our own little brand of leftism and ignore them." Lisa is speaking for the first time since Allison arrived. Toni's arm is resting on her shoulder and Lisa stares at it as she talks, gaining support from that contact.

"We don't have a brand of leftism, that's the point," Jill says. "At least, I hope not. What the paper's trying to do is provide a forum for discussion, not follow some party line."

"How can you have a forum when you won't even allow discussion?" Toni snaps. One of her clogs taps the floor in syncopated fury.

"I guess I'm worried about becoming their mouthpiece," Dennis says. "Here they send us all these rhetorical communiqués and expect us to print them, and then when we don't they're pissed. I guess I feel that terrorism is dependent on the media and—"

Magda interrupts him in an authoritative voice. "What I think and what I've said before to Toni is that, it's okay, it's great for the *Times* to print stories about the Cutting Edge. For them it's a big story and gets people to buy the paper. Nobody thinks because they feature the bombings on the front page that the *Times* is a dangerous organization. It's different for us. How can we print an objective news story on terrorism when nothing else in the paper is objective? If we write an article condemning their tactics, we run the risk of sounding more conservative than we really are. On the other hand, if we come off sounding at all supportive, we could easily be accused of being a terrorist group ourselves. I, personally, don't want the FBI coming down on my head."

Toni looks around at the nodding heads and blurts out in her nasal voice, "Oh shit, you're all so fucking afraid of committing yourselves to anything. The whole Left is like that, sitting around and talking and writing all the time about how the government is screwing people over, but as soon as somebody tries to protest—"

"If that's the way you feel about it," says Magda icily, "why don't you join them? I'm sure they'd be glad of the company."

"She just wants to write about them, Magda," says Lisa. "Where do you get off trying to be the dictator? This is supposed to be a collective."

"I'm opposed to having an article about them in this paper. That's all I have to say. My feeling is that everyone else agrees. Would you like to have a formal vote?"

"Lately you've been telling me that I should be writing for someone else," Toni says, getting up. "Maybe I'll see about it."

"You don't have to go, too, Lisa," Magda calls out bitterly as the two women start for the door.

"I can't work with you, I just can't."

"I'll phone you tomorrow, Toni," Jill shouts after them. And then worriedly to Magda as the door slams, "You don't really think they'll quit, do you?"

"How should I know?" mutters Magda, scrubbing around in her pocket for matches to light the cigarette she has produced from thin air. "Why did Lisa have to go too? Are they Siamese twins now or something?"

Allison can see that it's Lisa's defection that bothers Magda most. She's probably used to fighting with Toni like this, fighting and making up somehow. But Toni supported is a more serious matter.

"I think you're right, Magda," says Carl. "I mean, I think we're all right not to want to deal with the Cutting Edge. If they don't respect our politics, why should we respect theirs?"

"Toni made me feel like a coward," Dennis breaks in suddenly, his face flushed under the freckles.

They're all silent a moment. Then Magda says, "Well, we still have an issue to get out this week, unfortunately, and there are a lot of things to get settled. Do you think four of us can do what seven did last time?"

There's no answer, but four heads bend over the contact sheet once again.

Allison decides it's time to go if she wants to see Katey and Ben before they're asleep.

"And what do *you* think, Allison?" Magda asks as she gets up.

Allison shakes her head. "Me? I don't really know. There's something to both sides, I guess. I'm just glad I don't have to decide."

Three: Wednesday and Thursday

Allison stands in her kitchen eating leftover rice and vegetables from the refrigerator, wondering if she has time to gulp down a beer before going to the shelter, listening to Ben and Katey describe their days at school. The babysitter has already given them their dinner and is in the living room watching TV.

"Well, do you think that was fair?" Katey asks patiently.

"What?" Allison turns on the burner and sets the teakettle on it. She won't have a beer, she'll have some of those Folger's Crystals instead; she needs something if she's going to get through the evening. It's been a terrible day, busy as hell, with Holly alternately weeping and resolving. They called the police department early this morning; the cops weren't much help. Yes, they could try and get a restraining order, but in the meantime they thought Holly should get a new address. . . . This confirmed Holly's belief that no one could help her and even Allison began to see how hard it was going to be. She'd meant to call Legal Services, but Holly had taken the afternoon off to apartment hunt. . . and Allison worked so hard she's even gotten home late.

"Mom! Aren't you even listening?"

"I'm sorry, Katey, I. . . now. . . what about your teacher?"

"She made me stay after school because she said I was talking, but I wasn't talking, it was Linda, she talks all the time."

Ben interrupts, "Mom, I need that money for my uniform by Friday. That's the last day!"

"Okay, Benji, I hear you, you'll get it." The water is taking forever to boil. Forget it, it's seven-fifteen, and she doesn't have time for coffee.

It's not until she's out in the car again that Allison realizes she never responded to Katey. Goddamnit, Wednesdays are always like this. I will not feel guilty that I got home late and that I'm going to spend the evening away from them. I see them more now than I used to when I was a waitress.

Still—that look in Katey's eyes when she said good-bye. That terrible resignation. She's already eight, and like her mother small and plump. Boys probably make fun of her as they had of Allison at that age. And now the teacher, Katey's staunchest ally—always telling Katey how smart she is, how pretty—makes her stay after school. Because Linda talked.

Katey is eight already and Ben is ten already and when *has* Allison ever spent much time with them? It was better when Allison was going to vocational school. She was home to greet them in the afternoons. They had time to do things together. Now, with the business. . .

Then what the hell am I doing spending my free time with other women and their children?

Allison pulls up in front of an ordinary two-story wooden house on a quiet street. Every room is lit up behind curtains, but the house is far enough back from the street to be unobtrusive. This house has been a shelter for battered women for eighteen months; it was the first and is still the largest, though in the past few months two other houses have been opened.

Allison parks and gets out of the car a block away from the house. The sky is clouded over, out here, away from the central part of the city where she lives, the sky, the earth, everything seems darker, heavier, quieter. They say it's one of the safest areas in Seattle, but she always finds the block-long walk from her car to the porch of the shelter more intimidating than walking several blocks downtown at midnight. It's the absence of street lights, the absence of sidewalks, leaving her to walk on people's lawns—the lawns themselves, dark, wet, wooded, and the houses, tucked away behind Douglas fir, always silent, muffled.

Allison wraps her long, bulky sweater more closely around her shoulders and walks up to the door. She's regarded through the peep-hole a minute before the bolt is turned and the chain dropped.

In the beginning, the need for security struck Allison as excessive. The house rule that said: "Keep doors locked at all times. Only designated persons will open the door. Children should never open the door. Downstairs windows should be kept secured." It only took one incident to convince Allison that such strictness was necessary.

About a year ago a man followed his wife after she went to get help at Harborview Emergency. He somehow managed to keep track of her through the several car trips to the shelter. In the middle of the night, after all the volunteers had gone home, there was a terrific banging at the door. Threats to blow the house up. The woman's husband insisted that he had a bomb and that he was going to destroy them all if his wife didn't come out. She came out while someone else called the police. She said she thought she could talk to him. When the cops arrived she was almost unconscious. Several of the other women left the next day. No one was able to persuade them that this house was any safer than their own homes.

Karen lets Allison in. Karen is the youngest of the counselors, a black woman who was herself, briefly, a battered wife. She was one of the first to come to the shelter when it opened a year and a half before. Now she's getting a degree in sociology and working four nights a week at the shelter.

She is a dark brown woman in her mid-twenties, with a keloid scar almost ringing one eye, a reminder of the broken lamp her husband gave her as a good-bye present when she left. Her head, with its closely napped hair, is beautifully shaped and her long neck accentuated by enormous brass hoops in each ear. As usual she looks a little breathless, having only arrived a few minutes before Allison. She comes straight from school every evening; she and Allison are mutually sympathetic and despairing about their heavy schedules. Tonight Allison looks at her and pretends to huff with exertion as she takes off her sweater in the hall.

Karen laughs and nods. "Almost a full house tonight, Al," she says cheerfully. "Only room for one more. But let's hope we don't get one."

This shelter has room for ten women and their children. It is crowded with beds and cribs and cots. For a while they even had a hammock, before too many children piled into it one night and it collapsed, bringing away part of the ceiling.

From behind Karen come the sounds of TV and argument. The children, all under twelve, are grouped in front of the set, changing the channel back and forth. Several women are sitting on the stairs talking. Others stand in the kitchen, jiving, making popcorn. Some of them look familiar to Allison from last week. There are a few she doesn't recognize, though—for instance, the older woman dressed so nicely, who sits in a corner of the living room, knitting. She looks like somebody's grandmother, except that she has a large welt along the side of her face and her foot is in a cast.

Most of the outreach work—the talking to lawyers, the job referrals, the mechanical details of helping women put their lives back together— goes on during the day. There are three paid counselors available at the house then. During the evening there is only Karen and a rotating crop of volunteers, like Allison, who work one or two nights a week.

Allison hangs up her sweater and goes into the living room. She greets the older woman and tries to restore order among the kids. Privately she sympathizes with their argument; if everything on television is terrible, how is it possible to settle on just one show, and not be tempted to keep switching the dial, until they all run into each other? Still, she is able to help them settle on one station by the simple adult expedient of saying she'll have to turn the set off if they don't.

The older woman says, "It would be nice if there were more games for them to play." She speaks quietly and rather timidly.

"You're right, of course," says Allison, sitting down beside her. "It's just that they're used to TV. . . we don't really try and change much here."

"Do you have children, dear?"

It's absurd, but Allison does feel she's talking to her grandmother, long dead, and has a strong impulse to tell her all about Katey and Ben. Not that it's a bad thing to do under the circumstances. Allison brings out her wallet stuffed with photographs.

"If only I had my purse," sighs the woman. "I have some lovely photos of my grandchildren."

"Does anybody know you're here?"

"Heavens no," the woman says evenly. "The family's scattered every which way. I suppose I'll end up going to one or the other of my children's houses, but I thought I'd wait until my face looked a bit better. I can always lie about the ankle." She gives a bleak chuckle. "Nobody likes to admit she made a mistake, especially the third time around, with two fine husbands behind her."

Allison hesitates, then asks, "How did it happen, do you mind talking about it?"

It's rare to see such a well-dressed, obviously middle-class, older woman at the shelter. They usually have more at stake, more to lose by abandoning their situation. No, that's not true, Allison corrects herself; every woman who leaves the financial security of a man has a lot to lose.

The woman hesitates too, handing back Allison's photos.

"Oh, dear, I hardly know where to start."

"It's all right if you don't want to talk about it."

The woman nods and knits a few rows in silence. When she finally speaks her voice is at first almost inaudible and rushed. "He was a friend of my late husband's; he was the executor of the will, in fact. Mr. Madden had only recently lost his wife, too, through cancer. We felt we were in the same boat. He seemed quite well-off, besides, and I had practically nothing after the hospital bills. . . . I couldn't say I loved him, but he had been a friend and seemed, as I say, quite well-off. Oh, it seems so terribly mercenary, doesn't it? I suppose I only got what I deserved, in a way. . ."

She runs one finger down the crusty scab on her face; tears form and collect in her crow's-feet. She must be at least sixty, Allison thinks and is horribly pained at the idea of her suffering, at her thinking she got what she deserved.

"It started quite soon, the beating, I mean. He was a drinker, you know, I didn't realize that or I never would have. . . If there's one thing I can't stand, it's a drinker. Neither of my first two husbands ever drank. I myself can't. . ."

Allison puts an arm around Mrs. Madden, who is crying in earnest now, but softly, with her head turned away so that the children can't see her. Her voice is practically a whisper.

"No one had ever hit me since I was a small child, and that was only when I had been very, very bad. I didn't know what to do. He couldn't be reasoned with. I'd never seen him like that, so angry. . . he called me. . . names, you know. . . awful names."

Mrs. Madden shakes herself slightly and accepts a Kleenex. "You don't know what a relief it is to tell somebody, after all this time."

"How long did it go on?"

"Dear, I'm ashamed to tell you. Two years. But he wasn't like that all the time," she adds quickly. "And then he would be so kind, afterwards. . . . Now I understand that's quite common, I mean the kindness afterwards, so confusing, you really want so much to believe that he's telling the truth, that he'll never do it again. You see, it was all connected with his drinking and he didn't do that every night. He only became really drunk once in a great while, two or three times a year, so I was never prepared. It wasn't like some of the girls here, whose husbands beat them every week regularly. It seemed spontaneous. One night he wouldn't come home until quite late, I would have gone to bed, and the next thing I knew he would be shouting and punching me, even as I lay there."

"Did you ever tell anyone?"

Mrs. Madden has recovered herself and now sits stiffly upright, smoothing her woolen dress over her knees. "My dear girl, I didn't know who on earth to go to. Since then, I've heard that women have gone to their pastor and have been told that they're not being good wives, that they're making their husbands justifiably angry. . . but I'm not the church-going type. I didn't feel I could tell my friends. . . . Usually he hit me where it didn't show, so I never had any explaining to do."

Mrs. Madden touches her welt again and looks down at her casted foot. She laughs a little, softly. "Actually, it's rather funny, dear. I broke my ankle myself. I fell down the porch steps."

Allison's heart contracts in anger. "Was he chasing you?"

Mrs. Madden laughs again, picking up her knitting and absent-mindedly regarding the pattern. "No, dear, it's funny, as I recall it now. Of course it wasn't then. He had locked me out of the house after striking me in the face, and I was trying to get back in. Yes, I was really trying to get back *in* there, when I tripped over the mat and fell down the stairs. Fortunately, for it was quite late by then, our neighbor was out walking his dog. Some time I'll have to thank him properly. He could so easily have believed my story about forgetting my key. He didn't, thank goodness. He wouldn't take no for an answer. He packed me right up and took me to the hospital. It was there they found that I had a broken ankle."

Mrs. Madden stops smiling and the ball of yarn falls to her feet unnoticed. "I didn't even know that shelters like these existed. I wasn't sure what would happen if I told somebody about being beaten. I suppose I thought I would have to return to the house with the police or some such thing, and I couldn't face that. So for quite a long while I wouldn't say much. They kept asking me where I got the big cut on my face—it had started to swell up enormously by then, you see—and I kept saying I fell, I fell and hurt myself on a piece of furniture. So it was about four a.m. and I had been x-rayed and all, and they had put a cast on my foot and a couple of stitches in my face, and I was sitting by myself in an exam room wondering how I was going to get home again, when a nurse came into the room and said very simply, "We believe you've been battered by your husband. Is that true?"

"Well, my dear, I just broke down then, at that word 'battered.' There was a poem I used to know with the line 'battered in soul and mind' and I suddenly thought of it, and thought, yes I have been battered, terribly battered. And so I told her. . ."

"And now I'm here," finishes Mrs. Madden abruptly, recovering her ball of yarn.

"I'm glad you are," says Allison warmly. Every story is harrowing in its own way, but they all affect her equally. She is thankful, simply thankful, that this woman has gotten away.

"My dear, can I get you some tea?"

Allison jumps up. "No, I'll get it."

Mrs. Madden reaches for her crutches. "And you say you're trying to help us help ourselves. I insist; this is my home for the present, why don't you be my guest?"

"I'll come with you then," Allison compromises. "Even the most well-meaning hostess can't carry two cups of tea with crutches."

They go through the hall, past Karen on the telephone. She signals Allison to wait. Mrs. Madden continues; she is spry on her crutches, Allison notes from the back, but older bones don't mend as well as young bones, nor do older hopes. What will Mrs. Madden do, a woman who has made her living in marriage for forty years?

"Yeah, somebody will be there in twenty minutes," Karen says and hangs up.

"Another pickup?"

"Yeah, this one's from the free clinic." Karen shakes her head so that her long brass earrings brush against her cheeks. "Have you noticed that they're sending us most of our women these days?"

"Sure seems like it. Any children?"

"One, they said. Eighteen months. I hope you won't mind picking her up?"

"No." Though it will make her late tonight, especially if the car is late, as the clinic cars often are. No one is allowed to be dropped off directly at the shelter. The pickup point is several blocks away.

Allison calls her baby-sitter. The TV is loud in the background. No, she doesn't mind staying an extra half hour. Katey and Ben are in bed now.

"Can they sleep with the TV on that loud?"

The baby-sitter sighs. She is seventeen. "I'll turn it down."

Allison hangs up, thinking that tomorrow, for sure, she'll have to do something nice with the kids, take them somewhere, or just sit and listen to them.

She goes into the kitchen, drinks a cup of tea with Mrs. Madden and helps finish off the popcorn. Then she puts her sweater back on and walks the three blocks to the pickup point.

The sky is completely clouded over now and the wind carries with it a few raindrops and the promise of more. Allison shivers and remembers suddenly that she forgot to ask Emmie if Holly was home yet. Probably not, or the television wouldn't be on so loud. Did she find an apartment? Tomorrow, tomorrow for sure, they've got to see about doing something to get rid of James once and for all.

There's no one waiting for her at the corner. Allison crosses the street and circles the block, slowly at first, then faster and faster until she's almost running. She can't help it; she's afraid to be out on these suburban streets at night, and the area around the shelter is forever associated in her mind with the threat of male violence, however safe this neighborhood is supposed to be. As she runs, she goes over in her mind her conversation with Holly. She keeps seeing Holly with James, clenching her teeth, her eyes filled with tears, as he bends her back and enters her. Not rape. Oh, god, what if it were Holly she was going to meet, Holly with bruises or broken bones? Tomorrow, no matter what, or how busy they are, she'll call Legal Services.

Allison runs, puffing, furious with herself, determined to change. This goddamned business. It's always tomorrow. . . tomorrow I'll see my kids, tomorrow I'll help Holly, tomorrow things will be better, tomorrow I'll change the world.

There's a car waiting, the familiar clinic van, when she gets back to the pickup corner. The rest of the street is dead silent. Allison, her chest heaving from the unaccustomed exertion, goes up to the driver's side of the van, exchanges a few words and takes an envelope. Then she crosses to the passenger's side and opens the door.

The woman who gets out is small, with a limber and springy step. She's very young looking, round-faced, pretty in spite of her injuries. Her features are—no other word for it—cute. Turned-up nose, cupid's-bow mouth and long-lashed hazel eyes. Her skin under the street-light is wan and fish-belly blue, except the area around one eye which is black-green and puffy. She is dressed in a black polyester pantsuit, and a peeling plastic handbag droops from her shoulder. She doesn't have a suitcase; she hands a grocery bag to Allison while she hefts a sleeping infant into her arms.

"This is Mary Larson," says the driver. "And Joe."

"Allison Morris." Allison smiles, thanks the driver and motions Mary to follow her down the street. The car doesn't pull away, but waits just in case, somehow, they have been followed. A standard procedure, but Mary turns her head and stares at it as she and Allison walk away.

"What's she waiting for?" she demands suspiciously. "Does she think I'm going to give you the slip?"

"No, it's just in case. . . you know, your husband or your. . . somebody was following you. It happens."

"I see you're an old hand at this." The young woman's tone seems deliberately coarse and offensive. "What are you, some kind of counselor?"

Allison counts silently to three, reminds herself that not everyone sees her as a ministering angel and that this woman has just been through a hard experience. "No, I just volunteer once a week. During the day I run a print shop."

"Oh," says Mary. And then, "Is it much farther? He's heavy."

"Another couple of blocks. Do you want me to carry him for a while?"

"Sure." She gives him to Allison, and he is heavy. "I feel like I've been carrying him around for hours."

Taking this as an opening, Allison asks carefully, "When did all this happen? Tonight?"

"I'm fucking tired of answering questions," snaps Mary. "Are you going to put me through the third degree, too?"

Allison counts to ten this time, opens her mouth and then closes it. Fine, not another word. She shifts the boy to her other shoulder. Heavy, but nice. She remembers when she could carry Katey around; it's been a long time.

Mary twists her head to look at the car again. "Christ, she's still there. They really want to make sure I get there, don't they?"

"She'll be there until we get to the house," Allison says evenly.

"Christ." In disgust, then, "What kind of a place is this, anyway? Who lives here? Is it all rules and regulations like a girl scout camp?"

"There are rules as long as you stay here. Security, mostly. In by a certain time at night, no going out afterwards, no visitors, no phone calls. During the day it's a lot freer. There are counselors then. They can help you find a place to live, a job if you need one, or Welfare."

"I can hardly wait." But as she says this, Mary is less offensive than before, more weary. Allison's heart goes out to her. Starting over, admitting you made a mistake, never going back—it affects different people different ways. Some women that she picks up are almost giddy with excitement, others are depressed and teary. A few, like this one, are abusive out of fear. How would I be, Allison wonders.

"You ever beaten up?" Mary asks, as if thinking the same thing.

"No. I was married though. I got pushed around in other ways, still do." But even as she qualifies her "no," Allison feels the old guilt: I don't know what it's like; no one has ever laid a hand on me.

Mary, too, is contemptuous of her answer. "You're just the sympathetic bleeding heart then? Or do you get a vicarious thrill out of seeing us poor victims?"

"It's vicarious, sure," Allison shoots back, allowing her irritation out for the first time. "But that's not necessarily bad. I'm a feminist. For me it's interconnected. This is the extreme, all right; the women here are casualties from the war between men and women that goes on all the time, they're the physical examples of what men do to women psychically every day. It just shows on them. But all women are carrying around black eyes inside."

"Aren't we righteous, then?" mocks Mary. "So what do you see the purpose of these shelters being? Little liberal way stations of relief? Or are you teaching women to fight back? Are you teaching them about the economic causes of their oppression?"

If you're so up on the political questions, why are you here with a black eye? Allison wants to sneer, but she restrains herself, seeing the shelter a few feet ahead. Instead she answers, "Women can decide for themselves whether it's radical or liberal; frankly, most of them could give a shit. All they want is a place to go, and that's what we give them. . . . This is the house, anyway."

They turn up the walk.

"I'll take him again," says Mary. When she has him in her arms again, she puts her cheek next to his round head, his soft baby hair.

Allison rings the doorbell. The bolt slides open and Karen says, "Come in. Welcome."

"Good-bye, Mary. I'm going home now. Good luck."

Mary stands in the lighted doorway, nods. She looks afraid suddenly, trapped. Her hazel eyes go right through Allison's. "Thanks," she says. "I'll need it."

Not your typical battered wife, thinks Allison on her way home. Tough, and with some kind of political bent. Not that any battered woman is really typical. In her year at the shelter she's seen all kinds: some, like Mrs. Madden, see it as an unlooked-for refuge; others will use it as a jumping-off place for a whole new life; still others, and Allison is sometimes cynical about them, come regularly enough for it to be a home away from home, from which they return to their old lives refreshed and ready to do battle again, if not with their past lover or husband, then with a new one. It is these last women who have integrated violence most thoroughly into their lives. Most women abhor violence; when they finally realize that they don't have to put up with it, they don't. But a lot of others continue to expect it as a natural thing. They don't come across as victims so much as temporarily worsted adversaries. Allison imagines that they get in some good blows from time to time.

There's a class division all right, though not always. For instance, in her own marriage, middle-class to the core in spite of their student poverty, physical violence would have been unthinkable. Tom had other ways of keeping her compliant and they always ran to the underground, withholding technique. Silence, no sex, or quiet threats of separation. "If you don't like the way I am, Alli," he would say, "there's no reason for us to stay together." Putting the burden on her to decide to go her own way (with two children, of course), plumping the myth that they were rational, free adults, instead of a woman and a man bound together by numerous economic ties, including the maintenance of two small children. She never would have left him, so fearful was she, so needy of a husband; he had to leave her before she could realize (but had she ever really realized?) that she could make it on her own. No, he had never had to beat her to make her see things his way. Why, indeed, ever resort to physical violence, when, like Tom, you held someone's life in your hands like the puppet master holding a cross-stick and wire?

Yet there were plenty of other middle-class marriages where overt violence was a fact of life. You didn't see those women in the shelter much; Mrs. Madden was a rare exception. When a cycle of violence is never acknowledged, it's a lot harder to break out of. The idea of battered women's shelters was still so new that most women had never even heard of them, didn't know there was a place to go. If there was one on every other block, though, and women knew about it, it would be full every night.

It's raining hard now and the windshield wipers on her Volvo can hardly handle the downpour. They need to be fixed. Tomorrow, Allison thinks and then sighs, slows down and peers carefully forward.

Holly's car is out in front when she pulls into her driveway. Allison is relieved and pleased. It's been nice these last two days to have someone to come home to. Will I ever live with anyone again? She has to laugh then. To come home from a battered women's shelter thinking about the joys of coupledom, that's a joke.

Holly leaps up from the sofa, rubbing her eyes. "I must have fallen asleep," she says, then sinks back down. "I sent the baby-sitter home. What time is it?"

Allison feels the weight of her own tiredness, the events of the evening press down on her, when she looks at the clock on the wall. "It's late, almost eleven. I could use a beer. Want one?"

"Coffee?" asks Holly hopefully.

"It'll keep you awake. . ." Holly hangs her head, rubs her eyes again. "But, sure, I'll get you some." Allison tries to keep the maternal tone out of her voice as she asks, "How'd it go? Did you find anything?"

"Yeah, I gave them a deposit. I can move in tomorrow."

"What's it like?" They are both in the kitchen, Holly leaning around on the counters, eyeing the Folger's Crystals as if she would like to eat them out of the jar, Allison moving busily between cupboard and refrigerator, refrigerator and stove.

"It's not that great, it's okay. . . small. . . the kitchen probably needs to be painted, it's kind of blackened. . . I could just mix the coffee up with some hot water, 'stead of waiting for the kettle," she suggests.

Allison represses a groan, drinks deeply from her beer glass. "Suit yourself."

"It's what I usually do," Holly apologizes, turning on the tap.

"Tomorrow. . ." Allison says dreamily.

"What?"

"I'd love to shut the shop down, just for a day, and get caught up on everything. Do you ever feel that way?"

"All the time." Holly drains her cup and makes ready another infusion. "Maybe we should. We could say there had been a death in the family."

"We have so much work to do though. . ." It's unlike Allison to even be considering such a thing, it must be because she's so tired. Childish to revolt against your bread and butter. And there'll be that much more for them to do Friday, if they don't go in tomorrow. "No. . . you can, if you want, take the day off, why don't you? For moving."

"I won't if you don't," Holly counters, in one of her rare disagreeing moods. "You take too much on yourself, Allison."

"I have to," Allison bursts out, meaning: You won't.

"I can't take it as seriously as you. I just can't. I don't even want to try. It's already enough of a prison as it is."

It is a prison, Allison thinks, sagging into her chair. "It'll get better," she says weakly. The beer makes her feel like crying. It will never get better, and Holly doesn't even know the half of it.

* * * * *

Thursday

I'll just drop this off for Mrs. Madden, thinks Allison, and then I'll go home and take the kids out to a movie.

It's the end of a long day. In the end Allison and Holly both took the morning off to move Holly's things. After one o'clock Allison left Holly to finish up and went over to the shop. She meant to call Legal Services first thing, but the phone was ringing and, and. . . well, she never got around to it. She found herself half wanting to accept Holly's view: that James wasn't out to get her; he was just lonely, and when he was lonely, he thought of Holly. Today Holly's fears were cheerfully rationalized; she made jokes and was full of energy about her new place. She didn't want to call Legal Services, but made no attempt to stop Allison. . . and Allison hadn't.

I'm getting so I don't want to deal with anything more than the usual everyday stuff, thinks Allison, ringing the bell of the shelter. I'd rather pretend things are all right.

Mrs. Madden is showing one of the older children a simple knitting pattern.

"Oh, Allison," she exclaims when she sees the gift. It is a thick skein of coarsely spun wool, something Allison had lying around the house from a time when she imagined greater domesticity. "What a lovely present. I'm almost ready to start something new and this will be perfect."

Mrs. Madden looks so perfectly grandmotherly herself that Allison has to hug her. "I knew I'd never use it, it was just going to waste. What did you do today?"

This morning Mrs. Madden filed an assault charge and then called one of her daughters in Phoenix. "I don't know why I was so afraid to tell her, Allison. She not only invited me to stay with her for as long as I like, but she's coming up here to help me get things settled."

"Call me before you go," says Allison. "Let's keep in contact."

"I will, and thank you, dear, thank you for everything."

In the hall Allison meets Karen. "How's what's her name, Mary?" she remembers to ask.

Karen raises one of her finely shaped brows; the other is ragged from scar tissue. "Joe fits in fine, kids that age always get adjusted long as they can eat and everything. But that Mary is a strange case—I don't think I've ever seen anybody, so, you know, keeping to themselves. . . . I swear, she just hides up there in that room, she don't want to come down for nothing. The counselors during the day have been trying to get her to look for an apartment, but she don't want to go out of the house, even. She just reads or writes things down on little pieces of paper. She's got some envelopes and some stamps, maybe she's writing letters, who knows? We'll give her another day to settle in. Can't force her to talk. Funny girl. Know what she did today? Bleached her hair. . . makes her look completely different. But I've seen that before, I guess. When women want change, they want *change.*"

Allison is about to tell her about the acrimonious conversation she had with Mary last night, but someone else comes into the hall. "Guess I'll just go on up and say hi."

"Good luck," Karen nods.

Mary shares a room with Joe. The door is closed. No crime in that, though it's not usual. Most women are more sociable, want to be with others, after feeling isolated so long.

"Come in," Mary says finally after Allison has rapped a couple of times.

Allison pushes the door open slowly. Mary is sitting cross-legged on one of the beds, her newly bleached hair drawn back tightly into a bun. Karen was right, she does look completely different. She looks even younger than the last time Allison saw her, dressed in a borrowed house-dress with frills around the collar, her legs shaved, her toenails painted. Except for the black eye, going green and yellow around the edges, Mary looks like a college sophomore sitting on her dorm bed. She can't be more than twenty, Allison thinks.

"Hi. Remember me? Allison?"

"Sure." Mary looks indifferently in her direction. "What do you want? I thought you only volunteered one night a week?"

"I stopped by to see someone else. It may be hard for you to believe, but I do take a personal interest in the women I meet here."

"Oh, it's not hard for me to believe. You volunteer types are all alike."

51

"Fuck you" rises to Allison's lips; turning to go, she almost steps on an envelope on the floor. Automatically she scoops it up and hands it to the woman on the bed. It is addressed to Magda Jones, c/o the *Seattle News*.

"Oh, do you know Magda too?" she says without thinking.

Mary has gone all white around the blackish patch of eye; she stares down at her painted toenails. "No, not really. . . I mean, I used to know her. . . a little." With an angry movement she jams the envelope under her pillow.

"Do you think it's safe to send something to her at the office?" Allison asks impulsively.

"Safe? I don't know what you mean. . . . Safe?"

I must be mistaken, Allison thinks, I must be going off the deep end, saying a thing like that. Still there is something tugging at the corner of her mind. This woman is different, she's not like the rest, she is here for a different reason.

Mary can't control her agitation. "You know something," she bursts out. "What do you know?"

"I don't know anything. I don't know who you are, I only know you're not our typical battered wife. That's all. How'd you get the shiner?"

"My boyfriend hit me," Mary answers mechanically. Color is coming back into her face, she looks as if her brain is bleeding with effort. Now she chooses her words carefully. "Magda is just somebody I thought I'd like to get in contact with again. I don't remember her address, that's why I'm writing to her at the *News* office." She pauses, then asks with a show of indifference, "You know Magda, huh? Very well?"

"Well enough," Allison answers shortly. She's disturbed, trying to think. It seems to her that she should know who this woman is.

"Is she in some kind of trouble for something she wrote? I mean. . . she's not being watched or. . ." Mary looks as if she wishes she hadn't said anything, but she can't seem to contain herself. Panic is burning her eyes; the black-ringed one looks fierce and frightened at the same time. "Why did you say that it wasn't safe to send her something at the office? Has she said something. . . is their mail being. . ."

"You're one of the people who bombed Safeway, aren't you?" Allison asks slowly, trying to take it in. "You're in the Cutting Edge, aren't you?"

Mary turns her head away. "I don't know what you're talking about."

"For godssakes, what are you doing in a place like this?" Allison walks over to the other bed and sits heavily. She can't get her emotions straight: *I knew she wasn't ordinary*; and then a flash of danger which spreads through her entire body, *a terrorist*; then, a painful anxious throb for the fate of the shelter; but underneath and running neck and neck, two unhappy thoughts—*This on top of everything else*, and *What can I do?*

With her head still turned away, Mary, or Deb, as Allison concludes she is, begins to speak. She is resigned, frightened, wheedling. The words spill out: "I didn't know where else to go—after we got separated, after the last bombing, Safeway—we were supposed to meet at a certain house. We were going to leave the state for a while till things cooled off. My baby, Joe, had been staying with my mom—she doesn't know that I'm involved with this. She thinks I was visiting friends in Oregon. I went and got him because I didn't know when I'd be back. But when I got to the house where we were supposed to meet—I had just gotten off the bus—I saw some men in suits coming out of the door. I knew something was wrong. I was so glad I had Joe with me, a woman with a kid never looks suspicious. We walked in the opposite direction."

"So how did you get the eye?" is all Allison can think to ask.

"I did it myself," says Mary/Deb, and both women shudder. "I banged my eye on a doorknob later in the day and went to the clinic." For the first time she looks straight at Allison. "I don't know why I'm telling you this. I'm probably hanging myself. I don't know who you are. . ." She begins to cry.

"I wouldn't. . . how could I?" Allison almost starts to cry herself. She sits on the bed next to Mary/Deb and awkwardly puts her arms around the thin, shaken body.

"If you only knew how terrible this last couple of days have been. Not knowing what's happened to anybody else, not knowing how much the cops know. . . who those men were. . . I mean, they may just have been real estate agents or something, I know the landlord is trying to sell the place. But I couldn't take a chance. The paper this morning didn't say anything, I've been listening to the radio; nothing. What if the rest of them think I've hidden from them? What if they've left without me? And having Joe. . . That's been the only good thing about being here, somebody is taking care of him. The rest of it's been shitty. I don't belong here and I can't stay."

"No, you can't." Allison's hold on Mary/Deb tightens. The arrest of one of the CEB at a battered women's shelter, Christ, that would destroy everything they've been trying to do. She's got to get Mary/Deb out of here, and tonight. She's got to be responsible for her. The adrenalin courses through her bloodstream with such force that Allison feels dizzy.

"Where can I go?" Mary/Deb is sobbing into Allison's shoulder.

"Joe." Allison tries to think. "Joe's got to go back to your mother. And you've got to leave Seattle, never mind about the rest of them. It'd be all over the papers if they'd been arrested."

"That's why I was writing to Magda. I thought she might have heard something about the others. Maybe they put out a communiqué or something. It's a long shot, but I don't know what else to do. I'm afraid to call up any of my friends in case they're being watched."

Magda again. Magda who doesn't even want to put anything in the paper about the CEB. "I can get you together with Magda if you want," Allison says doubtfully. "But you've got to leave the shelter tonight somehow. You can just say you've decided to go to your mother's. I can drive you. . . to my house. . . you can stay there tonight. But you've got to leave here. It's not fair to the other women. If something happens the publicity would kill us."

Mary/Deb nods and tosses her head. Some of her old flare is returning. "I guess I won't be sorry to get out of here. It's like an old big coffee klatch all day. Mixed in with a little third-degree Florence Nightingale now and then. Believe it or not, I hate lying. I thought this might be a real shelter, just some place you could creep away and lick your wounds, but it's more like a cross between church camp and soap opera."

Allison draws away from her, taken aback. She has to remember that this woman isn't just a poor waif in trouble, but a committed, and decidedly arrogant, revolutionary. "This shelter wasn't designed for people like you," she says. "It's not part of some underground railway. In fact, you're taking up space that some other woman really needs."

"Go ahead, call the FBI then," Mary/Deb sneers, rigid where Allison has pulled away. There are tears on her cheeks, but none in her eyes now. Having Allison where she wants her, she has hardened. She knows she will be helped.

Allison jumps off the bed. "Fuck you. Do you want help or not?" She knows she has no choice. But she feels like giving the woman a companion black eye.

Mary/Deb gets up too and stretches, blonde and petite. Her Cupid's-bow mouth breaks into a smile, the first Allison has ever seen. "Thanks. I can't tell you how good it feels to have somebody tell me to fuck off.

This is a sugar palace and I'm not really the Shirley Temple type, though they used to tell me I looked like her."

"I heard she was kind of a bitch, too," mumbles Allison, not ready to give in yet.

"Keep it up, we'll be great friends." Mary/Deb throws off her robe, revealing a tight, lithe body. She begins to haul on her black polyester pantsuit and goes to the mirror. "If I have only one life to live. . ." she cracks, smoothing back her peroxided bun.

"Christ, Jesus Christ," Allison sighs, standing in the middle of the room, hugging her body tightly.

"Lead on, Harriet Tubman. I'm ready when you are."

Four: Friday

"Deb's at your house, Deb Houseman? You can't possibly be serious," says Magda the next morning.

With more and more the unreal feeling that she is acting out a television cops-and-robbers script, Allison has driven to Magda's apartment in order to get some help. Over and over she tried to call her last night after getting Deb out of the shelter. Magda wasn't home. This morning Allison thought, how stupid to use the phone. Magda's line might be bugged. This isn't the kind of thing Allison ever worried about before.

It is seven and Magda is not an early riser. Allison has to bang loudly on the door before she hears moving sounds. When Magda finally opens the door a crack, she is wearing a blue and red cotton kimono and her small eyes are squeezed to dark slits in her face.

"Allison Morris, if you guessed what time I got to bed last night, this morning, I mean, you wouldn't dare. . ." But she automatically motions Allison in.

"I need your advice. Let's have some tea. Here, I'll make it, just tell me where a few things are." Allison advances purposefully to the kitchen; Magda trails after, swearing, still too sleepy to ask, What is this?

Magda's apartment resembles Magda's dress: layered, elegantly thrift store, a little too much of everything. It is mostly red—tattered Oriental red and black carpet, red velour drapes, a lion-footed sofa upholstered in worn red plush with a black and red afghan thrown over it. There are strange little walnut tables everywhere with art deco lamps, a fold-out walnut secretary with an electric typewriter, newspapers in piles on the floors, books stacked up on the quaint little tables, magazine racks full to bursting. The living room has the darkened secretive look of a Victorian parlor. . . or a Salvation Army brothel, except that the walls are covered with feminist posters. In keeping with the almost sexual atmosphere is a cut-glass decanter on the biggest table. And two glasses.

"Magda," Allison whispers as they go into the kitchen, a room so claustrophobic that the ceiling-tall cupboards look as though they're going to topple down any minute, "is there someone else here?"

"There was the last time I looked," Magda mumbles, not in the best of humors.

"I need to talk to you *alone.*"

"Allison, what the hell is this goddamned mystery?"

"Can we go out to my car?"

"I am not leaving this apartment. You can tell me here and now or I don't want to hear."

So, with her eyes on the closed bedroom door, Allison whisperingly chokes out her news.

"Deb's at your *house*, Deb Houseman? You can't possibly be serious!"

"Shhh."

"Just a minute," says Magda. "Stay right here." She wraps her kimono around her tightly and marches into the bedroom. Allison hears a man's voice—"What?"—then the bedraggled sounds of someone getting up and dressed. In a few minutes a tall, sleepy and unfriendly man walks out. He stares at Allison. "I'm sorry," he says in rather an unsympathetic way as he goes out the door.

Meanwhile the water is boiling. Allison fills the tea egg with Earl Grey and tilts the kettle over the cups. Magda comes out of the bedroom smoking.

"He left his cigarettes," she says with satisfaction.

"He told me he was sorry," Allison says. "What did you tell him?"

"Oh, just some story." Magda is impatient. "Well, what's this incredible thing about Deb?"

Allison takes a sip of too-hot tea and burns her tongue. "I had a feeling when I first saw her," she begins, and finishes up, "so I took her baby, Joe, back to his grandmother's last night. . . I don't have any idea how much she's on to Mary—to Deb."

"Did her mother have anything interesting to say?" says Magda in a note-taking voice.

"She was pretty calm, surprisingly calm, considering the circumstances—a strange woman driving up with her grandson like that. She just said she was glad to have Joe back. She didn't ask any questions about Deb. I started to tell her the story Deb had concocted, but she said she didn't want to know anything except that she was safe. So I told her that Deb was safe and would probably contact her before long."

"The mom's smart. She probably wanted to protect herself—it's easier not to know—in case of a grand jury or something."

"What do you mean, a grand jury?" Allison asks anxiously, trying her tea again.

"In case she was subpoenaed to testify about her daughter's activities. . . but I really don't know much about those kinds of investigations. . . they were going on back east, but not out here, at least for a long time. The FBI was using the jury as a special investigative unit in New Haven and Lexington to get information about the Left." Magda is still smoking. In her blue kimono printed with enormous red poppies she looks very exotic and professional to Allison. Magda's darkly ruddy hair is pulled back in a tangled swirl, the puffiness around her cheekbones is subsiding, leaving room for her tiny eyes to emerge again.

Dragging on the cigarette, Magda asks, "Well, what now?"

"Deb thought you might have some ideas about how to get in touch with the rest of the group."

Magda snorts. "Not me. . . we used to get their notes and communiqués pretty regularly, but there hasn't been once since the bombing Sunday night. . . . I might even be getting that one mixed up with another one. And anyway, it's not like they use return addresses or anything. Besides, I always throw their junk mail in the trash for the FBI. . ."

Allison sits slumped, staring at the dregs of her tea. "I told her I'd figure out some way to help her."

"Now, Allison, it's ridiculous for you to feel responsible for her. She knows plenty of people, she's been around, she's no innocent. I don't know why she thinks I can help her either. Christ. . ."

"What am I supposed to do, turn her out on the street then?"

"Look, you take a risk if you go around blowing things up that the law is going to catch up with you. Do you know what you're doing? You're harboring a fugitive. You could go to jail for that, Allison, lose your kids, your business, everything. And you don't even agree with her politics!"

Allison slumps even further. "I *told* her. . . Jesus, Magda, don't be so moralistic. I don't need your help. I'll drive her out of the city myself, that's all."

"And just leave her in Yakima or some place?"

"Why not. . . leave her some money. . . clothes. . .?"

"No, she needs to be hidden. And I know just the place—"

"I thought you—"

"—She can stay in Ellensburg with Paul. We got a card from him yesterday, he says the political level of the place is zero. . . that's perfect. . . I'll even drive her there myself."

Allison is dumbfounded at this change. Magda is smoking yet another cigarette and looks extremely pleased with herself.

"What's the catch, Magda?"

"No catch. . . I'll just interview her first, this morning, and then I'll transcribe it and write it up this afternoon. We can start for Ellensburg tonight."

"But that'll take hours. . . I'm so nervous. . . . Can't you interview her in the car?"

"Not if I want to get the interview in this issue. It's already Friday. It has to be typeset and laid out and at the printer's by Monday morning. Don't worry. . . driving at night will be better anyway."

"I don't understand. First you tell me I'm stupid to have gotten mixed up in this; now you want to do an interview and tell the world you know where she is, practically."

"It's different for me, Allison," Magda explains, a little condescendingly. "People expect things like that from a journalist."

"Why, though? Is it to show Toni that she's not the only radical on the paper?"

"Oh, Toni and Lisa quit after the meeting, didn't I tell you?" Magda starts for the bedroom. "I'd better get dressed. Would you make me some coffee." She laughs. "I wouldn't be surprised, though, if my motives were a little impure," she calls over her shoulder. "It's a scoop, in other words. A real scoop."

What to tell Holly? Allison stands in the badly lit hallway of Holly's new apartment building, banging on her partner's door without a convincing story in her head. Holly has no telephone yet.

When Holly finally opens the door, yawning, in a pair of men's pajamas, Allison blurts out the first thing that comes into her mind. A blatant lie.

"Katey's sick and I've got to take her to the doctor. I'll be in, but not until later. So could you get there a little early and open up the shop?"

"Sure I can. Oh, poor Katey. The doctor, that sounds serious. What do you think is wrong?"

It does sound serious. Why did she bring in the doctor at all? "Oh, it's probably nothing," Allison amends. "You know how kids are. . . they pick up things so easily. . ."

"I'll get dressed and over there right away," Holly promises, running her fingers through her lank golden hair. "I'm sorry you had to come over. They should be hooking up the phone today or tomorrow."

"Getting the phone company to come is worse than getting a doctor's appointment," Allison jokes. It's all too ridiculous, running around like this, banging on people's doors, telling them terrible stories. By tonight it will all be over, though. She'll make it up to Holly, somehow. And next week they'll start fresh, on an even keel. Will work hard and make up for everything. Things will be better. Allison feels the adrenalin which rushed through her body last night still swimming along in her bloodstream sedately, if adrenalin can be sedate. This heightened sense of life has begun to seem almost normal. She can't judge, can hardly comprehend, can only act step by step to work out some kind of ending.

Deb is asleep on the couch when Allison reenters the house. Starting up in a panic, Deb knocks over a cup of coffee at her feet. She is fully dressed, still wearing the sleazy black pantsuit; unmade-up, her face is dazedly young.

"It's only me," Allison says.

"Oh, hi." Deb slips off to the kitchen for paper towels and when she comes back, her face wears its customary cool, taunting look.

"Well, your kids got off to school all right, in spite of me trying to help them. I offered to make them some eggs or something, but they were smart and decided to have granola. I can't cook worth a damn."

"Were they surprised to see you?"

"Nah, kids these days are cool. The main action was going on between them, the usual morning fights. . . . But they're okay. . . you must be a pretty good mother, Tubman."

She insists on continuing to call Allison by that name, mocking Allison even as she praises her by the comparison. Allison wonders if Harriet had to put up with shit like this; hard to imagine that runaway slaves would be anything but grateful. Would they dare to lecture their savior on politics?

But politics is a nervous habit with Deb, and Allison is growing as used to it as she might a habitual twitching of Deb's upturned little nose. If it weren't for the circumstances, Allison might even find it invigorating. With a kind of bemused humor she thinks back to Tom's visit only a few nights ago. Then she'd stood on the other end of the spectrum, a crazy radical in her ex-husband's eyes, an apologist for revolutionaries who went around blowing up grocery stores to make the world more fair. With Deb, Allison stands revealed for what she is, a liberal feminist who, with home, car, business and moderate views, represents the staidest elements of alternative society.

But, suddenly businesslike, Deb is asking, "So, what did she say?"

"She doesn't have any idea where the others might be, but she thinks you should get out of Seattle, too, and fast—she's willing to drive you over the mountains."

"Magda?"

"But on one condition. She wants an interview first."

"An interview! Are you shitting me? For that reformist little rag of hers? Hell, they haven't printed a thing we've sent them."

"I thought you'd leap at the idea." Allison slumps into one of the armchairs. "Don't look at me like that—it was Magda's idea. The whole thing is just making me nervous."

Surprisingly, Deb begins to laugh, showing her dimple. "Why not, if she really wants to. It's no risk for me, I'm already underground. It's a risk for her, but if she wants to take it, why not?" Deb jumps up and begins to pace excitedly. "The main thing is, it would show the others that I haven't betrayed them or anything. They'd see it and know that I just couldn't make contact with them, that I was hiding somewhere."

Allison wonders, not for the first time, who these others are. How many there are and what hold they have on Deb. How the thought of disappointing them has a stronger grasp on her almost than the idea of getting caught.

"Where's she planning on taking me after the interview?" Deb pauses in her pacing.

"Ellensburg. . . she has a friend there you can stay with."

"It's a long ways away. . . fuck, you can't imagine how stupid I feel. We should have had a contingency plan. . . I shouldn't have gotten so freaked out when I saw those two guys coming out of the house. Paranoia like that causes you to make mistakes."

A knock at the door makes them both jump.

"It must be Magda," says Allison, peering through the peephole to make sure. She opens the door and Magda, dressed as simply as Allison has ever seen her, in jeans and a sweater, strolls in with a notepad and tape recorder.

"No taping," Deb says right off.

"I knew this wouldn't be easy," Magda sighs to Allison. Then she gives Deb a good look. "Nice disguise," she comments. "I wouldn't have recognized you on the street."

Deb's hand flies to her peroxide bun, as if she's almost forgotten what it looks like, then drifts to her cheek. "You still look the same, though." She manages to make it sound like an insult.

"I'll go make some coffee," Allison says quickly and leaves the room. Better I should leave the house if they're going to start like this, she thinks. And why not? Why should I hang around and listen to more political bullshit, listen to them try and one-up each other? While waiting for the water to boil, she makes a phone call to Holly at the shop.

"Oh, Allison, how's Katey?"

Christ, this is where lying gets you. A daughter sick enough to be taken to the doctor is sick enough to have her mother stay home to take care of her. Of course Allison can't just pop over to the shop after a lie like that. Think fast.

"Uh, we're waiting to see the doctor. But she seems better. When I get her home, I'll probably just let her sleep and then come on over. How are things going?"

"Fine, don't worry. You know, I really think I'll be able to manage if you don't come in. There's not much printing to do. I can handle the counter."

"Well. . . okay." She doesn't want Holly to think she doesn't trust her, for godssakes. "I know you'll be able to handle it. . . but maybe I'll try and come in later anyway, so you can do some printing."

"Okay, but don't worry, okay? Tell Katey hi. Maybe I'll drop by tonight and visit a little with her."

Christ. There's nothing to do but agree, for now. Later she can think up some excuse. Perhaps by some miracle Katey really will get sick at school today.

Brooding and disgusted with herself and her guests, Allison scrapes the last of the Folger's Crystals from the jar. This has really been the week for coffee drinkers. She'll have to buy some more. She's got to leave the house. Maybe she could go to the store.

"But I'd destroy the tape right after I transcribe it," Magda is cajoling Deb as Allison comes back into the room. Magda is sitting on the sofa, shoes off and feet curled under her, smoking a cigarette from the rapidly emptying pack her friend left behind earlier this morning. Deb is still standing, though she has stopped pacing. She seizes one of the cups in Allison's hands.

"I've got to go out. . . to do some errands, and then to the shop," Allison announces. "So help yourselves to food or whatever. I'm sorry there's no more coffee." She hands the other cup to Magda.

"Oh, it shouldn't take too long," Magda says airily, waving her cigarette toward the tape recorder lying suggestively on the couch beside her.

"I've got to see you destroy the tape afterwards," Deb says.

"Fine," says Magda. "We'll have a little ceremony tonight before we leave."

"See you both later." Allison grabs her parka and makes for the door. "Good luck."

They nod, then turn back to each other. Allison's last impression of them is of two pugilists squaring off in the ring for the first round.

Now, where to go and kill some time? Allison drives aimlessly for half an hour, then finds herself downtown, near the market. She decides to park and walk around, maybe pick up some vegetables. It's raining, not hard enough for an umbrella, but not quite softly enough to disregard it altogether. Allison pulls the hood of her parka closely around her face and makes her way up a wooden staircase.

The Pike Place Market is constructed on the side of a bluff overlooking the Sound. A rickety, strung-out collection of buildings and sheds, it clings precariously to the cliff, looking, from below, as if it might crash down at any minute. A few years ago developers wanted to tear the whole thing down and put up a bunch of high-rises. The market, while thriving during the early part of the century, had become more and more of a deserted relic. Truck farmers had stopped coming in to sell their fruits and vegetables; their customers, moving out to the suburbs, had discovered the delights of supermarket shopping.

She pauses at the top of the steps and looks out across the gray and busy water. Ferries, like ungainly birthday cakes, cross and recross, from island to port and back again. A few pale sailboats struggle in and out among their wakes while a tanker laboriously puts in at a far dock. Across the harbor is West Seattle, rising green and misty, the first landfall of the early white settlers.

Turning back to the market buildings with the noise of reconstruction going full blast, Allison thinks the renovation is a perfect example of a good cause which has turned into a Cause, not only liberal and respectable but also, in the end, profitable to the corporate powers. Not that anyone would have thought it would happen this way in the beginning. The big-time investors had been ready to go ahead with their plans to raze the old buildings when a few people had gotten together to stop them. The Friends of the Market, as they called themselves, had so far swayed public opinion that a referendum had been passed, calling for renovation instead of destruction. Hadn't that been cause for rejoicing? Seattle was to preserve its flavor and its history.

Yet now, those same few people are fighting the construction a few years later, arguing that the renovation is keeping the market but destroying its quality. Once the city officials and investors got behind it, renovation became a catchword for dismemberment. Rickety wooden staircases are being replaced with concrete steps—who can argue with that? But when the seamen's taverns and all the strange and useful little shops the market harbored are replaced by boutiques and gourmet specialty shops, isn't there something wrong?

But the renovation goes steadily forward; parts of the market are blocked off intermittently to allow for reconstruction—when they're opened up again, some of the old shops are gone and new ones have taken their places. Everywhere are the sounds of tearing down and rebuilding. Allison plugs her ears and wonders.

The market controversy was not something that she was ever involved in, though she voted in the referendum. So why should she worry? Yet it strikes her that the same forces of cooptation and liberalism are at work here as everywhere. It's the same with the shelter. City and county officials are talking about the need for battered women's shelters, meaning that they need to be put on a more bureaucratic, controlled footing and not just left to individual groups of women to coordinate. Well, isn't that good? Allison challenges herself. We need lots of them—funding, staff and publicity. We pay taxes, don't we, all of us women, battered or otherwise? So shouldn't the government give us what we need?

Yet she imagines that the same thing will happen with the shelter as has happened at the market. Once a need is officially recognized, some of the life and vision goes out of it. When it's a question of people fighting for what they want, there's a chance for people to feel they're really taking control of their lives. As soon as bureaucracy steps in, everything goes cold. The shelters will have to be overseen by the city or the county, only licensed staff will be able to work there, and somehow, Allison believes, it will all get tied up with Welfare and HEW. The women who come to the shelters won't be treated as if they're doing something courageous; they'll become part of another machine to grind them down.

Don't be such a fucking pessimist, she reprimands herself. The market's still here, isn't it? That's the important thing. It's still almost the same. And the shelter idea will be almost the same, too, only better funded and staffed. Compromise, compromise, compromise. If you won't, you're arrogant, idealistic, elitist. If you will, you're in danger of losing everything you want. Is it better then to give in, to give up, to start something else, or to hang around and try and make sure they don't take away from your project what little meaning it has?

If Allison were someone like Deb, she wouldn't even have to ask herself a question like that.

After a long while, damp and chilled, she heads into the shelter of the market buildings themselves, warming herself at the sight of ruddy squashes and sun-heavy pumpkins. On an impulse she buys a pumpkin large enough to be a fine jack-o'lantern. Katey and Ben will love it. She has to put both her arms around it to carry it away, but surprisingly the weight doesn't bother her. Instead it makes her feel more like a part of the marketplace, carrying a piece of its rich color and sumptuous growth; people smile at her as she dawdles along, admiring her choice.

Allison stops for a cup of tea in one of the old restaurants, not yet renovated, and is lucky enough to get a table by the window. She places the pumpkin across from her like a very short companion with its head on the table. The waitress, for a joke, brings two cups.

"Just what every woman needs—a man who don't talk back," she says.

Allison prefers to think of her vegetable as a lady. Ms. Pumpkin, she silently addresses her, what would you do if you were me?

On this gray morning, with the rain swirling like mist against the cool windows, Allison feels the need to do some summing up. It has been so long since she actually took the time to think about her life. Day to day, her mind is like one of the lists she compulsively scribbles: do this, do that, and then cross it off.

Perhaps it is fear which has suddenly erased her mental page of lists. Up until yesterday the most serious thing on her mind was the second loan, the possible repossession of the xerox machine. That, and worry about Holly and James. Today, those problems are nothing compared to the possibility of jail or worse for helping Deb.

I am doing something illegal, Allison tells the pumpkin. I am a criminal. I am in opposition to the State.

Nonsense, the pumpkin responds serenely. You were thinking of the shelter. What else could you do?

But I don't necessarily believe that what she did was wrong. It's in me, too, that urge to destroy property, to fight back. I've just never acted on it.

And you never will, says Ms. Pumpkin with a touch of harshness. It's only a fantasy. What good does it do?

How long are we going to wait to do something about the take-over of our lives?

Now you're just talking rhetoric, the pumpkin reproves her. You know better than that. Struggle is day to day, things don't change over-night.

I shouldn't be in business. I should be working to change things.

I thought you wanted to be self-sufficient? I thought you wanted to prove that you could support your kids? The pumpkin is getting bored with this discussion. She rolls her eyes toward the window as if she would rather be talking about the weather.

What's better? Allison demands. That they should grow up to have the comforts of a bourgeois home or that they should grow up in a better world? And would you please look at me.

The pumpkin grimaces slightly against the strictures of her tough flesh. You make me tired, Allison, really. Running into Deb should have destroyed some of your illusions about revolutionaries. What's so special about her? Is she a better person because of her commitment? Is she the kind of person you can admire and emulate? Is she really the kind of person you would like to be? No, she's nasty and dogmatic, and she's lost without her cadre. She's dependent on you now to get her out of this mess, you and Magda, and she's going to be dependent her whole life long. Even if she doesn't get caught, and she's going to sooner or later, what kind of influence will she ever have? People don't respond to that far-left kind of action. Maybe some did during the Vietnam War, but not now. The time for heroics is over. Work at the shelter full-time if you want to change something. Or start something new. But don't whine at me about how you should be terrorizing the State without a focus or plan. That's just bullshit.

"How're you and your friend doing over here?" the waitress wants to know.

"Oh, we're just talking about social change," Allison smiles. "What do you think about bombing as opposed to other forms of protest?"

The waitress gives her a funny look and moves away.

You've got to do better than that, Ms. Pumpkin says.

I know.

Pumpkin clasped again in both arms, Allison leaves the restaurant. The waitress gets a big tip.

Holly looks disappointed to see Allison come into the shop.

"How's Katey?" Her voice is almost reproving.

"Asleep," Allison says briefly. She goes to the desk and takes out the books. "I'll just be here a little while."

"Allison, do you trust me?" Holly asks from behind a veil of hair. She is bent over the press, but her tone is strong and determined. She has obviously been thinking this out.

What now? "Of course I trust you, what do you mean?"

"Sometimes I get the feeling you're afraid to leave me at the shop by myself."

Why does everything have to come to a crisis at once? Allison feels the distance between them like a thick and congealed pudding. Nothing is spoken of, nothing can be; nothing is resolved, nothing can be. They stand in the same relation to each other that they always have and always will. Can't they just accept that?

"I don't trust either of us here alone," she tries to joke. "We're like two halves of something that has to look like a whole."

"Doesn't that ever bother you?"

"Sometimes. Not today. I just want to do the books, Holly." Her voice is dangerously near tears. She can't even muster enough energy to feel righteous. What she really wants to do is to tell Holly the story of Deb and Magda. And she can't do that.

"I'm sorry, I'm really sorry." Somehow the tension has vanished; the pudding has turned liquid again, though it is still difficult to wade through. "I'm just being silly." Holly churns her hair with her fingers, her face screws up comically. "I guess I was just on some kind of power trip. Wow, I thought, I'm the big businesswoman today. Got the whole shop to myself. I was running around on a little power trip. And then you came in. I don't know what I was thinking of."

Relaxing, Allison admits, "I'm like that too, sometimes. It's funny how it goes up and down. Sometimes you want to prove you can do it all yourself, other times you couldn't care less. Today I'm in the couldn't-care-less mood. . . I'll just stay over here in this corner and count my beads, okay?"

Holly crows. "Oh sure. Something happens, you're going to be right in the middle of it. I know you! But that's okay. In fact, I'm glad you're here now."

"Holly, you twit!" They both laugh and it is over, or at least post-poned. No crisis here today after all. Well, it will probably always be like that; up and down, both of them insecure and doubting the other. I'll think about it more later, Allison decides, beginning to rack up figures. When this is all over.

There's no one in the house when she returns. "Ben, Katey," she calls into the half light, hearing a forlorn quaver in her voice. A thin rain is falling, it is unusually windy. The wind blows away her calling as she stands on the porch; she can hardly hear herself; she is frightened by the glowering sky, the empty house. "Katey, come home. Benjamin, Ben!"

Did she take them hostage, has everyone been arrested?

"Oh hi, mom. . . You're home early," says a little voice behind her. "I was in the back yard. I think Benji is still playing football in the park."

"Katey, sweetheart. Hi!" She hugs her daughter urgently. "There's nobody in the house. Did my. . . friend leave somewhere?"

"Dunno," says Katey, wriggling loose, uninterested. She has been playing at some imaginative game in the garden, perhaps at being queen or president, and her mother's embrace is somehow humiliating. "She wasn't here when I got home," she adds before running inside.

So they got away all right and in plenty of time. Allison slowly follows her daughter into the house. It's all over now. Suddenly the humor of the whole situation seizes her: Allison Morris, bourgeois moth-er of two, small-business owner, political coward, harboring a fugitive in her own home. And no one will ever know. She walks dazedly through her living room, smiling.

While the three of them are eating a makeshift dinner of noodles and fried zucchini, the doorbell rings.

"I'll get it, I'll get it," screams Katey and runs for it.

Allison's fork freezes in mid-air. She hears Magda's voice.

"Hi, Katey. Is your mom here?"

Before Katey can lead Magda to the kitchen, however, Allison is in the living room, still holding her fork, with a frightened stare.

"Katey, go back and finish your dinner. I thought you left already?"

"How could I leave without Deb?"

"But she's not here, Katey told me she wasn't here when she got home from school. I thought. . ."

"Not here? Where is she, then?"

Magda slams the door angrily, melodramatically, behind her. Allison is furious and thwarted, too. Damn Magda and her interview; if she hadn't farted around the whole day writing it up...

"I knew she didn't trust us," mutters Magda, bouncing into a chair, her many-petaled skirts flouncing. "I could tell, the way she kept making cracks about the paper and me."

"I would've gotten nervous, too, waiting around the whole day inside... and anyway, why should she have trusted us?"

"We've gone *out of our way* to help that bitch, at the risk of...."

"That's hardly sisterly."

"You bet it's not."

The two women glare at each other. Magda is the first to laugh. "Sisterly, shmisterly. We helped her as much as she wanted to be helped. We should be glad that we're not more involved than we are. As it is we could be in big trouble for just talking to her if the circumstances ever came out. We should be glad she let us off the hook. And we would be glad, if we didn't want to feel like goddamned heroines or something."

Allison sighs ruefully, relaxes and rolls onto the rug. "It was pretty exciting, you have to admit,." She stretches her arm and leg muscles, lets her neck relax. "She could come back, you know."

"She won't."

"Mom, aren't you gonna eat?"

"Yeah, I'm coming. Magda, you want some dinner?"

"Sure."

Later, after a few beers, a few TV shows, no phone calls, eating popcorn in front of the fire, Magda rummages in one of her pockets and pulls out a tape.

"I guess we'll have to have our burning ceremony without her." She holds up the spool and regards it thoughtfully. "This is one of the hardest interviews I've ever done. I had to edit out all the personal arguments and attacks. Christ, was she defensive. She took me to task for the *News* and for everything else wrong with the Seattle Left. All that had to go."

"I'm looking forward to reading it."

'Well, it should be on the stands by Monday afternoon. I can't believe how surprised Toni is going to be."

"I've been thinking about Deb all day," Allison says a little dreamily, watching the flames flicker up over the alder log. "Going back and forth in my own mind about what made her join that group, what she wanted to accomplish."

Magda snorts. "Beneath that hard exterior, as they say, beats the heart of a scared little girl. Psychologically, I guess it's pretty interesting., but politically she doesn't know her head from her ass."

"She just carried out to an extreme what a lot of us think."

"And went off the deep end. Allison, she's nuts." Magda begins to unravel the spool of argument in her fingers. "I'd love to keep this for history's sake. . . the typeset interview is as pale as a ghost next to it, but I guess that's what Nixon thought, too, and look where it got him. Nope, here goes." She tosses the spool into the brightly burning fire. Its thread catches first and burns like a dragon's tail; then the rest of it begins to smolder and melt.

They watch it burn for a moment. Then Magda says, "Well, I know why I got involved in this, for me it's just journalism and I don't mind admitting it. . . but how come you did, Allison? You don't seem like the type."

The autumn fire casts a warm glow over Magda's wide face as Allison turns slowly to her. She is drowsy from beer and is thinking about bed. "I don't really know. I could say it was the shelter, and of course that was the main motivation, but it's more than that. Maybe, like you said, I wanted to be a heroine. Maybe, in some way, I identified with her. She did what I know I'll never be capable of."

"I don't know about you, Allison." Magda lights a cigarette. "Lucky it's all over, and we're no longer involved. God, I'm glad I didn't have to drive her to Ellensburg tonight. I'm exhausted."

"I'm glad it's over, too."

They watch the voices of Deb and Magda fade from argument to cinder while the fire flares up anew.

PART TWO:
JOURNALISM

There is a moment of truth when you are overcome by sheer astonishment: "So that's where I'm living and the sort of people I'm living with! So this is what they're capable of! So this is the world I live in."

Nadezhda Mandelstam, *Hope Against Hope*

Five: Questions

Magda is getting going.

Magda is puttering.

Magda, the late sleeper, is, at two in the afternoon, up. She is performing small, nonsequential tasks having to do with her apartment and her person. In her blue and red kimono, she has finally decided to start an herb garden on her kitchen windowsill. She's had the seeds all summer, but never got around to planting them. Now it's October and they probably won't grow very well, but better late than never. It pleases her when she finally commences carrying out a plan; it pleases her to cross things off the agenda she has propped, like a blackboard, up behind her eyes. Sometimes things don't get done for months or years, but she never forgets them and in fact thinks about them regularly. Just a while ago, as she lay in bed admiring the sun on the wallpaper, so bright it rendered the ridiculous horse and carriage pattern almost invisible, Magda thought about her herb garden, the packets she bought last April in the market.

Yawning, she arranges the bright seed envelopes on the kitchen counter. basil, thyme, rosemary, sage, marjoram. What else should she do today? Call Lisa and Toni and clear up the misunderstanding. It's one thing to fight, but the paper needs their help and Toni's money.

Toni may be jealous that Magda got the interview, but she'll have to admit that Magda did what she, Toni, wanted. Wait'll she sees the paper on the stands today. The bold headlines: *AN INTERVIEW WITH THE CUTTING EDGE*. What it actually says will be boring to most people, but it will sell. How the sun pours in, though, sprucing up her kitchen as no new paint job could ever do. She'll have to go out into the sunshine, take a walk, walk along the streets where the paper is being sold, and admire it in the boxes—the bold red letters on the cover. They decided at the last minute to skip the photographs of the market (Toni might be pissed about that) and not to use any photos at all; instead, just the words, filling the page, announcing the fact.

Sunny, but cold as hell. Her feet are freezing. Magda runs back into her bedroom and searches under the bed for her slippers. Then she throws herself on the unmade bed and closes her eyes. If she tries very hard, Magda can almost smell what's-his-name's, Sam's sweat and semen from a few nights ago.

To think she'd been seriously considering whether she should move to San Francisco as he was doing.

"Contacts, contacts," Sam said. "You need 'em desperately if you're a journalist. You can't get 'em in some out-of-the-way burg like Seattle."

They had stayed up late, drinking wine and talking very seriously about their careers in political journalism. Magda, of course, had to lie a lot to keep up.

Sam was from Boston and had worked on the *Phoenix* and the *Real Paper*. He'd never had a class in journalism, had started out reviewing records and ended up with a regular column (she said, uh-huh, she'd read it, lying confidently). A change in editors had bummed him out and, besides, he didn't like the East Coast much anyway, too cold and sedate. . . He was sure San Francisco was the right place for him, rather than New York. It had to be one of the two, right?

He was just passing through Seattle. Magda met him at a party and invited him home with her. She told him about the *News*, which he hadn't read yet (she didn't offer to show it to him), and exaggerated her importance in the world of Seattle journalism. Bragged modestly about the investigative articles she'd written, talked about plans she had; she thought of moving on too. . . Of course, she'd been drunk, and that was before this interview.

Magda hadn't dared to tell him much about her past jobs. Since graduating with a degree in journalism from the University of Kansas six years ago, she'd worked in Kansas, Florida, and Connecticut, writing restaurant reviews, features, weather reports—well, just about everything, except any kind of political writing."

"Politics, I didn't even know what the word meant, outside of election time," she could have told Sam, but she didn't dare confess how ignorant she'd been. Before moving to Seattle over three years ago, she'd never worked on an underground newspaper, never been in a demonstration, never even written about one. She had hardly been aware of the Sixties.

Punching the pillow back into shape, Magda is disgusted with herself. Of course he could have been lying, too. But she suspects not—too many of the damned details ring true. Why should she feel guilty, though? It's not a crime to have been apolitical. What does he expect? Here she is from this poor, totally conservative, "if a girl goes to college, it's only to get married," midwestern family. . . She used up so much energy resisting their moral and cultural values that she'd had none left over to begin to formulate something new.

Rich kid, hippie, Magda thinks vengefully. If Sam had been a woman, she could have told him, "Sex was all I was interested in, boyfriends, that is, love. I was always in love." It was to follow her boyfriend to college that she'd tried for and won a scholarship to the University of Kansas over her mother's objections. It was because of another boyfriend that she'd started to work on the college paper, and because of a one-time fiancé that she'd moved out of Kansas, following him to graduate school in Florida.

She doesn't mind telling this kind of stuff to other women—they can laugh and groan and swear about it because they've all had their paths twisted and turned for love of some jerk. But Magda knows she's too proud to tell the same stories in the same way to men. She wants to sound as purposeful as they do—to say things like, "After I finished college, I decided that the next step was. . ."

Until recently, though, Magda hasn't thought in terms of "next steps." It isn't that she isn't ambitious, she knows she's horribly ambitious, a perfectionist who throws herself into everything she attempts. She became the best writer on her college paper the same way she learned to write the best restaurant reviews the *St. Petersburg Daily* had ever seen, but until recently her choice of place, lifestyle, profession, was never dictated by self-interest. If her boyfriend, fiancé, lover, was moving on. . . she did, too, leaving everything behind.

Magda plumps the pillow vigorously one last time and straightens the covers. She hasn't been really in love with a man since Paul. Never again will love be a reason for going, staying, or choosing a job. She doesn't know what will, but it won't be a man.

Still, as she pulls on two pairs of socks in addition to her slippers, she can't help realizing that one reason she was so pissed at Deb for disappearing was that she had been looking forward to seeing Paul again, dropping a terrorist fugitive in his lap for him to deal with.

They haven't been lovers for months now, but Magda is still affected by his departure. In spite of all the quarreling, in spite of the mutual abuse they heaped on each other, in spite of their triangulated infidelities, Paul still remains, in her mind, the symbol of the kind of man she would like to get close to. He was, after all, the first man to introduce her to political ideas, the first to give her life a larger context.

"My mentor," she called him when she was in love with him in the beginning. "My mentor," she can still call him, but with ironic scorn. She has far outstripped his paltry politics. These days he's no better than some hippie back-to-the-lander, moving to central Washington to get away from the turmoil of leftist politics. He says he needs to study and reevaluate some of his ideas. What does he think he is, a Russian revolutionary going off to Siberia to think? Magda knows better.

When she first met him, Paul overwhelmed her with his knowledge. He was a socialist, primarily interested in the revolutions of the Third World countries. He knew Spanish, he'd been on one of the first Venceremos Brigades to Cuba. With money he'd made in an Alaskan cannery he'd spent nine months in South and Central America. He was the paper's authority on Chilean refugees, Argentinian guerrilla warfare, and the fascist economies of all the rest of the dictatorships.

At first Magda worshipped him; she read all the books he gave her, she went to every benefit for the oppressed that he organized, she even gave one of his slide shows once when he was sick. But that was before she found her own political bent, before she began to accuse him of being a bleeding-heart internationalist, more concerned about events in far-away countries than what was happening right here at home. He found her newly discovered interest in labor just as hypocritical. Some things he said still rankle. He accused her, for instance, of exploiting her grandparents.

"When I first knew you," he said, "you were a nice middle-class girl whose father was a dentist before he died. Suddenly all we hear about is that your grandparents were meat packers in Chicago and that your mother had to raise you on a dental hygienist's salary. Suddenly you're working class. Now where do you get off with that bullshit?

"Have you ever worked on an assembly line? Have you ever been in a union? So what if your goddamned grandparents were meat packers? Mine worked in a sweatshop in the Bronx, but that doesn't make me working class. You've worked on newspapers or been on unemployment since you got out of college. My interest in the 'little brown people,' as you so respectfully call them, comes out of knowing what their lives are like. You wouldn't know a worker from a hole in the ground."

Magda called him a "tourist to the Third World."

He called her "our working class heroine."

It's better that he's gone. Their arguments were disrupting the paper. Still, and still. . .

I am, too, working class, Magda thinks resentfully. What does Paul, what does anybody know about it? They hear "dentist" and they think, oh, professional, but her father was born poor, had worked like his parents in the packing plant until the war came and with it, the chance to go to school. He was only a year out of dental school at the time of the accident. All the equipment, bought on loan, was sold to a new partner in the office. Her father'd had no insurance, all his savings had gone into the office. The house was mortgaged to the attic. Her mother, his assistant, had kindly been kept on by the new tenant.

She's still with Dr. Hubert, whom she adores, years later. Magda has always wondered why she never married him. He did ask her once. Things would have been so much more comfortable for them all. But no, her mother had to go on baking him bread and picking up his clothes from the dry cleaner, just like a wife but without any of the economic benefits. Poor and proud and forever loyal to her first husband.

What do you know about it, Paul Kravitz? Sweatshop, huh? A brief interlude in the rabbinical tradition, nothing more. And now your family lives on Long Island.

The sun has faded off the bedroom walls, leaving them shadowy and splotched, the pattern again so idiotically apparent that she thinks of painting. A nice cool blue, for instance. But that's on another list, in the future, and maybe she'll move before that. Meanwhile it's getting on three and she hasn't done anything with her herb garden yet.

Just then the phone rings and Magda rushes over to it as if she'd never had a phone call before.

"Toni, hi!" The proud New England goddess brought to her knees—by curiosity, Magda hopes.

Toni doesn't waste any time. "All right, what's the story?"

"Story, what story? Oh, you mean the interview?"

"Of course I mean the interview. How did you get it?"

"I plead a journalist's right to protect her sources. At least on the telephone. You want to meet me for coffee, or better yet, a beer, in an hour?"

"Sure. Why not?" Does Magda imagine it, or is there something respectful in Toni's nasal voice? She'll have to watch it; it would be too easy to gloat and get Toni mad again. The best way to keep Toni around and contributing to the paper is to treat the whole thing casually, as if anyone could have done it.

"In an hour then. At Pete's."

And now for those herbs, or she'll never have a garden. Magda rummages around for the little disks of squashed dirt, lines them up in a plastic egg carton, and drenches them with water.

Toni has a lot in common with Paul, which is probably why Magda was attracted to both of them, and why she has such ambivalent feelings about them now.

For a while, with Toni as with Paul, but especially with Toni, unreconcilable tension has found an outlet in sexual attraction. For a brief, three-month period earlier this year all the animosity between them, before and since, balanced out into the passion of opposites for each other. Or maybe we aren't so opposite after all, thinks Magda now, busy with her tiny garden.

There are words to describe them, adjectives which could be toted up on either side of a sheet of paper like antonyms, but which, given a slightly different twist, could easily become synonyms. On Magda's side would be (according to Toni): "cynical," "ruthless," "fickle," "prosaic." On Toni's side (according to Magda) would be: "stubborn," "dogmatic," "jealous," "insistent." Balanced out, and they had been in a brief and inexplicable flash, they came together to describe two women who had a pretty good idea of what they wanted and how to get it.

The moment when they drew together like two positively charged ions, released from the laws of nature, had been startling and wonderful in its intensity. One moment they had been arguing, the next wrapped in a tight embrace. Each one's strength had been a mirror of the other's, their lovemaking was like a dam breaking. "This is why we've gotten so angry at each other," Toni said. "It's really love." Magda agreed, she had never felt so equaled.

Suddenly romantic, they had envisioned what a strong front they would present to the world, they would work together in tandem, no longer separated by petty arguments, but reveling in each other's strength. At meetings they supported each other's views fervently; they worked together on articles; they planned the entire future of the paper.

For weeks they went on like this, animosity transformed into passion. When the inevitable quarrel came, the big one, they were mutually astounded. "You love me, why are you disagreeing?" Magda asked. "Because you're *wrong.*

Immediately, overnight, over a minute, the miraculous bond was broken. They were ranged on opposite sides of a river so wide that neither could imagine bridging it, much less that they had bridged it once and so marvelously. They were enemies as before. But worse than before, because each held the other responsible for the breach.

Magda can be objective like this, but she also firmly believes that it was all Toni's fault. If she hadn't been so damn stubborn, she often thinks. Goddamn rich kid, trying to push everyone around.

Magda has a strong case, the only case, she feels. Toni comes from an old, moneyed family. She went to private schools and Radcliffe, where she majored in art history. Her politics began out of a mixture of guilt and benevolence and she hasn't moved much farther. She wants the world to change, for there to be such equality that there will be no more rich people like herself and her hateful family—but she wants the change to occur according to her lights.

It enrages Magda that Toni spreads a different story, an entirely different story of their break based on her own "pure" lesbianism and Magda's casual bisexuality, when the real and overriding split is a class one. Magda knows now that Toni expected her to act like a respectful servant. It wasn't the fact that Magda slept with someone else, that was unimportant; it was that Toni thought her money entitled her to the last word.

The wafers of dirt are nicely plumped up in their deeply scalloped carton. Recklessly Magda opens all five packets at once, clutching them in one hand and ripping off their tops with the other. It's too bad there are so few wafers; she can only use a few seeds from each packet. So tiny, like little ant feces in the palm of her hand. Then she makes an indentation in the spongy bit of earth and plants. All too soon she's done. Why, she could go on planting for hours. She sees in her mind a Millet painting, pictures herself in a kerchief and apron moving up and down the furrows. Funny that she never wanted to help her mother with their garden at home. In fact, she'd been positively remorseless about the flowers and vegetables in that small plot of land. However much her mother begged her to water it during the hot summer days while she was at work, Magda (she had been Maggie Ellen then) had not, would not. None of the other neighbors had gardens, just a few rose bushes and neat green squares of lawn. Only her mother was trying to raise carrots and peas, a few pansies for the dinner table.

Magda places the egg carton in her windowsill. I will water you, she promises the nascent herbs in a burst of sentimental feeling, as if to make up for all the plants she once let shrivel up. She is thinking of her mother, of her mother's efforts to decorate their old pine dining table with flowers from the garden. Toni professes to hate her parents. It had always shocked Magda a little to hear her go on about how evil they were. Magda might have laughed at her mother for her beliefs and pretensions, but now that she sees what her mother went through to raise her and her sister. . . Ma, I'm sorry I didn't water your plants, she has the sudden urge to tell her, but just then the doorbell rings.

Oh hell, Magda is still wearing her kimono. She feels slatternly to be caught in it at three in the afternoon. Even in front of someone she knows.

But it is no one she knows. It is two large men, one dough faced, blue eyed, balding, the other with pitted, post-acne skin and a bristly black moustache.

"Magda Jones?" Dough-face inquires briskly.

She nods, knows even before he flashes his badge, and wants to slam the door. The FBI. Could she really have believed that they wouldn't pick up on her interview?

"We just want to ask you a couple of questions? Mind if we come inside?"

She feels him moving toward her. Down the hall one of her neighbors is coming out of his apartment. He looks at them curiously.

"I have nothing to say," Magda says as firmly and as rudely as she can, and then shuts the door on them. She runs into her bedroom, as if she expects them to break down the door. But nothing happens; they don't even ring the bell again. Instead, she hears footsteps walking away

She lies flat out on the rumpled bed, as if she were preparing for her own funeral, and stares at the ceiling. Well, it's finally happened to her. And she handled it well. She remembers a drawing she saw in a radical paper somewhere. It showed a man closing the door on two rather menacing plainclothesmen. She has done the same thing. It just goes to show the power of graphics. Now that it's over, she's almost pleased with herself; but what if it's not over? It probably isn't over. They'll come back. They'll stake her out, follow her, trump up charges, arrest her, and when they have her in the stationhouse, torture her. How could she have been so stupid as to interview a fugitive under her own name? No wonder they want to talk to her. Jesus Christ.

Magda lies rigid as a fallen tree, the pillow over her head. She wants to get up and put her clothes on, sure that clothes will help her get a better grip on the situation. It makes her feel so tacky to have opened the door to the FBI in her kimono. The problem is that she was planning to take a shower before dressing, and now she is strangely afraid. They will burst in with machine guns. . . and, well, she doesn't want to take off her clothes, much less be naked in the shower if they come back.

But she promised to meet Toni at four. You twit, she admonishes herself. Get up, for godssakes, they're not coming back. Would Toni be hiding under her pillow? Magda doesn't know if Toni would be or not, but the thought that Toni might not is an idea compelling enough to rouse her into action. She puts on jeans and layers the top half of her body with turtleneck, plaid shirt, vest, and sweater. She hides her hair under one Indian printed scarf and ties another around her neck. She pulls on knee-high boots that give her another three inches and makes her feel tall and warriorlike. Thus armored and with a growing momentum born of self-contempt for her fears, Magda snatches up her big canvas bag and leaves her apartment.

No one is in the hall, no one is in the lobby, no one is in the back seat of her car. Magda tries to keep her head lifted and not shift her eyes furtively from side to side as is her natural response. But once in her Valiant, she can't seem to help her eyes from flicking to the rearview mirror every few seconds. Does that dark sedan at the corner have two men in it? Then, quick, turn left here, right here, throw them off the track. Never a very conscious driver, Magda weaves an erratic and overlong path to Pete's Tavern, where she is relieved to see Toni's car parked outside.

Toni is at a back table with a pitcher of beer and two glasses in front of her. Her pale blonde braids are caught up severely on either side of her thin face, servant girl style, except that with a nose like that she will never be mistaken for a servant. Everything else in Toni's face is subjugated to the perfect curve of the nose: the narrow lips, the washed-out hazel eyes, the wispy brows. The nose has character, more beaklike than Roman, but still with a commanding air. Toni speaks through her nose, too, which gives it even more prominence.

She greets Magda with an interested but restrained hello. I can be just as cool, Magda thinks, though it's on her lips to blurt out the news about the FBI.

Magda eases herself onto a bench across from Toni and pours herself some beer. "Well, you see what happens when you go away for a while," she attempts with a show of joviality.

"I didn't go away. I was right here."

"I wanted to call you," Magda protests, "but you'd made it so clear that you were quitting. . ."

"Well, I'm not," Toni snaps. "You know me better than that." Her voice rises with aggravation. "Someone should have at least called me to tell me what was going on."

Magda risks a shrug and finishes off her first glass. It's always dangerous playing games with Toni; on the other hand, it's just as suspicious to be honest.

"I mean, I've been identified with the paper for so long that naturally people will think this has something to do with me. I'll have to take responsibility, too, for whatever consequences there are."

This is probably not a good time to bring up the FBI visit. Magda tries the tack of flattery instead. "You were probably my biggest influence, you know. I mean, everybody on the paper really thought about what you said at the meeting. . ."

"Well, that's a surprise." Toni's thin brows lift slightly, but Magda can tell she's pleased.

". . . so when this opportunity came up, I thought I'd better grab it for the good of the paper."

That's laying it on a bit thick, but Toni is relaxed and even preening a little. She loves to be right; rather, she knows she is right and appreciates people recognizing that fact.

"So do I get to hear the circumstances or not?"

Magda pauses, glances around, then says sincerely, "You're the one person I would tell." This in itself is risky, but seems to be the only way she can mollify Toni: to put her on the inside, make her part of it. She begins with the story of Allison knocking on her door in the early morning hours and builds to the climax, "And when I went to pick her up, she was gone."

"Gone!"

"Gone." Magda drinks deeply from her glass. The beer is going to her head and she feels warm and expansive. The windows of Pete's Tavern have a band of red glass running along their top frame; the afternoon sun streaming through them lights their table and hands with a rich cranberry glow. Magda feels supremely self-satisfied. It's all over, or almost all. There is the question of the FBI, but that can't be serious. They can't prove anything against a journalist.

"Allison's that woman who came to the meeting, right? Funny, she didn't seem like the type to get involved in something like this."

"Type, what type is that?" In spite of herself, Magda can't help flaring a bit. She may have thought the same about Allison, but when aristocratic Toni begins to talk about types, Magda is always suspicious. Still, in recognition of newfound harmony she softens her voice. "To me, it seems fairly simple. Deb turned up at the shelter and Allison knew she had to get her out of there. The only thing she could think of at the time, short of dropping her out in a field like a stray dog, was to take her home. The interview was my idea, but I was willing to drive her out of town."

"Even though you disagreed with her politics. . ."

". . . Even though I disagree, yes."

"Well, your disagreement certainly made the interview interesting."

"You liked it?" It's been so long since Toni praised her that Magda can't help flushing. Or maybe it's the beer. The sun's refracted red warmth continues to enclose their table, rendering the moment close and tangible. She wants to reach out to Toni in gratitude for her praise.

"Yes, I really did. There were only a couple of things. . ."

She should have known that Toni would find something to criticize. Jealous bitch. It's impossible, it's just impossible to talk to her without feeling these sudden stings. But wait a minute, relax, listen to the criticism, maybe it's not so bad. Remember, Toni must be placated if the paper's going to continue.

"Well, for instance, when you asked her about her background. . ."

"Toni, it's not like I had two weeks to prepare the questions. It was totally impromptu. . ."

"I *know* that. All the same you were revealing your political ignorance– you could have taken her up on her Marxism, made some connections between her study groups and the concept of armed struggle. You could have asked her. . ."

"I'm not going to take this." Magda sets her glass down heavily and glares across the table. The red glow has departed, and Toni has never looked more washed-out and haughty than she does now in the dim light of the tavern. "You're always so fucking critical. First you get me to tell you everything and then you pounce on me because my ideology conflicts with yours."

"Your ideology? That's a joke." Toni half rises in her chair and looks around for her purse. "You don't have any ideology—you're just an opportunist, and your interview shows it. You have about as much grasp of theory as a turnip."

"That's enough, goddamn it. I'm sick of you and your goddamned richbitch faultfinding. Nothing is good enough for you, no one and nothing." Magda stumbles, can't find the words. "You, you need to go live in some kind of radical convent, that's what you need to do." Anger is welling in her throat, tears in her eyes, and she wants to punch that cold, skinny blonde statue standing there in front of her. Instead she jumps up and walks out of the tavern.

All the way home she lashes into Toni. The danger of tears was minute and has passed, giving way to strident threats: this is it, this is the last straw, she can have her fucking newspaper. I'm quitting. This is just what I need to push me out and on.

Back in her apartment, Magda feels woozy and tired. She is making herself a cup of coffee preparatory to deciding her future when the doorbell rings.

"Who is it?" she calls cautiously.

"Allison."

Thank god. Magda opens the door, pulls Allison in, and doublebolts the door again. "You'll never guess who. . ." Then she notices Allison's face.

Allison's eyes are red and her mouth is quivering. "They came, they came inside and they. . ." She breaks down sobbing.

"What? Allison, who came? What happened? Was it the FBI?"

"Yes, and some other people. An agency, plainclothesmen. The Alcohol, Tobacco, and Firearms Division, they called themselves." She stands shivering in the middle of the room, her round face crumpled. She is wearing a sweatshirt and her work overalls, once white, now streaked with ink. She is shaking and crying so hard that she can hardly get the words out.

"They came to the shop, they said they wanted to speak to me. There were customers at the counter. I said I would talk to them outside. They said they wanted to ask me some questions and I said, about what? They said, we think you know. I said, no, I don't know what you're talking about. One of them said, we know you're a single mother with two kids. It would be a shame if you couldn't take care of them. I said, tell me what you want, I have to get back to work. The other one, who hadn't spoken yet, was scary-looking, with a big black moustache— he said, now don't get upset, we just want to ask you a few questions about a woman named Deborah Houseman. I said, I don't know a person by that name. They both just looked at me. I didn't know what to do, what kind of authority they really had. We were standing outside the shop on the street and people kept walking by and looking at us. I can't help you, I'm sorry, I said, and I was going to go back into the shop. Then the first one pulled out a piece of paper and said, this is a search warrant. It's for your house and we want you to come with us."

"Did you go? Didn't you try and call a lawyer?"

"It didn't occur to me. All I could think of was Katey and Ben and how they'd be home from school. They had a search warrant and I couldn't think straight. All I could think of was Katey and Ben. I wanted it to be over before they got home."

Magda has pushed Allison into the red velvet armchair with lace doilies all over it, and is hanging over its back. "What were they looking for, what did the search warrant say?"

"Guns, firearms, bombs, things like that. Of course they didn't find anything, but they ransacked the whole house. . ."

"The tape, was the reel still in the fireplace?" Magda draws in her breath harshly.

"No, thank god. I remember looking at it this morning before I went to work and thinking, no big deal, then I went over and picked it up. I carried it in my pocket the whole day."

"They didn't search you then?"

"No." This sets off another wave of crying. "But I was terrified that they would. I've been wanting to throw it away—all the way here—but I thought they might be following me."

"Oh, Christ, do you think they were? Allison, it makes me nervous that you came here, I mean, I'm glad you did, but the Feds were here too, earlier. They must have gone straight from me to you."

"They were here, too?" Allison looks around as if she expects to see one of them behind a door. "Magda, what have we done? How did they find out?"

"I thought it was just my interview." Magda begins to pace the room. "Either Deb squealed or it was the shelter. Have you called them? Is there anyone you can ask?"

"No, I mean, I haven't called them. I haven't talked to anyone except the babysitter—I asked her to pick up Katey and Ben and take them home to her house. I came straight here. I haven't even called Holly. I have no idea what she thinks—she was out of the shop when they came, and I just locked it up without a note." Allison has stopped crying and shivering. Her round face is pale and creased; slumping, she looks far older than she is. Even her halo of brown hair is dull and grayed-out.

Magda is still pacing, but drawing a kind of invigoration from the exercise. "Those fuckers can't do this to us. I'm sure it's illegal.We'll get a lawyer right away." She grabs for the phone book. Already she is thinking of leads for an article in the next issue of the *News:* "No sooner did my interview with one of the Cutting Edge hit the stands than the FBI dispatched two of its most trusted men to. . ." Or: "It's not that I had anything else to do that day. I would have been glad to answer the questions of the two burly men who tried to push their way into my apartment. . . ."

Already the incident is assuming the proportions of myth in her mind. The two men are now both "burly"; she is almost beginning to think they did try to push their way into her apartment. When someone from the Lawyer's Guild answers the phone, she discusses the case with detached brevity and even humor. Already it has begun to seem as if it happened to somebody else, someone who is the subject of a story. If only Allison wouldn't look so white and frightened.

Six: At the Lawyer's Office

Magda and Allison are keeping their appointment with the lawyer the Guild has found for them. Already they have more to tell her than that the FBI questioned Magda and tore apart Allison's house.

This morning before Magda was even awake (she had her alarm set for nine o'clock in order to make the lawyer's appointment at ten), there was a strong rapping at her door. She should have been more wary, should have asked who it was. But groggy and guilty, she only imagined that she'd overslept and that Allison was waking her. She opened the door to have a piece of paper thrust at her by a man with a badge.

She took it and then slammed the door, though it didn't matter, for he was already walking away and didn't seem interested in talking to her.

The paper invited her to appear before a grand jury investigation on Friday. She was subpoenaed in order to testify.

The same thing happened to Allison.

"They're moving fast," says the lawyer, Bess Weinstein. "I wish I'd been able to talk to you yesterday."

Magda suppresses a desire to snap at her. But it's her own fault. They could have talked to a lawyer yesterday evening, but Allison insisted on having a woman. Magda agreed; now she wishes they'd taken anyone.

Bess is the same age or perhaps a little older than Allison, though better kept, thinks Magda, glancing at Allison, who looks pounds heavier in a pair of wool pants and a short coat than she does in her overalls. Bess is tall and athletic-looking. She looks as if she puts on a matched warm-up set in the morning and runs briskly around Green Lake. Now she is wearing a calf-length gabardine skirt, an expensive pair of knee-high leather boots, and a tailored blouse with a short pullover sweater. Her light brown hair is short and feathery across her broad forehead. She has a wide mouth, nervously chapped, and a large authoritative nose. That's the word for her, in fact, "authoritative." Like Toni, she has the air of money—not the idealistic, high-strung East Coast sort of money, but the West Coast, liberal-socialist sort. From California probably, Magda thinks harshly.

Bess takes off the oversize glasses she's been looking over the subpoenas with and says in a warm but businesslike way, "Now, suppose you tell me how this all started."

"Well," Allison and Magda both begin and then glance at each other. God, but Allison looks terrible. She is absolutely packed into her clothes, but her face has a drawn, skinny look under her mound of frizzy hair. She looks dumpy and starved at the same time, and like she hasn't had any sleep for days.

"Go ahead," says Magda.

"I work as a volunteer at this shelter for battered women," Allison sighs.

How *could* Allison have gotten involved in all this, Magda wonders as she listens and looks at the strained face of the woman next to her. She's not a radical, never has been. When Magda was her neighbor, she used to spend a fair amount of time in Allison's kitchen—but their talk was usually of men, rarely of politics.

Allison's lifestyle is potentially political, Magda has to admit, raising two kids by herself, but she has a hard time thinking beyond herself to the world outside. Allison is a middle class woman who has had to work all her life, who was saved from upward mobility when her husband left her, but who still dreams constantly about making a better life, i.e., a middle class life, for her children. Her whole existence revolves around those kids. Being in business is obviously driving her crazy, but she keeps at it because she wants to give her kids more. . . and maybe to prove something to her ex-husband. But what if the business becomes really successful? That's what she's pushing for, isn't it? How is women's capitalism better than men's? And then there's Allison's constant volunteering: five hours a month at the co-op, one night a week at the shelter. She used to go around the neighborhood and collect money for the cancer drive; she used to call people up and urge them to vote for the school levy. She's always giving bits of money and large chunks of time to any organization that sounds the least bit cooperative. A capitalist volunteer, a timid liberal-feminist who used to talk about not voting, but ended up on the side of the Democrats and the liberals every time. A guilt-stricken do-gooder who used to say things like, "We need to work with what we have," and "Socialism will never come in our lifetime. . . probably. . ." At least that was the gist of one of their conversations, and it doesn't seem, in the brief time since they've become reacquainted, that Allison has changed much. How had she managed to get involved with Deb?

Bess Weinstein is undoubtedly wondering the same thing; though she allows Allison to tell her story without interruptions, she raises her straight eyebrows when Allison says, simply, "So I just brought her to my house."

"And where do you come in?" the lawyer asks, turning to Magda.

Magda is slightly hurt that she has to ask. But perhaps Bess just hasn't seen a copy of the paper yet; it's only been on the stands less than one day. A little dramatically, Magda hands her a copy of the *News*, admiring as she does so the bold red type on the cover.

"Oh. I see." She gives Magda a curious look. "You interviewed her, then?" At Magda's nod, she puts on her glasses and turns to the interview. She reads silently and quickly.

"Very interesting." She laughs a little when she finishes. "No wonder the grand jury wants to talk to you. . . . I suppose you know you were taking quite a risk," she tells Magda.

Frankly, Magda was hoping for an admiring word, but full of bravado, she says, trying to match Bess' briskness, "It's a risk I wanted to take. As a journalist I feel I have a right to make facts available, give other sides. . ."

"Oh, you're a journalist?" Bess asks mildly. There's no trace of mockery in her voice, but Magda flushes. She feels illegitimate and exposed in front of this self-possessed young woman sitting behind her neat little desk.

"She's been working on the paper for years," Allison says in surprise. "Don't you read it?"

For years. . . at that Magda feels even worse. How could she have given her life to this rag, this two-penny sheet of garbage? In Bess' hands, the shoddy, amateur quality of the paper has never been so evident.

"Yes, off and on." Bess laughs composedly, removing her glasses. "I guess I just don't look at the names. . . Magda, Magda Jones, yes, that does sound slightly familiar. . ."

Magda knows she is lying and hates her. At the same time she is cowardly enough to want to excuse herself. "I've written for a lot of straight papers, but the time came when I found I'd rather be poor and write what I wanted than work for the establishment press."

"Oh, I agree," says Bess warmly. "Isn't that what we're all trying to do?" She glances around at her small office and laughs.

Allison laughs too, but Magda is glum. At least she has an office. In spite of having held out with Allison for a woman lawyer, she now wishes that they'd chosen someone else. She knows one or two lawyers socially, both men, who at least seem to respect what she's doing.

But Allison is talking again. "This is all just freaking me out. The whole thing. It's been going on almost a week and I'm a nervous wreck. I'm worried about my business and about my kids. They don't know what's going on at all. . . . And I've had to miss a couple of days of work. . . I don't think I even understand what a subpoena means. How could anyone find out that she was at my house? Nobody at the shelter knew who she was. She was at my house less than a day and I have no idea where she is now. . . ."

"Did you tell anyone she was there?"

Allison pauses and glances nervously at Magda. "Well, I told Holly, my business partner."

"Allison, you said you wouldn't tell anyone!"

"I didn't tell Holly who she was, only that there was a woman who needed help and couldn't stay at the shelter any longer. I had to tell her something because I'd gotten involved in a huge lie about one of the kids being sick. . . . It's impossible to keep secrets from somebody you have to work with day in and day out."

"Did you tell anyone at the paper?" Bess interrupts to ask Magda.

"Not where Deb was." But then Magda remembers her conversation with Toni. But Toni would never, it's impossible. "Well, I did tell Toni, but that was at the same time they were raiding your house, Allison."

"There are several things we can do." Bess extends her long blunt fingers with their well-kept nails to tick off the options. The gesture reminds Magda of a schoolteacher's habit: keep things simple for the children, count them out. "First of all your problems are somewhat different, depending on how much the prosecutor and his friends know, and they can be defended differently. Magda's position is simpler, owing to a series of rulings on the First Amendment and a journalist's right to protect his or her sources. Recently it was decided that the attorney general has to approve all subpoenas served on journalists. I doubt that they've had time to do this. So we can probably get the subpoena quashed on those grounds—this isn't to say they couldn't subpoena you later, Magda.

"Allison's position is more serious, I think, at least right now. We're at a disadvantage because we don't know how they got their information. If you think you may have been wiretapped, we could try to quash the subpoena on that ground—illegal wiretapping. There may be something we could do about the search warrant. I'll have to get a copy of it and we can compare what they said they were going to take with what they took." Bess begins to make notes on a pad of paper in front of her. "But I think the most important thing for me to do is to talk with some other people about the whole grand jury process. I've never had a case like this before, though I've heard of several of them on the East Coast lately. What worries me is that this might be the start of a whole series of subpoenas. They obviously want to find out as much as they can about the Cutting Edge."

"What are they going to do. . . the grand jury, I mean?" Allison asks. She's beginning to like and trust Bess, Magda thinks. . . . Damn the self-confidence of these rich people, these professionals. Just when Magda believes that *she* has gotten it together enough to meet any situation, along comes someone with real, with born arrogance and makes her feel like an idiot, a powerless upstart. She's still smarting from Bess' innocent question, "Oh, you're a journalist?"

"What's happened in the last few years is that the grand jury process has been used against the Left, as a way of making people give information against their will, and on penalty of jail, to the federal prosecutor. You're not actually on trial for anything or accused yourself of illegal acts—the prosecutor is just using you to gather information to build a case against somebody else. This isn't to say you couldn't be indicted later on the basis of other evidence."

"Couldn't we just tell them we don't know anything?" Allison wants to know.

"Once you start to talk, you have to continue, according to the rule. It's complicated and I will have to talk to other lawyers, but I think the safest thing to do, the only thing to do, is to keep quiet and take the Fifth."

" 'I will not answer on the grounds that it may incriminate me,' " explains Magda, noting a slowness on Allison's part, but Allison is merely thinking hard. "Yes, I know, Magda," she says. Magda flushes. All right, she won't say another word. But Bess smiles encouragingly at her.

"Have your heard about use immunity?" she asks Magda.

"Isn't that when they supposedly give you immunity from prosecution, but you still have to testify?"

"Yes," Bess says, and Magda can't help feeling pleased that she has answered correctly. That's what Bess reminds her of, a very proper, kindly, authoritarian elementary schoolteacher. And Magda was always an "A" student.

"But what happens if you don't testify, even then, if you still take the Fifth?" Allison asks anxiously.

"Well, I suppose they can, they probably will, find you in contempt of court. . ." Bess begins.

"They could send you to jail, in other words," Magda finishes.

"But I can't go to jail. Where would Ben and Katey go, what would happen to the print shop?"

"Ben and Katey are your children?" Bess asks gently, but Magda notes that she is writing it all down. "How old are they?"

"Eight and ten. She's eight and he's ten." Allison is close to tears. Or maybe it's because she hasn't had any sleep lately that her eyes are red and watery. Probably she's thinking about her ex-husband and what a big stink he'll make about the whole thing—isn't he some big shot at Boeing? Will he try and take the kids away? Is this a justifiable, bona fide example of bad motherhood? But now Bess is asking her, Magda, something.

"Do you have any?"

"Any what?"

"Children."

"Me? Oh. No. Do you?"

Bess smiles slightly, showing her expensive teeth. "One," she says, surprising Magda, whose eyes automatically flick to her ringless left hand. "I'm divorced."

"So am I," mutters Allison, "and he'll kill me when he finds out that I've been subpoenaed."

"It's no crime to be subpoenaed," Magda says heatedly. "Just tell him to fuck off."

"As a matter of fact, Allison has committed a crime of sorts, a federal crime," Bess interrupts with a touch of sternness, "by having this woman in her house. It's called 'harboring a fugitive.' And you have, too, Magda. Remember, loyal citizens that we are, we're supposed to report the whereabouts of known criminals to the authorities. Failure to do so is a crime—misprision of felony." Her tone has become ironic, though.

"What would you have done?" Allison demands.

"I'm a lawyer, so it's a little different for me. . ."

"Oh great—you're a lawyer and Magda's a journalist, but what about me?" Allison asks bitterly. "I'm nobody."

"Well, if it makes you feel any better, I might have done the same thing. It's pretty understandable that you didn't want to involve the shelter in any publicity, and that you weren't ready to turn her in just because you recognized her. It's lucky for both of you, you know, that she left the house. Otherwise, it could have been even more complicated than it already is."

Magda, who has secretly been feeling the same thing, rebels a little at this cold-hearted dismissal of Deb. "I hope she's safe, wherever she is."

"Yeah," sighs Allison. "I could have almost liked her. . ."

There is a pause, and then Bess begins to write rapidly on her yellow pad. "Today's Tuesday and you're scheduled to appear Friday morning, so that doesn't give us much time. What I'm going to do is call some other lawyers, in New York and New Haven, who've been connected with grand juries. If you wouldn't mind, I'd like to get another lawyer involved in this case, specifically to work on Magda's end of it. . ." She looks inquiringly at Magda.

"Fine." Magda thinks spitefully, I hope it's a man.

"Other than that, my best advice is to contact everyone you know and try to get a support group together. Begin educating people about what grand juries do, how dangerous they are for the entire community, get as much publicity as you can. You're lucky you work on the paper, Magda."

"But it doesn't come out for another two weeks. . ."

"A special edition?"

"Hey, remember I have a print shop. All you have to do is write it, Magda, and we'll print it. We can plaster this town." Allison is looking much cheered, but Magda feels that she won't begin to breathe freely again until she's out of this office, away from Bess' benignly self-confident eye.

"Let's meet for a briefing tomorrow night, okay?" Bess suggests. "Here at, say, seven? Then we can go over our strategy."

Allison is effusive in her thanks, Magda less so as they leave the office.

"Isn't she great? I'm so glad we have her." Allison enthuses as they wait for the elevator in the staid marble hallway. "I guess I just like her calmness about the whole thing. It helps."

"She makes me feel about ten," Magda bursts out. "Like we're naughty little girls who got involved in something too big for us."

"Well, aren't we?" sighs Allison as the elevator arrives.

Once they are out of the building, however, Magda's spirits lift. Phone calls, posters, speeches, stirring indictments are really her element. The grand jury hasn't got a chance against her pen. After all this is over, everyone in Seattle will know who Magda Jones is.

They first plan to go right to the print shop and begin working on the flyers, but then Magda decides she doesn't know all the facts. It would be better to pick up some information at the library, if she can find any, or at the *News* office, in newspapers from other parts of the country where there have been grand jury investigations. Accordingly, they embrace and get into their separate cars.

Only Carl and Dennis are in the *News* office, but they are loud enough in their surprise to almost satisfy her. Magda throws herself like a Barrymore into one of the bulging armchairs and announces theatrically, "I've been subpoenaed."

"What?"

"Subpoenaed!"

Dennis looks up from the camera he is working on and Carl from the morning newspaper. Of the two, pudgy, goateed Carl is the one she trusts most. He is new to the paper and always takes her side. It's sometimes boring, but always comforting. Magda hasn't gotten to know him very well yet, though she's sure he would like it. All she really knows about him is that he used to be a creative writing teacher in the Midwest somewhere, and is now employed part-time at the library. He writes poetry. Magda has never seen any of his poetry nor does she want to; she has a horror of what she names "la-dee-da" literature. She is always urging Carl to eschew his florid descriptions when he writes an article. He snickers back that he's going to put her into a novel someday.

Dennis, on the other hand, is someone much closer to her in temperament, and for that reason they are always fighting, but good-humoredly. With his red hair and auburn beard, he is a feisty arguer. Intermittently they have been lovers, which keeps them on good terms.

While Carl sits almost dumbstruck, Dennis fairly leaps out of his chair. "Subpoenaed? For what? The interview?"

"It's the grand jury. They want to find out some things about the Cutting Edge."

"Magda, I knew you never should have done it," says Carl, but his puffy-lidded eyes are admiring.

Magda feigns nonchalance. "What else could I do? I had the chance... and *certain people*"—she rolls her eyes—"seemed set on having something about the group in the paper."

"When do you have to appear?" Dennis asks.

"Friday morning. . . . Another woman, Allison Morris, has been subpoenaed too. . . . We have a lawyer already, but we need to do some publicity, get a support group together, things like that."

"Allison? Wasn't she the woman who was here a couple of times last week? What's the connection, Magda?"

"It's all circumstance. I'm afraid I can't tell you anything more." She is a bit lofty here.

"Jeez," says Carl. "Magda, can I do anything to help?"

"Sure." She puts him to work ferreting through their stacks and stacks of old alternative newspapers, looking for articles about the grand jury. "I'm going to the library for a couple of hours and then I'll be back to see what you've found. Allison and I are going to put together a flyer this afternoon and post it in as many places as possible. . . . Dennis, do you think you could call some people for me?"

"The newspapers, you mean?"

"No, I'll talk to them myself. You call, you know, friends, groups, everyone should know about this as soon as possible. . . . We may be only the first. They could start investigating a lot more people."

"Okay," agrees Dennis, though he puts down his camera with some reluctance. "See you in a couple of hours."

By the time Magda finally arrives at Last Minute Printing it is six o'clock. She's had a busy day and feels more fulfilled than she has for a long time. After leaving the *News* office she stopped in at each of the daily papers and gave a reporter a brief rundown of the facts. She emphasized her own subpoena as resulting from a courageous piece of journalism. She wasn't quite sure how to explain Allison's subpoena other than to hint darkly that it could mean the start of a witch-hunt in the community. She pointed out, however, that Allison was a single mother, a respectable businesswoman with two young children. The man at the *Globe* was impressed with her knowledge of the grand jury; he had someone take a picture of her and said he would try and get the story in the morning paper. The reporter at the *Times* did even better, though he didn't get her picture; he promised that he'd get a short in the late edition of that afternoon's paper. Both promised to cover the court appearance on Friday.

Flushed with success, Magda then spent an hour or so at the Main Library, digging through the stacks to find books and magazine articles on the history and process of the grand jury. With that information and with the stories Carl had managed to pick up from the alternative papers, Magda was able in another two hours to write up the material for two flyers—one to be posted and the other to be given out at the rally (Dennis was ensuring there would be one in front of the courthouse). With great dramatic intensity she read aloud her efforts to Carl and Dennis. All three of them had become terribly excited about this organizing effort.

So it's with a light and energetic rap that she knocks on the door of the print shop. Allison comes to let her in; another woman—Holly, Magda supposes—is hovering in the background.

"Hi!" Magda calls to her and hugs Allison. She feels larger than life, an avenging angel. "Allison, things are going so well. The *Globe* and the *Times* are both going to do stories. There's going to be a rally at the courthouse on Friday. And I have some great copy."

"Magda, this is Holly," Allison says, rather dully, as the tall, wraith-like woman floats toward them in the artificial, too bright light of the shop. The woman smiles uncertainly and then glances at Allison with a tight despairing grimace. Allison meets it, tries to look encouraging and fails.

"Is everything all right?" Magda demands, almost impatiently, for they are spoiling her triumphant entry. Don't they care that she has good news? Or has something awful happened in the meantime? Another FBI visit, the return of Deb—oh no, not that. "What is it, what's wrong?"

Holly takes a step forward, as if out of a lineup, as if hands are pushing her forward. "I don't know how I can explain this, how I can..."

"You didn't talk to the FBI or anything did you?"

"I didn't *think* I was. . . Well, let me tell you how it happened and you'll see. . . I was married to a man named James. We split up about three years ago. For a while he moved away, but then he came back. I try to stay away from him as much as possible, because he's always trying to hit me up for a couple of bucks. He's into dope, is always out of a job. . . like that. So I never tell him where I'm living or working. All the same, somehow he manages to find me."

"And do you give him money?" Magda interrupts.

". . . Usually, if I have it. . . that's the only way I can get him to stay away for a while. Though lately, he's been wanting something different—to get back together." Holly begins to twist the scarf around her neck, unconsciously tightening it like a noose. Allison reaches over and gently stops her.

"Okay, well, what happened yesterday was that early in the morning while Allison was out picking something up, James came into the shop. I had just moved"—here she glances at Allison with pleading in her eyes—"but he must have got this address from my landlord somehow. So I said I would give him some money if he'd go away, but he didn't want that. But he wouldn't leave, either. He just kept hanging around. He said he wanted to get to know me again. He kept saying things like 'Nice shop you have here,' until I thought I was going to go crazy. I'd been printing but I didn't want to leave him alone at the front of the shop, so I was pretending to do some figuring, hoping Allison would get back soon. Well, then two men came in. . ."

Magda looks quickly at Allison, who grins weakly.

"How was I supposed to know?" Holly looks desperately from one to the other. "They said they were from the Small Business Administration and could they just ask a few questions about how we were doing and such? Well, okay, I said, even though it seemed like terrible timing. I didn't want James listening in and finding out any more about us than necessary. . . . But what could I do? I thought I *had* to answer them. So I gave them all the information they wanted, about the kind of work we were getting and about our bank loans. . ."

Allison groans loudly here. "If they fuck us up with the bank. . ."

Holly stares at her helplessly.

"What happened then?" Magda prods.

"They asked more questions, like where was Allison Morris and did she still work here? Some stuff that seemed personal, but how did I know? They seemed to have it all down on their little pads of paper. Like, didn't Allison have kids? Was she still living at the same address? Like that. Then they looked around a little at the shop and thanked me and left.

" 'I would say that the Feds are mighty interested in your partner here,' that's what James said right after they left. 'What?' I said. 'Those men are from the SBA, are you crazy or something?' 'Look,' he said, 'those guys are agents or I've never seen no agent in my life, and believe me I've seen one or two. Come on, give, what's she done?'

"Well, of course, then I remembered the woman Allison had had at her house. I didn't know who she was, Allison just said that a woman from the shelter who'd had a little trouble with the law had stayed there one night. I was scared. I thought, no way am I going to tell him what I know, which is nothing anyway. But standing up to James is impossible, that's why I keep moving away. I. . . I told him." Holly's face twists up in anguish. "All I could do then was promise to start seeing him again if he kept quiet."

"I still don't understand why you didn't tell me this yesterday," Allison says, taking Holly's scarf away from her before she can strangle herself with remorse.

"I didn't want you to worry."

"We're both so worried about getting the other one worried."

"Jesus Christ," Magda murmurs. "This is too fucking unbelievable, the whole thing is just unbelievable."

But now Holly is sniffling and she and Allison are holding each other in a death grip, both of them muttering at intervals, "I'm sorry, I'm sorry."

Magda sinks into a chair, still holding the copy for her flyers. She is thinking hard about everything she's heard. When Allison and Holly have calmed down a little, she says decisively, "I'm not sure if this is any comfort in the present circumstances, but I can't believe that it was James who tipped off the Feds. If they knew enough to come to the shop looking for Allison, they must have some kind of other, previous information. It *must* have been someone at the shelter. . . I'm sure of it."

Allison, still with an arm around Holly, nods her head slowly. "Much as I don't want to believe it, someone must have mentioned to somebody that it was me who drove off with Deb. But I'm sure they didn't know who they were talking to."

Holly is beginning to hiccup. "If only James weren't in on it, too," she hiccups, bleating out the word "James" and making them all laugh, though a bit hysterically.

"It's all my fault," Allison says. "If I'd helped you last week, none of this would have happened. . ."

"Oh no, Allison, *I* should have been stronger. . ."

Magda looks from one to the other, weariness overcoming her. Are they going to go on with their apologies forever? For, like it or not, she's stuck with them. Subpoenas make strange bedfellows all right.

She sighs. "I could sure use a cup of coffee after all this. How about you, ladies? We've still got the goddamn flyers to get out tonight."

Seven: The First and the Fifth

Magda has never, no, not once in her life, had insomnia. All the same she's taken to spending the night at Allison's. It's more than a matter of conserving time, more than presenting a solid front—it's that she's afraid to be alone when darkness comes on. Holly, too, has abandoned her new apartment for Allison's house, though she goes to the shop each day with a renewed terror of meeting James.

She and Magda trade off the couch and the floor. Allison's kids think this camping out is fun. They want to sleep on the floor in their sleeping bags! Magda secretly wishes that Allison would let them, so she could have one of their beds; even with a carpet under her, even with a sofa, she wakes up stiff in the morning. But Allison, good, responsible mother that she is, keeps trying to maintain some kind of routine: a hearty breakfast in the morning, packed lunches, dinner in the evening, and bed promptly at nine o'clock. Magda has to admit, though, that Allison's strict adherence to meals and sleep is keeping all of them together. Holly is a nervous wreck, worrying about James and the shop and her part in the subpoenas, which nevertheless exclude her. And Magda, while often exuberant, is more often so frenziedly busy that she would forget to even wash her face if Allison didn't tactfully point out a spare washcloth.

Every day before Friday's court date has brought some new development, something to complicate their situation, and Magda feels somehow more responsible than any of the others for fitting each new piece of the jigsaw puzzle into a coherent whole. She wonders if it's her journalistic training that pushes her to keep trying to make sense of things, or whether her whole life has been like this—an attempt to force facts into meaning, or, if not meaning, then logical order and credibility to the outside world. Facts and their relation to each other are what keep her preoccupied during the day and up at night after everyone else has gone to sleep.

Facts like Deb's mother being subpoenaed to testify on the same day. Facts like Allison's conversation with Karen at the shelter which revealed that someone had called the shelter looking for a woman fitting Deb's description. Facts like the death of one of the CEB, not Deb, but a man called Ted Shovik, apprehended on the freeway for speeding, according to the police report, and shot for resisting arrest when he pulled a gun.

Magda has been trying to write a story for the *News*, but every day the story changes, as does her place in it. For one thing, she lives in daily expectation of her subpoena being dropped. Wallace, the lawyer Bess brought in to help her with Magda's case, is supremely confident that she'll get off. Believing him, she fluctuates between hope and a kind of annoyance. If her subpoena is dropped, she'll lose her place in the thick of things; her story will have to come from outside instead of inside.

Because of Ted Shovik's death the day before, the rally on Friday has a different atmosphere than planned. Dennis organized speakers and called up every group he knew, while Holly and Allison and Magda spent all Wednesday putting up flyers on telephone poles, in coffeehouses and taverns, at the university and in laudromats. But none of them expected such a big turnout, almost two hundred people, or such a grim one. Instead of a group of concerned citizens coming together to protest a symbolic death of civil rights, the Left community is out in full force to mourn a real death. The mood is still one of outrage, but underneath is a current of paranoia and righteousness. The posters and banners protesting the subpoenas are almost outnumbered by those calling for the end of the police state. "Pigs = Murderers" reads a typical sign.

Though Magda never knew Ted personally, she recognized his name from previous demonstrations and groups she had dealt with in the course of writing for the *News*. There are others at the rally, however, who worked with him as far back as the anti-war movement. No one seems to be asking what suicidal impulse drove him to join the Brigade; most people at the rally seem to be in support of his actions, or at least sympathetic to them. Now that he's dead, he's a hero.

The atmosphere can't help but unnerve Magda a little and anger her at the same time. Another fucking male revolutionary taking precedence over a more serious thing like two—three—women being subpoenaed by the grand jury. Or perhaps it's just that her own moment of glory has been diminished by his death. She would like to be the hero of the day.

Dennis speaks first, using the bullhorn, and then a woman who talks about the subpoenas in New Haven and Lexington. The next speaker asks for a moment of silence for Ted, but someone else jumps up and grabs the bullhorn. "We won't be silent any more." It is supposed to be Magda's turn to speak, but the man harangues the crowd for ten minutes or more with feeling and rhetoric, before Dennis can hand the bullhorn over to Magda. The shouting and calling out of the crowd have knocked her prepared speech right out of her head. As the police move closer to breaking things up, all she can manage to shout is something inane about the grand jury being the legal arm of the police state. It's not exactly what she meant to say, but it strikes the right chord and is greeted with cheers and clapping. As she hands the bullhorn back to Dennis in some confusion, Bess appears by her side, smiling tensely, looking very professional in a wool suit and ascot, saying, "It's time to go in now."

Dennis has promised a vigil outside the courthouse while the session is in progress, but already Magda sees people beginning to drift away. . . to school or to their jobs. At the same time she notices with a start of fear and awe how many cops are standing around—big, heavyset men in crisp blue with holsters at their sides. It doesn't take much for her to become paranoid at this stage and she avoids their eyes as they stare at her curiously, measuring her physical dimensions or coldly sizing up her potential for criminality.

It's on the way into the stately courthouse that Magda, calming now from the excitement of being up in front of so many people, so visible, becomes aware of the people walking with them. One is a tall young black woman with beautiful and ornate silver earrings and a scar over her left eye. She walks along with Allison and a hovering Holly, speaking in a quiet yet charged voice, telling to Holly the story she already told Allison at the shelter Wednesday night. Allison has said that Karen feels responsible for the subpoena. Responsible and pissed, too, that someone would give a stranger Allison's name, would reveal that it was Allison who took Deb away from the shelter. The woman Fed had apparently posed as a lawyer, had said it was imperative she get in touch with Mary Larson.

"I don't know why 'lawyer' is such a magic word around there," Karen is saying. "When I hear 'lawyer' I get suspicious right away."

Magda wishes Bess were near enough to hear that.

"At least nothing has come out in the papers about the shelter yet," Allison says. Magda notices how she draws Holly toward her and Karen, holding her hand in an encouraging way, absolving Holly of all responsibility for talking to James.

Magda feels suddenly a little excluded; she looks around for someone to talk to and notices an older woman with a thin and intelligent face walking slightly in front of her, accompanied by a lawyer-looking man. Can this be Mrs. Houseman, Deb's mother?

Since she read in the paper yesterday that Deb's mother also had received a subpoena to testify today, she has had mixed emotions. The calculating part of her mind knows that the more people subpoenaed, the better for their collective case, yet she also feels afraid of the noose tightening around Deb's neck. There is to her no contradiction in wanting Deb to remain free while disagreeing with everything she stands for. Especially after the headlines yesterday: *ARMED TERRORIST KILLED ON I-5*. The details of Ted Shovik's death are still maddeningly obscure and frightening. Did they know he was a member of the CEB when they shot him? That they do now, and that the newspapers are exonerating the police in his death, raises the stakes for all of them.

Until this moment, however, it hasn't occurred to Magda to feel much sympathy for Mrs. Houseman, but at the sight of her thin straight back, her half-turned, weary face, she feels a rush of compassion. At least Magda and Allison had some idea of what they were doing, but Deb's mother is only a relative. She must be terrified. Thinking that her daughter could be murdered outright like that, at any time.

"Mrs. Houseman?" Magda calls out impulsively.

The woman turns with a jerk, stares her straight in the face. "Yes?"

"I'm Magda Jones. . . and I'm so sorry." She catches up with her and the lawyer.

"How do you do?" Mrs. Houseman murmurs. Her face has a watchful look and she says nothing else.

Magda, too, is suddenly at a loss for words. Perhaps this woman holds her somehow responsible for what has happened to her daughter. Perhaps she lumps Magda with the terrorists who have taken Deb away from her.

The lawyer steps in and introduces himself, however, in the awkward pause, just as they reach the elevators. Bess and Wallace catch up with them there, and all three lawyers begin to talk quietly among themselves while Magda falls back with Allison and the others. She notices that Allison is avoiding Mrs. Houseman completely. Of course she has to—it wouldn't do for anyone to suspect that they've met before.

Allison instead begins to tell Karen about the phone call from Tom. "This was late Wednesday, after I got home from the shelter. He started out all right—he said, I read about you in the paper this morning. I've been trying to reach you all day. Where've you been, are you all right? I said I was fine, that I'd been out of the house most of the day putting up flyers. What kind of flyers? he wanted to know. For the rally in front of the courthouse Friday morning, to protest the grand jury's fishing expedition, I said, all calm and sweet.

"Then he started in. Allison, would you please tell me what the hell is going on? Why were you subpoenaed, what have you done? I told him that I hadn't done anything I was ashamed of. He said, if you haven't done anything, why are they subpoenaing you? Because they want to find out as much as they can about the Left in Seattle, I said, and I for one am not going to tell them a damn thing. His voice started to get louder and he said, you don't mean that you're not going to talk to them? If you're innocent, then there's no problem. Just tell them that you don't know anything. I had to give him a short rundown on the grand jury. I wanted to sound as smart as possible, because I knew that sooner or later he was going to get around to the question of the kids. And pretty soon he did. He said that the publicity didn't bother *him*, he could take old friends calling him up and asking—what's this about Allison being subpoenaed? No, *he* didn't mind his co-workers finding out that he had been married to some kind of criminal and his chances for advancement going down the drain, but the *kids*. What was going to happen to *them*, how were *they* going to cope with all this publicity at school, their mother a public figure of the worst kind? And where were the kids, anyway, and what was I going to do about them while all this was going on?

"I said, they were just fine, that they were home with me and going to school and leading a totally normal life just like they always had and would continue to do and would he please stop bugging me because everything was fine and it was all no big deal."

Bess has waited during this story to shepherd them into an elevator, while Mrs. Houseman and the two other lawyers have already gone up. She laughs with the rest of them over Allison's imitation of Tom's outrage, but suddenly turns somber. Allison, watching her, bursts out, "How big a chance is it that they'll send us to jail?"

"There's a good chance," Bess says evenly. "And it's very much up to how you want to handle it. You shouldn't feel pressured into making a decision you'll regret. If there is any possibility that your ex-husband will make trouble for you, or will try and take away your children because of this. . ."

"The bastard," Magda says.

"I can't believe that he'd do anything like that," Allison protests unconvincingly. "No, I don't want to think about it."

"Let's hope it doesn't get to that point," says Bess, leading along a polished corridor to the benches where Mrs. Houseman and her lawyer are already seated. "I'm really encouraged by all the publicity you've generated. The rally, the newspaper articles were great ideas. My guess is that they really don't have that much on you. A few rumors, the fact that Magda did that interview. . . No, if the case starts out like this, with people already protesting, then I'm hoping the prosecutor will see that it's not to his advantage to pursue it."

Allison looks happier and Karen gives her a hug, but Magda doesn't feel as sanguine, looking at the stiff form of Mrs. Houseman on the other end of the bench. Magda doesn't sit, but paces for a few minutes in front of them and then goes down the hall to smoke a cigarette.

Wallace joins her. This is only the second time they've met, hardly enough to form an opinion on, but still she feels a liking for him. If only he didn't wear his hair like that; bowl-shaped and floppy, it obscures the clean cut of his jaw.

"I'm feeling very confident," he begins. This is exactly what he said the night before last, the first time she met him.

"Confidence seems to be raging like an epidemic among you lawyers," Magda cuts in a bit sharply. "Did you hear that pep talk Bess was giving Allison? It's a pile of shit. Of course they have something on her, they could practically arrest her right now with the information they have, for aiding and abetting a fugitive."

"Well, why haven't they, then?" Wallace counters. Really, she likes his style, arrogant of course, but without any of the professional distance Bess puts out. He treats her like she might even know what she's talking about.

"They subpoenaed Deb's mother, didn't they? That to me is pretty sure proof that they know who they're dealing with. They probably know who every single person in the Cutting Edge is. Look how they murdered that guy Ted yesterday." She can't help shivering, though she doesn't identify with him at all.

"How do you know they knew who he was? It was probably just a routine speeding ticket when he freaked out and pulled a gun. Those people get paranoid in a situation like that."

"I suppose you deal with the criminal element all the time," Magda says after a minute, not wanting to think of the man dead on the edge of the highway. Wallace is also sober.

"Not really. I haven't been out of law school very long. . ."

He looks at her with a self-deprecatory smile and she can't help smiling back. Something flares up quickly between them, but Wallace glances over at the group on the bench and restrains himself. "No, when

I said I was confident, I meant about your case. I'd be surprised if you ever had to come back here."

"I'll come back to cover the story if nothing else."

"Who are you planning to write it for?" Wallace names a few national papers. "I bet they'd be interested."

"I bet they would," Magda answers evasively. She'd been thinking of the *News* of course; why does she always think of the *News*? This is a hot story, she could use it to break out of her mold.

A deputy appears in the corridor in front of the bench.

"Allison Morris? Please follow me."

They all stand up and each in turn hugs her solemnly. Magda barely makes it back to her in time to whisper "good luck."

"Give it to 'em good," says Karen.

Five times Allison goes through the heavy wooden door and returns. The first time back she is shaking.

"You're right, it *is* intimidating," she mutters at large. She looks paler than before, or maybe it's only the strong lighting in the corridor. It makes all of them look a little peaked, thinks Magda, putting a hand to her cheek and glancing at Wallace.

"What's it like?" asks Holly. This is the first time she's spoken since they entered the courthouse. She looks worse than any of them, tall and ungainly, hunching over a book in the corner.

"It seems huge. . ." Allison begins, but there's no time to elaborate; the deputy is watching her severely.

"What did they ask you?" Bess asks.

"My name. I told them that, and my address. Then they asked me if I knew Deborah Houseman." She glances quickly at Mrs. Houseman, who stares at her shoes.

"Now just go back and read them this." Bess gives her a piece of paper.

Four more times Allison returns and Bess tells her the same thing. Out in the corridor they are mostly silent. Holly twists the ends of her scarf and tries to read; Magda smokes up half a pack of cigarettes, stubbing them out in the ash tray before they are finished. Karen finally begins to talk to Mrs. Houseman about the weather, but both of them keep breaking off and staring around. Wallace and the other lawyer stand a little apart, talking shop. Only Bess seems completely unconcerned; she reads from legal papers with her briefcase open on her lap. Magda studies her covertly. She can't help remembering how when she was in her freshman year at college she wanted to be in a sorority. She finally struck up an acquaintance with a sorority woman in her English class and was invited to dinner at her house. Magda dressed up, perhaps she even spent some of her scholarship money buying a new dress, only to find the women around the dinner table all wearing expensively casual sweaters and skirts. She remembers how they all asked her polite questions, averting their eyes from her flounces. She wasn't able to eat a bite. She was never asked back. Thinking of this, Magda smooths her Mexican shirt and stares down at her printed skirt. Dressing inappropriately is a habit she got from her mother, but she has cultivated it ever since, as a way of flaunting her style. All the same, well-dressed women her own age, like Bess in her tailored suit, still have the power to make her feel a little ridiculous.

While Allison is still inside the courtroom, several people from the rally, including Dennis and Lisa and Toni, join them on the bench.

"There you are," exclaims Toni. "They didn't even want to tell us where you were. We've been hunting all over. Is Allison inside?"

Their presence restores Magda. Not only are they casually dressed, but she knows, in spite of their differences, that they respect her. Self-confident once again, she explains what is going on and introduces them to Bess.

Then Toni takes out a notepad and begins to write. With studied off-handedness, she informs Magda in a whisper, "I'm going to write an article for *Challenge.*"

"No, you're not," Magda immediately snaps, though in a low tone. "I'm going to."

"You can't, Magda, you're one of the participants."

"So what? I know what's going on at least." Before Wallace first brought up the idea, the most Magda had imagined was a two-page spread in the *News*, written from a personal angle. But for the past fifteen minutes she has been plotting how she will get her story into the big Left periodicals, one of which is *Challenge.* She won't allow Toni to profit from this.

But Toni has never looked more aristocratically disdainful. Her thin beaked nose quivers. "You can't be writing for them, Magda," she explains in a whisper, as if to a child, "because I am. I called them up yesterday, and they said they'd be very interested in a story on the subject."

I should just punch her out and be done with it, Magda thinks, I should rip her notebook in half and. . ." There are other papers and magazines," is all she can manage.

And now Allison comes out for the last time. "They dismissed me," she says to Bess. She sags into place beside Magda. "He kept asking me what I had to hide and they all stared at me, and all the worst kinds of things kept occurring to me, like what if something happened to Katey and Ben and what about the women at the—"

"Could you excuse us, please?" Bess says loudly to the others. She takes Allison part way down the hall and motions for Magda to follow. She is the severe schoolteacher as she says, "Now, I know it's hard, but you've got to be careful. Don't bring up the shelter, for instance. I'm worried about it, too, especially worried that they might try and sub-poena someone else who works there who would tell them something."

"Margaret Ellen Jones," the deputy calls out.

Everyone looks around.

"My driver's license name," Magda says airily. "It even takes me back."

"Remember," says Bess. "We'll do the same thing with you as we did for Allison."

"Yeah, yeah," Magda mutters and sweeps through the door, past Toni and all of them.

Once inside, however, she is frightened. It *is* a huge room, and it seems filled with people. There is a large mahogany table in the center surrounded by jurors, with more of them lining the walls. There seem to be many more than the required twenty-three. A man who must be the prosecutor is the only one standing. He motions Magda to sit down at the one empty chair at the table. Next to her seat is the court stenographer, a slack-faced man with a curiously alert posture; he has his hands poised over a little machine in front of him.

Mr. Hanford introduces the jury foreman without giving him a name. "This is the foreman, Miss Jones. I presume your lawyer has given you some idea of how the grand jury operates?" His tone is less biting than his words suggest; he looks irritable, but not malevolent, rather like he'd like to get it all over with soon. He is middle-aged, about forty-five, and is not particularly well-dressed for a lawyer, Magda thinks. He is wearing a suit that is too light for October and a rather faded shirt. His back hair is long and brushed forward to hide his bald spot.

"Yes," says Magda. She tries to concentrate on the details of the room; the tall windows, the ornate seal high above a set of double doors at the back, the muffled atmosphere of investigation.

"I'm going to ask you some questions and I hope you'll be able to give me some answers."

Magda wants to study the faces of the jurors, but she feels too acutely conscious of their eyes on her to do much more than stare at the furnishings. In spite of herself, she keeps glancing at the dainty hands of the stenographic recorder, poised to take down her every word, should she speak.

"Can you tell us your name, Miss Jones?" he asks, absurdly redundant.

She tells them, wishing she could force her voice louder; it seems strangely to want to sink back down her throat halfway through "Jones."

"And your address, please."

Then suddenly Magda can't remember; is she supposed to tell them this or not? Would this force her to answer all of their questions?

"Your address, please, Miss Jones. Do you *have* an address?"

She hears a couple of people behind her titter. This is terrible, to put people behind her where she can't see them. She'll show them. But now, just now, she can't quite remember her address. She has lived in so many places. What if she tells them the wrong one? She feels her armpits pouring sweat; what an odd sensation, as if a dike wall sprouted leaks.

"Your address, Miss Jones."

"I refuse," she stammers, knowing that these words are somehow the beginning of something important, some important sentence that will free her from this ordeal. But before she can get out the rest, she sees the stenographer's fingers pause, and in that pause, all the rest of the words fly out of her mind.

"You refuse to give your address, Miss Jones?" The prosecutor mocks her dispiritedly, inviting the jury to join him. "On what grounds, may I ask?"

"Grounds," that's the word; and then it comes to her and she spits it out before the words can escape her again. "I refuse to answer on the grounds that it may incriminate me."

Except, that's the Fifth Amendment and isn't she supposed to be taking the First? She stumbles on, "I mean, I'm a journalist and I. . ."

The prosecutor, surprisingly, stops her. "All right, all right, that's enough. You are excused for the present, Miss Jones."

Magda stares at him, not understanding. Is this all, then?

"You may go, I said."

Slowly she gets up and walks to the door. She opens it to find even more people from the rally crowding the hall. They all seem to make a rush for her. She feels someone's arm around her waist; someone else is hanging on her arm. She shakes them off and goes over to Bess and Wallace.

"What a strange experience," Magda says wonderingly. "My brain just shut down or something."

"What did they ask you? Don't you have to go back?"

"No, they dismissed me, too."

"What did they ask you?"

"Just my name and address. I didn't give them my address." Magda pauses; she can't quite bring herself to say she forgot it. "I didn't want to tell them anything. He let me go."

"I knew it," exults Wallace. "He knows he can't get her, so he's not even trying."

"That's all for the two of you today," Bess says slowly. "We'll see what they pull next."

"Mrs. Mary Houseman," the deputy announces. The thin woman in the well-pressed, shabby dress ignores them all as she walks stiffly past.

Allison and Magda look at each other. "I keep forgetting we're not the only ones," Allison says miserably.

"She's going to take the Fifth, too," Bess says to console them. "She's got a good lawyer."

"She doesn't look like she wants to have anything to do with us," Magda notes. "But we could support her, too."

"She'll have to deal with it in her own way," Bess says. "Do you want to wait for her?"

"We should. . ." Allison begins, but their supporters are urging them away.

"Let's have a drink to celebrate," Dennis proposes.

"Come on, Allison," Magda says. "Let's get out of here before they change their minds."

"You go ahead. I want to wait for her."

Magda is borne away by a tide of friends and supporters; looking back, she sees Holly and Allison sit back down on the bench, as if prepared for a long wait.

Another day, Magda thinks grumpily Monday morning as she lurches up from her sleeping bag on the floor at Allison's. Nothing happened over the weekend, but today something is sure to break. From here she can see the clock on the dining room wall. Eight o'clock. Ugh. She glances over at Holly, a long lump on the couch. Holly wouldn't wake up even though a dozen kids were running back and forth through the upstairs bedrooms. Holly can sleep through anything. Magda used to think she could too, but that was before she began to stay at Allison's, back when she'd just had to contend with traffic outside, garbage collectors, and doors slamming in other parts of the apartment building.

"Magda," says Allison, coming into the living room, fully dressed in a crisp pair of cords and a flannel shirt. "You're up."

Magda glowers at her from the floor.

"You look like a crocus or something, emerging from the earth."

"I feel like a piece of shit." Magda struggles to stand up from the sleeping bag. "Holly and I stayed up talking for a while after you went to bed."

"Hi, Magpie." This is Ben, running downstairs and through the living room.

"Hi," Magda croaks like a bird. This is an old joke of theirs, but today it sounds authentically high and croaky.

"Did you keep drinking last night?" Allison asks sympathetically.

"Don't remind me. . . I threw the bottle away before I went to sleep. I hate waking up with empty bottles around, it's so end-of-the-road, don't you think?"

"Have some breakfast with us, you'll feel better."

"Ugh, nothing to eat. . . no, I think I'll go home for a while, sleep a little more and then take a shower. . ."

"Sounds good. I'm going to try and make it to the shop today. I think I'll just let Holly sleep. Remember that we have a meeting with Bess and Wallace at two, though."

"Right. I'll be there." Magda fumbles for her clothes and staggers into the downstairs bathroom.

"Hey!" says Katey. She is on the pot, indignant.

"It's only me."

"Go away, I want to be alone."

"Oh, all right." Magda picks up one of her socks which has fallen to the floor and stumbles out again. Modesty in an eight-year-old? Was she like that when she was eight? No, of course not. She and her mother and her sister lived in a small house, with two bedrooms and one bath. They wouldn't have thought of being modest, shielding themselves. "We're all girls, here," her mother used to say. They traded clothes, advice, make-up. . . You couldn't shut the door on anybody, much less lock it.

Upstairs, in the second bathroom, Magda shuts the door and locks it.

Back in her own apartment again, Magda sees that her herb garden is not doing well. She's been in and out for the last week, but has forgotten to water it. Maybe it's not too late, though, maybe the seeds have returned to dormancy temporarily in their little dry balls of earth. Magda waters them thoroughly, then takes her mail into the bedroom and falls into bed, fully dressed. She is so exhausted that she's not even sure whether she has a hangover, or whether it's not just accumulated tiredness knotting itself at the back of her neck.

How much did they drink, anyway? A couple of beers with dinner, and then some rum afterwards. Later, she and Holly had finished up the rum, somewhere in there, though, they'd had a few more beers. . . . Well, don't think about it. Worth it though, talking to Holly. . . . She hadn't realized before what an interesting woman she was, she'd kept so quiet before. Holly said she admired Magda because she was a writer. I've always wanted to write, Holly said, and then later, she admitted that she did write, short stories and a journal. But they're not very good, she'd laughed.

Holly's hair is blonde, like Toni's, but darker, richer. Had Magda touched it? She feels as if she had. . . How had Holly ever gotten hooked up with that guy James? That was something Holly could write about— coming home to find somebody out cold with a needle in his arm, or the stereo gone. Beautiful hair and eyes. . . Toni is washed out next to Holly.

Magda wakes to the phone ringing, still clutching her unread mail.

"Hello?"

"Magda? It's me, Toni."

"Oh. . . hi. . . I just woke up." She rubs her eyes, sees that one of the letters in her hand is from Paul. She hadn't noticed it before, had thought it was all bills and junk mail. Paul.

"Magda?"

"Yeah, I'm here. . . just a little spaced, sorry."

"Maybe this isn't a good time to call you."

"Yeah, it's okay, it's fine. Go ahead, what is it?"

"Well, you don't have to sound so impatient. I just called to talk."

"Sorry, I didn't mean to sound impatient," Magda says impatiently. "I guess I've just been talking on the phone too much, you know, relaying information mostly, that kind of talking. . ." What *does* Toni want? Magda begins to tear open Paul's letter.

"Well, I guess what I wanted to talk about was. . . well, the question of careers. . ."

"*What?*"

"Okay, I'll tell you. I'm feeling guilty about what I did to you. . . getting the okay from *Challenge* to write up your case. I just thought of it as a way of advancing myself, I mean, I knew the background, the people involved. . . You know I've been trying to get into a national magazine for months. . ."

"No, I didn't know."

"We haven't been talking much lately. . . maybe we could start again. . . . I think you want to get out of the *News* as badly as I do, at least I hope you do, I'm not really sure. . . Magda?"

("Dear Magda: I could hardly believe your letter, much less what I've been hearing from other people. You subpoenaed? How could you be so stupid, to go around interviewing some terrorist groupie?")

"Huh? Yeah, I'm here."

"Well, don't you think it would be better if we started working together, giving each other leads, reading each other's stuff. . . I'm serious, I want a career in political journalism, I want to be a free-lance journalist. . . I don't want to stay stuck in Seattle all my life and I know you don't either."

"Look, Toni, I appreciate your concern, but I've got other things on my mind just now. . . the little matter of a grand jury subpoena, for instance. I may go to jail, and if I don't, the FBI is going to be watching me pretty closely."

"You're *not* going to jail—it'll never get that far."

"That's what you say. . . . You wouldn't go to jail, not with that family of yours backing you up, I don't have any kind of name of any important relatives."

"My family has nothing to do with it." Magda can hear Toni breathing hard, trying to control herself. "I'm just saying you won't go to jail, it's impossible. You can fight it."

"If I'm fighting it, how can I have time to write about it?"

"Writing about it is another way of fighting it." Toni is no longer trying to control herself; her nasal voice, as Magda notes in bitter satisfaction, is rising angrily. "Jesus, Magda, why do you always treat me as if I'm your enemy?"

"I'll talk to you later, Toni. I'm busy right now." Busy being attacked by Paul from a sheet of paper.

"Oh, go fuck yourself."

Why do they all hate me, why is nothing I do good enough for them? They don't have the grand jury breathing down their necks. . . . She crumples Paul's letter into a ball and throws it across the room; she follows suit, landing on the sofa in a wadded heap of tears. "How could you be so stupid—interviewing a terrorist groupie?" A woman can't be a serious revolutionary, according to Paul, a woman can't be a serious anything, not even a serious fuck. Magda certainly wasn't a serious fuck to him, she wasn't a serious anything.

And Toni too—Magda will never measure up to Toni's standards, it just isn't possible. As she lies on the sofa, Magda can see it all—Toni a famous journalist in a few years, while she, Magda, a much better writer but without the connections, struggles on at the *News* (if the *News* can exist without Toni's money), unrecognized, unpaid, unread. . . .

The phone rings again.

"Hello," Magda answers, rather wobbly.

"Are you all right, Magda? This is Holly."

"Oh Holly, it's nice to hear your voice." Magda begins to cry again. "No, I'm not doing too well. I feel awful, my head hurts and nobody likes me." Of course, as she says this she has to laugh a little. "Just feeling sorry for myself, that's all."

Holly's voice is deeply soft on the other end. "I hope you don't feel bad about last night. . . I called to tell you how much I liked it. . . like talking to you. . . and everything."

As far as Magda can remember, they just kissed a few times, nothing to get excited about. She hopes Holly isn't taking it too seriously.

"I liked talking to you, too. . . . You've had such an interesting life."

"Me, are you kidding? You're the one! Well, I don't want to bother you, I just wanted to let you know. . ."

"Thank you. . . listen, do you have a minute? I really need to talk to somebody. Can you come over?"

"Well, I should go to the shop. . . but maybe for a little while. . . ." She sounds so happy that Magda is touched. Some people like her, after all. After they've hung up, she picks up Paul's letter on the way to the bathroom and drops it in the toilet.

"Don't you fucking presume to tell me what to do," she mutters as she flushes it down.

Eight: Immunity

Holly stretches out on Magda's blood-red sofa, lanky in jeans and a too short sweater, her blonde hair like gold in the mid-morning sun. She is wearing very strong-looking hiking boots, well-scuffed, which she's careful to keep off the velvet.

She doesn't judge Toni or Paul, but neither is she unpartisan. She makes sympathetic noises while Magda, fresh out of the shower and in her kimono strides back and forth in front of her. Holly's presence is immensely soothing to Magda. This is what she's been needing—someone to talk to, someone who will just let her talk, let her spill it all out, how bad she's been feeling, how let down, how pressured to do the right thing.

"I can't tell you how good it feels to get it all off my chest," she says when she is through with her story. "I get to feeling paranoid when I have to keep things bottled up."

Holly blushes. "I thought, I guess I thought you and Allison talked all the time."

"No, no. . . I like Allison a lot, of course. But she's so. . .business-like, she keeps things on the track."

"I know. But I think it's that she's had to become that way, or-ganized and everything. I admire her so much, keeping her kids together, starting a business—you know it was her idea, and then all the stuff she's involved in, the shelter and the co-op and everything."

"Yeah, I know, it's great," breaks in Magda, feeling a little put out. She doesn't want to talk about Allison and her guilty volunteering. Of course Magda feels better having gotten everything about Toni and Paul out in the open, but. . . has she really made Holly see how impossible her situation is? No, probably not—it would take days to explain—but right now she's exhausted and it's time to get ready for the meeting with the lawyers.

All the same, it moves her to see Holly sprawled out on her sofa, her hiking boots hanging over the side, absurdly big at the end of her thin, straight legs. She has a young, sweet face; she is much younger-looking than twenty-six. Magda can understand the maternal impulse Holly inspires in Allison; in spite of having been the one to pour out her troubles, Magda feels almost motherly, too. She also feels large and dramatic, wearing her kimono, like an opera singer, her big breasts slightly revealed.

She goes over to Holly, full of her own power. "Thanks for listening to me spout off."

"Oh no. . . I mean, it was interesting," Holly says, choked and whispery.

Magda kisses her, meaning it to be a light kiss—the way they kissed the night before— a light, sweet, good-night kiss. Holly's response surprises her; Holly shudders, makes a deep kind of noise in her throat, and suddenly she has Magda's kimono open and her face between Magda's breasts.

Magda pulls away. "If I didn't have to get to this damn meeting. . ." she jokes, but she too is breathing a little faster than usual. She rewraps her kimono.

Holly sits up straight, not looking at Magda. "Yes, I've got to get to the shop."

They are both awkward, trying to get back to where they were a few minutes before. But at the door Magda once again feels powerful and sexy, and extremely pleased with herself. "See you tonight?"

Holly nods, hardly looking at her, but smiling.

In front of the elevators in Bess' office building, Magda sees Allison, and her first thought is to make a joke about her new conquest. She hasn't had a woman lover since Toni and she's excited. Holly's blonde hair, her wide mouth, her trustfulness. . . she never would have imagined it, but now that it's happened, Magda is smug and amused. Forget men. . . women are, in every way, finer, softer, more responsive, more receptive.

Magda opens her mouth to speak, but Allison cuts in first. "Well, did you get it?"

"The subpoena."

"Another one? No."

"Then it's just me," Allison says bitterly. "I'm the one they want. They've dropped you." Her round face is tight and anxious; she leans into a corner of the elevator.

"So, they're going through with it," is all Magda can think to say. She should feel pleased that she's free now, but strangely enough she is a little peeved. "When do you have to appear?"

"Wednesday."

"So soon. . ."

"Magda, I could be in jail by the end of the week!" Allison flails her arms suddenly as if even the elevator makes her feel claustrophobic. "I'm just not prepared."

Magda grabs her arms and holds. There is nothing sexual about it and yet for an instant Magda feels profoundly shaken. That this is not a play, but real; that Allison is going to suffer out the consequences of her ignorance and idealism.

"We'll think of something, the lawyers will. It will be all right, don't cry." But even as she consoles Allison, the moment of true feeling passes and all Magda can think of is the dramatic possibilities of the action, the story it will make.

The lawyers' faces reflect the concerns of their two separate cases: Bess is the more upset, of course, while Wallace struggles to hide his satisfaction over the outcome of his successful maneuvering. The discussion turns immediately to the possibility of Allison's imprisonment.

"Might as well go to prison," Allison remarks morbidly.

"Why do you say that?" Bess wants to know. Today she is wearing another pinstriped shirt with a small black tie. Her earrings are tiny pearls. She is crisply sympathetic, but disapproving of such fatalism.

"I'd get away from Tom at least. He's been calling or coming over every night since he heard."

Magda finally met Tom Saturday night, when several of the *News* people and the support group were sitting around in Allison's kitchen. They were discussing publicity about the grand jury and drinking beer when the doorbell rang.

"It's Tom, I bet," muttered Allison. "Somebody else answer it, please. Give me a minute to get ready."

Magda volunteered, swaggering over to throw the door open. Outside stood a tall, well-tailored blonde man.

"Hi. Are you the FBI or Allison's ex?"

"I'd like to speak to Allison, please. Is she here?"

"Yeah, come on in."

Allison introduced him rather solemnly to everyone around the kitchen table. He shook hands with the men, trying hard to be genial.

"Kids around?" he asked.

"No, they're at a friend's watching TV."

Magda saw something flash between them, then Allison said, "Well, how did I know you'd want to see them? You didn't call to say you'd be coming over until an hour ago—"

"Allison, I've tried calling you many times—here, at the shop—you're never there, either. I don't know where you are. I don't know how you can stay in business if you're never there. . ."

"Look, do you want to go into the other room? I'm sure my friends don't want to sit in on a pseudo-business discussion between us."

So Magda didn't hear the rest of the conversation, short as it was. Only about ten minutes after Allison and Tom left the kitchen, they heard the front door slam and Allison came slowly back in. Nobody wanted to ask her about it. "He'll get over it," she said, taking her place once again at the table.

But obviously he isn't getting over it. Besides suggesting to his bank officer friend that they go ahead and repossess the xerox machine, he is threatening to take her to court in a custody case. Allison tells them this dully, almost uncomprehendingly; she says "children," not "Katey and Ben." Her voice is full of flat despair.

"Maybe I could talk to him" Bess suggests.

"Oh, would you?"

Oh, would you? Magda echoes to herself nastily. Oh, would you, kind, sweet Bessie? Sweet-talk or stiff-arm my ex-husband into giving me and my children the right to exist?

Magda turns to Wallace. "What's going to happen to me now?"

"Nothing, I hope." He is matter-of-fact and cool, not like Bess with her pretense at womanly sympathy. He *is* a little wimpy-looking, with his carefully trimmed bowl haircut and his wire-rims, but she feels comfortable with him. And grateful. Hasn't he been the one responsible for freeing her? Magda is still surprised that she feels so let down. Did she want to go to prison for her stupid interview? No, but it would have been nice to have remained in the game a bit longer. Somehow it has all been too easy.

"Nothing," Wallace repeats, "except write those articles and get the word out."

"Right. . . Allison, I know it doesn't help, but I wish it were me instead of you."

"Don't worry about me," Allison says, smiling gratefully at her. She has recovered herself. "I've talked to my mother and she's agreed to come and stay with the kids for however long I'm. . . away. As for

115

the business, well, we may lose it, but. . ." she chokes a little on the words, "I'm determined to see this thing through. Whatever happens."

"I admire you more than I can say," Bess approves.

Magda casts an ironic look over at Wallace, but even he is staring in admiration at Allison.

"What are you doing tomorrow night?" Wallace asks Magda as the two of them leave the office.

"Helping Allison prepare, I guess. . . . It's funny," Magda goes on, not realizing at first that her lawyer is, in fact, asking her for a date, "I feel so let down. Passed by. I know it's irrational but it sort of pisses me off that the prosecutor didn't think I was important enough to keep on the hook."

"You're a funny woman," Wallace laughs, pushing his bangs away from his eyes. "You'll do more good out of jail, you know."

"Oh, I know. . ." With a start, Magda understands that he is interested in her, that his question was a question about seeing her separately from the case. Well, isn't this interesting. First Holly, and now Wallace. Though nothing may happen with either of them. . .

"About tomorrow night. . ."

"Yes?"

"I'm free."

That evening, back at Allison's house, Magda and Holly make dinner for the five of them. Afterwards Magda urges Allison to take the kids to a movie. Katey, Ben, and Holly, who has been on the verge of touching Magda all evening, look at her gratefully.

Allison hesitates. "I thought you wanted to go to the shop and finish that new flyer?"

"That can wait until tomorrow. It's almost done, isn't it?"

"Yeah, mom, let's go to a movie!"

"Okay," Allison smiles wanly. "I guess I don't need much persuading. I think I'd like to just sit and think of something else, for a change."

Magda and Holly wash up the dishes while Allison and the kids get ready to leave. In low tones, they discuss the case again. Allison has said little to Holly about what happened, and of course at the dinner table there was no discussion about going to jail. "I'm going to tell them," Allison said. "Pretty soon."

"And Mrs. Houseman's been subpoenaed again?"

"Yes. That's even harder to imagine—her going to jail."

"You know, we waited for her after her court appearance, but when she came out, she walked right by us."

"That's what Allison said. I guess she blames us somehow. But our publicity is helping her, too."

"How do you feel, now that you're off?"

Magda shrugs. "It's a victory, isn't it? At least that's what Wallace says. . ." It's on the tip of her tongue to tell Holly about him and his invitation, but she holds back. No sense making complications before they exist. She wants to go through with whatever happens—with both of them. Will anything happen, though? While she was amorous earlier today, now, in spite of the fact that she's engineered Allison out of the house Magda feels hesitant. She and Toni just fell into each other's arms; she can't quite imagine that with Holly.

Holly, however, is hardly hesitant. As soon as Allison and the kids are out of the house, she says, more forthrightly than Magda suspected she was capable of being, "I'm very attracted to you."

Magda laughs, a little uneasily. She feels very conscious somehow of her big breasts under her sweater and vest, remembering how Holly pulled open her kimono this morning and kissed them. Reaching out to touch Holly's silky hair, she drops her dish towel. They both bend for it and knock heads. That breaks the tension.

"Want a beer? Want to take a beer and go into the living room?"

Holly smiles, she has a lovely wide mouth, a full lower lip. "Sure, I'll get them."

On the living room sofa Holly asks, "Are you, I mean, do you, well, are you attracted to me?"

"Yes," says Magda, unusually at a loss for words.

"I guess you've been with other women?"

"Yes, a few."

"I haven't been with anybody since. . . James. Before I was married, I, uhm, used to kiss my girl friend. In junior high." Holly giggles; her courage in pursuing this dangerous subject is making her slightly punchy. "I guess this sounds stupid?"

"No, no." But there is an awkwardness. They are neither touching nor not touching on the sofa. Magda drinks her beer in quick gulps and says nothing. She is wet inside her pants. But she feels as if Holly is waiting for her to make the first move.

"The women I was with were lesbians," Magda explains, surprised at how small and breathy her voice is. What she means is that they always took the first step. They knew what to do; they kissed her and put their hand between her legs. After that it was easy. She doesn't tell Holly this, though, and wonders at her own passivity. Maybe it's that she doesn't really feel attracted to Holly.

"I've never known any lesbians," Hollys says. "My friend and I didn't think like that. We didn't have any boyfriends, so we kissed and pretended the other one was a boy."

"Ah yes, gotta have a man. . ." They both laugh, and for a minute it seems as if anything and everything might happen; then the moment is gone and they are both as stiff and far apart as ever. Magda looks at the clock; already Allison has been gone half an hour. This is ridiculous, she thinks, you can't just talk yourself into a sexual experience. All she has to do is say, Look Holly, I really don't feel like getting into this. And they could turn on the television or something. . . . She tries to think about the flyer, the possibility of Allison going to jail, Wallace, everything she has to do tomorrow. She feels the tenseness between her legs subside.

"Want another beer?" Holly asks.

"All right."

While Holly is gone, Magda gets up and turns on the TV. She's searching for the program guide when Holly returns. Nothing doing, Magda has decided, and is determined to ignore Holly's discouraged look. "This might be good," she suggests, pointing to the screen.

"I hate TV."

"Oh." Magda wavers a minute, then turns it off and lights a cigarette. The thought goes briefly through her mind that she could get into an argument with Holly ("Think you're too good for mass culture?"); instead; she sits down heavily in a chair across the room and picks up the paper again.

There is a long silence. Allison must have been gone an hour by now. God, another hour and a half to get through. Why did Magda ever suggest a movie, or why didn't she go, too? Nothing is going to happen with Holly, and what's more, Magda doesn't want it to.

"What did you do with your lesbian friends?"

Magda puts the paper down and looks across the room at Holly, tall, knobby, blonde, silky, upright on the sofa with her big hands clenched together.

"Holly," she says. "I think it's a mistake."

"You *said* you felt attracted to me."

"I know, but. . . I don't know if I really do."

"I just asked you what you did with your friends. Can't you even tell me that?"

"Okay, I guess. . . Well, there was Nancy. . ." Magda thinks of Nancy with her swimmer's back and her short plump thighs, and the throbbing starts to come back into her groin. "I'll get us another couple of beers and then I'll tell you," she murmurs desperately.

In the kitchen Magda takes out the last two bottles from the carton, then closes the refrigerator and stands leaning against it. She doesn't know what to do; she doesn't know how to do it.

Holly comes into the kitchen behind her and puts her arms around Magda's shoulders. "I don't want to make you feel bad."

"I feel terrible. I feel like an adolescent. I don't know what I want."

"I know what I want," says Holly, turning her around. "I want to know what comes after the kissing." With terrible earnestness she pushes Magda up against the refrigerator and begins to kiss her.

"Well, now you know," says Magda, still breathless as they lie in Allison's room, on her bed. Holly lies next to her, her long body flushed and damp. Her legs are still apart, the dark blonde hair between them soaked.

"Uhm." Holly stretches luxuriously. "Isn't this a great bed? Let's ask Allison if she wants the sofa tonight."

Magda laughs, slowly coming back to herself. "I don't know if we should tell her."

"Why not?"

"I don't know."

Holly rolls over and takes one of Magda's nipples in her mouth.

"Holly, we've got to get up. I don't know how long we've been here, but Allison and the kids. . ."

"I know, I know. I just want to do it a little more, okay?"

How can Magda say no? She hasn't felt so good in weeks. All the tension resolved, her body relaxed, floating. She feels ready to come again, and wants to.

The front door opens. "Hello, hello?" calls Allison. The kids are already running up the stairs.

Both Magda and Holly leap out of bed. Holly closes the bedroom door, then Magda opens it hastily to call, "We're upstairs, down in a minute."

They jump into their clothes but are still half-dressed when Allison opens the door.

"Oh," she says, trying not to look at Magda's bare breasts and Holly's legs. "Sorry." She closes the door.

"Oh God," Magda mutters. "I knew, I just knew this would happen." For some reason she feels almost angry at Holly and leaves the room without her.

Katey, plump and curly-haired, is standing on one leg outside the door. "What were you guys doing in there?"

"Giving massages," says Magda airily. "Do you like massages?"

"What's a massage?"

"Making your sore muscles feel good."

"Oh," Katey says uncertainly. "Like if you fall off your bike?"

"Right."

Allison is in the kitchen, putting away the empty beer bottles for recycling. "You could have at least saved me a beer," she says pleasantly.

"I'll run to the store and get some more," Holly says, appearing briefly behind Magda.

"You don't have to. . ." Allison begins, but Holly is already racing for the door.

"Actually, I'd rather have tea," Allison says, putting the kettle on. "You?"

"I'll wait for the beer," Magda sits on a stool and digs up a cigarette. "How was the movie?"

"Pretty awful, but the kids liked it." Allison reaches for a mug from the cupboard; stretching, one of the snaps on her overalls pops. She's definitely getting fatter, Magda thinks abstractedly, and pulls in her own stomach.

"Magda, I'm sorry I came in like that. I should have known. . . the door being closed. . ."

"Nothing to be sorry about."

Half-turned away, Allison says, "I didn't know that either of you were. . ."

"Lesbians? I don't know if we are. I mean, I've had. . . we just sort of fell into it."

"I think it's great," Allison assures her, her round face bursting with suppressed curiosity. "I was just surprised."

"Me too. I didn't know it was coming until today."

Allison sits down at the table across from her. "It's not you who surprises me as much as Holly. It all came flashing through my mind how little I know her. She keeps so much to herself."

Magda nods. She doesn't feel much like talking for some reason. She feels a little dazed.

"Do you want my bed tonight?"

"Oh no. . . I was thinking about going home tonight. Maybe Holly will come with me. Give you a chance to be alone with the kids. . ."

"I told them tonight. Sort of." Allison gets up again to make the tea. "Kids are funny, aren't they? They couldn't really take it in. They wanted to know if they would be able to visit me, then they wanted to know when Grandma was coming. I guess I can't really take it in, either. I somehow can't imagine not seeing them."

"How'd your mother take it?"

"Well, I suppose she's less supportive of me politically than enraged about the fact that her *daughter* is being harassed. I haven't told her all the details. She wouldn't want to know them either. She keeps saying, 'If your father were alive,' though what he could possibly do is your guess as good as mine. But she's been like that ever since he died. Why, I don't know. I can't remember her ever asking his advice, ever. . . . Have you told your parents?"

"I just have a mother, too, and no, not yet. I wanted to see what happened first. And it's not the kind of thing she'd read about in the paper. I guess I should call her. . . she won't understand a thing about it, of course."

"No." Suddenly Allison looks exhausted. "I have to pick her up at the airport tomorrow morning. I guess we can do the flyers after that?"

"Sure. Are you going upstairs? Good-night, then." Magda stands and they hug, in a weary kind of solidarity. In spite of everything they've been through, they have never really gotten close. They don't have that much in common, they don't think the same way. . . . I could have tried harder to get to know her, Magda thinks, but I didn't. And now she feels at the end of something. Allison will have to play her part alone. This good-night hug is more of a real good-bye.

Magda is waiting by the door when Holly comes in with the six-pack.

"Why don't you put that in the refrigerator and come home with me?"

It's flattering but a little terrifying to see how full of love Holly's eyes are. "Allison?"

"Allison's gone to bed. She understands."

Do I? thinks Magda.

But love is hardly on Magda's mind by the time they get back to her apartment. She has been seized with the desire to talk to her mother.

"Do you mind?" she asks Holly.

"Oh no, I'll just sit here and read. . . but it's so late. Won't it be almost midnight there?"

"She stays up late."

When did Magda last call her mother, anyway? Was it as long ago as Mother's Day? But she had sent a card in August, on her birthday. . . and there had been a few letters. . . . Her mother lives alone now that Audrey has finally left home. Still, Aunt Madge lives down the street and even Audrey is only ten minutes across town. It isn't that Magda feels sorry for her, her mother isn't the kind you'd feel sorry for. All the same she can inspire guilt. She holds strictly to convention; as long as Magda remembers birthdays and holidays, answers all her letters, her mother is satisfied. Let Magda forget to send an Easter card, though, and for the next six months she has to face recriminations in every letter, her mother calling up to say, "I hope you're not too busy to talk."

In the past all these cards and anniversaries were a source of contention, as Magda drove back and forth across the country, working for different newspapers. "You were in New Orleans, Maggie Ellen, and you didn't even send a postcard for my collection!" There was one year when Magda broke off contact completely, the year she came to Seattle, changed her name, and started working for the *News*. She didn't even tell her mother her phone number. Lately they've been on better terms; her mother is even planning to visit her this Christmas. And Magda keeps her anniversaries and holdays straight with the aid of a calendar she calls "Mother."

"Maggie Ellen! What a surprise, darling. I was just about to turn in."

"Hi, Ma. What's new?"

"Well, I don't know—the usual, I guess. Audrey's met a nice man, she likes him quite a bit. . . . Oh and say, your Aunt Madge went and bought a little foreign car, some little Japanese thing."

Aunt Madge is ten years her mother's senior, sixty or sixty-one. "Ma, she never goes anywhere. What's she going to do with a new car?"

"She does too get around. You talk as if she's died and gone to heaven. I never would have believed she'd buy such a *little* car, though. She said she was going to beat the gas prices, but I wouldn't feel *safe* in one of those little bugs, would you? They give you absolutely no protection, you know—somebody just taps you from behind and you're an accordion. . ."

Her mother has an Oldsmobile. Magda has an old Valiant. They discuss the merits of large versus small for some time. Magda turns her clock away so that it doesn't keep reminding her of a cash register. She should have called collect—her mother can talk for hours.

"Ma. . . the reason I called. . ."

"Is something wrong?"

"No, not wrong, but well, it's very interesting."

In general her mother doesn't find politics interesting. In fact, she finds the existence of rival points of view on important matters distressing. To argue about large and small cars is one thing, but to argue about the government is another. She is a Republican because she has always been one—it has nothing to do with voting, because she often forgets to vote, and nothing to do with the policies that come down from even Republican governments. It's like being white or a Methodist, a fact of existence.

Magda has given her mother a subscription to the *News*, but she doubts that her mother reads it. Though lately she has seemed less inclined to ask why Magda doesn't get a job on one of the "really big" newspapers. And even that was a step up from her previous line of questioning about marriage and children.

"Well, it's like this," Magda begins, looking quickly at Holly, stretched out under a newspaper on the red sofa. Is she falling asleep? What is she really asking her mother for anyway? Approval in some way for having done the right thing? She'll never get that; her mother has no conception of the political subtleties of the Left. All she will want to know is whether Magda is in any trouble.

"But you're all right now, aren't you?"

Better not explain that she could still be subpoenaed again if the attorney general gives the say-so. "Yeah, I'm fine. I'm just trying to write about it. . ."

"You'll send me a clipping, won't you, Maggie Ellen? You know I keep everything you send me. . ." her mother trails off cheerfully and vaguely, reducing Magda's experience to something she can put in a scrapbook. It's all fodder for the relatives; no one understands what she's doing, but they do respect the reality of a printed page. As long as Magda keeps adding to the scrapbook, she's still a journalist, still some kind of eccentric success. Would her mother want her to send clippings if she were going to jail? Probably not. Daughters in jail are best kept away from relatives' scrutiny and gossip. Magda can't imagine her mother swooping down like Allison's to lend support. She wonders, not for the first time, what her father would have said about what she's doing. Whether he would show any sign of understanding her politics—or whether he would be as right wing as her mother's dentist, Dr. Hubert.

When they finally say good-bye, however, there is an extra twinge of concern in her mother's voice. "You will keep me posted, won't you, Maggie Ellen? And please be careful. . . keep out of these things from now on. I know you just got dragged into it without knowing, but if you'd be a little more careful about your friends. . ."

"Okay, okay. Yeah, I'll be careful. I'll keep you posted." I'll send you a telegram every day if you want: "Still at large, Maggie Ellen."

Holly has fallen asleep, but wakes immediately when Magda bends over her. Her face is soft and young, her eyes the most startling dark blue. Magda wishes she felt more in the mood for lovemaking, not so weighed down by the past and her longing for the kind of understanding she has never had and never will. Holly really is beautiful, but after the phone conversation Magda is restless and irritable and sad. More than that, she has a desire to lash out in her frustration.

Holly picks up on Magda's energy as sexual, though, and pulls her down to her. She has half Magda's clothes off before Magda can resist.

She doesn't resist but her heart isn't in it. Even as she caresses Holly's body and listens to her moan, she thinks of the next day. Dinner with Wallace—that should be interesting. As Holly goes down on her, Magda gives into the impulse to imagine that it's Wallace's tongue, Wallace's fingers. That gets her more excited than Holly's eager and fumbling explorations, and she is strangely disappointed when she comes without the familiar hard thrust inside her.

"I can't believe you were celibate so long," she teases gently when Holly has finished and is lying spent across her body.

"I feel like I've been celibate my whole life long."

"What about James?"

"That was terrible, let's not talk about that."

"Why? What was he like?" Magda rearranges herself more comfortably so that she can admire Holly's long clean limbs, the way her pelvic bones protrude.

"Fucked me and went to sleep," Holly says shortly. "Like all men."

"I thought you said you'd never been with anybody else."

"Why talk about it? I had the usual experiences in the back seat." Holly sits up and hunches over. Her vertebrae stand out like a skeleton's. "But that's all over now."

Magda has a perverse desire to continue. "There are some men who can make you feel great. You should try one sometime."

"I'm not interested in men," Holly mutters, looking at the bottom of one large foot. "I'm a lesbian now."

"Well, I'm not."

Holly turns slowly, her great blue eyes filling. "Does that mean you're interested in someone else?"

"No, of course not." Satisfied, Magda? she thinks irritably. Now that you've hurt her feelings? "I'm trying to be honest," she adds, trying to soften her voice.

Holly blinks back tears. "I don't want to be with any men."

"I know, I know. I just want to be with you, too," Magda comforts her, holding her tightly. I'll break my date with Wallace, what can I be thinking of, to want to get involved with some man and hurt Holly? She's all I want, I should be satisfied.

All the same, when Magda finally drifts into a weary and uneasy sleep, it's Wallace she's dreaming of, Wallace with his man's arms around her, tight.

Nine: Seduction

She can never say what triggers it—the figure of a banker, maybe, in a three-piece suit, passing through black glass doors deep into some anonymous steel and concrete skyscrapers; a newspaper headline that screams *"MILLIONS"* or *"MILLIONS LOST."* It's nothing so simple as an attractive window display—or the word *"SALE"* blazoning across plate glass. Greed or even envy (waiting to cross the street on a corner crowded with stilt-heeled secretaries in velvet jackets) she would be ashamed of. It's something more; it comes out of anger, powerlessness, the desire to get them. Or get hers.

I should never go downtown, Magda thinks. She has parked her car and is walking to Wallace's office along a street of quietly ostentatious shop windows. She doesn't need more clothes, she's late anyway—still, she finds herself turning into one of the biggest department stores.

The escalator carries her up past walls of mirrors, but Magda stares straight ahead, unlike the other shoppers who steal quick and frequent glances at their reflections. It will be the same in the dressing room; she will undress, dress and undress and dress with blank haste, keeping her back to the tall mirrors.

She gets off at the second floor, passes automatically through section after section until she comes to a banner that reads "Funky Fashions." Already she is losing all discrimination, it always happens this way. She can no longer see the clothes as separate objects, each blouse, each pair of pants covering a possible body somewhere in the world. It's as if she begins to feel, rather than see, a maze of colors, a labyrinth of racks tracking back and forth across softly carpeted floors. She moves unerringly through the maze to the number thirteens.

This is ridiculous. I'm going to be late.

Her fingers rub and pull at the fabrics. She begins to drape silks, cottons, and wools over her arm. Such a small dent in the big store. As far as the eye can see—clothes and more clothes, and clothes still being made in factories, every day, to supply thousands of stores like these. Every time she comes to this store the stock has changed. Where do all the old new clothes go? Sold, or filtered down through sale after sale to the bargain basement, to the rummage table. But still, they can't all be sold! So many millions, billions of them.

It depends. Some days she looks only at the prices, ignoring everything less than forty or fifty dollars. Other days she grabs willfully, heedless of even like or dislike. She is no penny-pinching secretary to worry about color combinations and integrated wardrobes. A writer for a cheap rag, always on food stamps or whatever government allowances she can scrape up, here Magda can be as frivolous as the wealthiest society woman. She can snatch up lacy plum overblouses with yellow and green flowered skirts, never minding what is in her closet at home.

There are so many ways to do it. Sometimes she doesn't even bother to go into the dressing room, but simply tucks a blouse or a vest into a paper bag. Not today though: she has nothing in her hands, not even a purse. She tells the young woman in front of the dressing room hall, "I've got six." "Okay," the clerk smiles with a cursory look. Sometimes they count, but there are ways to get around that, too. Magda always wears so many layers of clothing that an extra vest is hardly suspicious.

Magda yanks the curtain closed and strips off her clothes. She is getting later and later for her meeting with Wallace. Good, let him wait, damn lawyer. If he could see his client now, standing in her underwear, slipping on a black silk blouse marked at sixty dollars, buttoning up every other button. . . . It does have erotic possibilities.

She began it in high school, on a dare. Or was it a dare? Yes, it must have been, for her mother had spared nothing to keep her and Audrey well-dressed. Her mother loved shopping and made friends with all the salesladies. "Nancy, what do you have in pink? Maggie Ellen looks so well in pink, you know." It was hard, stealing something right out from under Nancy's nose. "How are you doing, Maggie Ellen? All right in there? Sure I can't get you anything? I think that pink's going to be so sweet on you. Want me to come on in and zip you up?"

Yes, Magda could only have done it on a dare. Unless it was already a kind of getting back for the feeling of being pushed around.

Magda is sweating heavily now; she shouldn't have put on the black silk first, it will be stained forever. Well, so what? She can get another tomorrow if she wants. She knows she won't want. Every time she gets into one of these claustrophobic dressing rooms with their terrible three-way mirrors, the awful ease and stupidity of shoplifting almost overcome her. In order to calm herself down, Magda always has to promise:

"If I get out of here without getting caught, I'll never do it again. This will be the last time."

"What if you got caught?" people like Allison, yes, especially like Allison, say. "I'll never get caught." Magda knows that they really admire her; it's part of her image now, she can't give it up. She doesn't really want to.

And she can justify it. In round numbers. In square numbers, too. No doubt about it, anything you do to undermine capitalism is good. Allison is middle class, she wears downwardly mobile overalls; what does she know about clotheshunger, clothescontempt? Or Toni, or lawyer Bess in her quietly expensive, tasteless suits?

Magda fastens the last snap on the velour sweater. She brought in nine pieces, she can walk away with three. It doesn't matter which three, she doesn't like any of them anymore. She will take them home, jam them into her too-full closet. In a few months they will have absorbed enough of her smell and feel so that she can wear them, forgetting the dressing room. Or she'll give them away. Give this indigo velour to Allison, for instance. It would look good on her and she'll get a thrill from wearing stolen goods.

"Six," says Magda to the clerk, puffing and rosy.

"Didn't like any of them?" asks the woman sympathetically.

"No. None."

She glances at the clock on her way back to the escalator. Only a half-hour late—really, she's getting very fast. She can say she had trouble with her car.

Out on the street a cold wind tears toward her, through her layers of clothing, chilling the sweaty black silk against her skin. She automatically glances at the newspaper stand as she hurries to Wallace's office. *"MILLIONS,"* the headlines read. *"MILLIONS LOST."*

Magda runs up two flights of stairs and into the restroom where she hastily washes her face. She would like to change out of some of these clothes, they make her look uncomfortably bulky, but she has nothing to put the clothes in. At the last minute she throws one of the sweaters into the trash bin. If by some chance, Wallace has already left, she can retrieve it later; if not, then no great loss.

Wallace is waiting for her, however, not only waiting but evidently still busy behind his cluttered desk. He motions Magda to a chair while he finishes a phone conversation, and she sinks into it gladly, exhausted from her recent endeavors. At first she is empty-headed and her thoughts float rather than settle, but gradually the very fact of being in an office begins to focus them. Offices always do this to her. . . make her feel ambitious and businesslike. She imagines having her own office, putting a plant here, a print there, surrounding herself with books and magazines—and working, working. Using the phone, the typewriter in rapid succession. This proprietary interest comes, of course, from never having had her own office. She has always worked in news rooms or at home, has written her copy either in the stir and clash of the newsroom or late at night, sometimes lying on her sofa, with a bottle of wine nearby. Both these situations have their romance, but it's nothing compared to an office of her own. Although in theory she despises the idea of professionalism, the things that go with it—offices, telephones, a door to close—are what Magda wants most in the world. But how to get them? How to get them and still remain a radical journalist? How to close the door on her own office and not lose her anger against the professionals?

Wallace is wearing a suit and tie but looks as disheveled as his office. His bowl-like, Dutchboy haircut has been pushed into a more relaxed part; his wire-rims perch on his nose. Magda thinks she likes him better like this, more unassuming and less starched.

He smiles at her and goes on talking.

No sex, Magda warns herself. Absolutely not. Dinner someplace and then right back to Holly, who will be waiting up for her. She tries and succeeds in concentrating on the remembered smell and feel of Holly's body; when she has managed to banish the almost equally real feel of Wallace's body from her dreams last night, she sets herself to imagining again how she could get an office like this someday.

Thoughts mature. Though the idea of leaving the *News* has been with her intermittently for some weeks, only in the last day or so has it gained a new and stronger hold on Magda's mind. It probably began with that guy Sam and his move to San Francisco. It was clarified and given strength by the vision of Toni moving on, too. Getting an article in *Challenge*. This morning, while again attempting to write her article for the *News*, Magda drafted several letters to alternative publications, asking if they had any jobs available. She won't tell anyone, she'll just wait—but at least she's doing something, preparing in her own mind to leave Seattle, the *News*, and all it has represented in her life.

Wallace hangs up the phone and grins at her, showing two creases that could almost be dimples in his boyish face.

"I bought oysters," he says, "for oysters Rockefeller. And leeks to braise in wine. And a tremendous bottle of Johannesberg Riesling."

129

"I thought we were going out?" If he changes the scenario like this, introduces wine and oysters, it will be more difficult to get home at a reasonable hour.

"But I love to cook. I thought I said I wanted to make dinner for you."

Maybe he had. Or maybe "How about dinner tomorrow night?" has different meanings to different people. She has been tricked somehow, but pleasurably so. She does like oysters, and if it takes longer to make them, she can call Holly and explain. It is only a kind of business meeting after all.

Magda follows his car to the house where he lives with another lawyer, one of his partners who is out of town. The house is small, but well-furnished. Wallace dismisses the deep sea-green rug, the paintings on the walls, the expensive modern furniture, "It's all his. From his first marriage. . . she went to live in Europe. . ."

He leads her right to the kitchen, obviously remodeled to accommodate the tastes of good cooks, with lots of counter space, open shelves filled with gourmet foods (paté, chutney, gooseberry preserves, things in aspic) and hooks on the wall for an array of copper pans and skillets. He mixes them both a drink and rummages around for the oysters and oyster knife.

"This is going to be messy. Why don't you go and put some music on?"

Magda wanders back into the living room to the stereo. She feels completely taken in by the luxury of the place. None of her friends live like this; they huddle in shabby studios, with furniture from the Goodwill and dish collections from previous tenants. Their sheets smell like mildew, their toilets run, their faucets drip. When they have more than three people to dinner, everyone sits on the floor. Even Toni, who could afford a penthouse, lives in a run-down house in a neighborhood where rocks and baseballs go through the window and dogs shit all over the front yard. Allison's house is comfortable, but it bears too many children's marks: comic books in the bathroom, baseball bats on the couch. Magda has tried to make her apartment as nice as she can, but poverty limits her like everyone else. Her faucet drips too, and her kitchen is more like a closet than a place to prepare food.

Magda browses through the vast record collection, thinking, just once I'd like to live in a place of my own and have some money to make it look nice. Surely there has to be a happy medium. . . this place is a little ostentatious. . . but a thick rug on the floor and counter space in the kitchen, a few copper pans, a decent stereo. . . She places a jazz album on the turntable and takes off her shoes. The Scotch and water is strong, she's relaxed enough to lie flat, sip it, and listen to the music.

Is it impossible? Here I am, thirty in a few years, and still as far from living the way I want to as ever. And if I go to New York or some-place, I'll probably have to live in a worse place than where I'm living now. I've never lived in a *nice* place, she thinks with sad anger, forgetting that a few years ago she would have been down on the very idea. When she first came to Seattle, she threw away many of her notions of bour-geois comfort and tried to live like the rest of the people on the *News*. When she lived back east, she'd at least had some of her mother's china and a beautiful Navajo rug. In the first flush of her political enthusiasm she had given those things away.

"How're you doing?" Wallace comes in with an oyster shell in one hand. "Relaxing? That's good."

"I can help." Magda raises herself languidly. "Tell me what to do."

"Just come and talk to me."

He fixes them both another drink and settles Magda in a comfor-table chair near the counter. Magda finds it extraordinarily pleasant to be fussed over, to be taken care of. Everybody she knows is so casual. Not only do you end up having to cut up the salad greens for them, but you have to wash the dishes afterwards. She notices with satisfaction that Wallace's kitchen has a dishwasher. Political people usually have about as much notion of hospitality as scout leaders. . . it's all demo-cratic, pitching in to help. How charming to just sit and drink Scotch and watch Wallace expertly split the oyster shells with his broad flat knife. . . how would it be to live with someone who liked to cook, who was capable and intelligent, made enough money and liked nothing better than an evening at home. . . .

"How did you get into journalism?" Wallace asks her.

"This kind or the other?"

"What do you mean?"

"I used to write for a living." Magda is laconically defensive. "Now I do it out of political idealism."

Wallace smiles back at her irony. "Isn't it possible to do both?"

"A few people do. I haven't found the key yet." Should she go in-to it? Should she tell him about her fears or that her mind has slowly been changing, gearing up for a new challenge? Or will he pick holes in her too? "Have you always been political?" she asks suddenly.

Wallace is arranging the oysters on a baking sheet. "Was I born with a concept of social justice, you mean?"

"You know what I mean."

"Well, then, no. But I've been active for several years. Not in civil rights, I was too young for that—but I worked in the anti-war movement. Dropped out of school a couple of times, went to live on a farm, then came back and decided I could be more useful as a lawyer."

"There sure are a lot of people like you, then," Magda snipes.

"I'm sure there are—but what do you mean?" Now he is spooning a cool green mixture from a blender onto each of the soft gray bodies in their shells.

"Say—just say—that you weren't born in a large city, but in a little town in the middle of nowhere, say Kansas. Say you were raised by a mother who only wanted you to get married, so you wouldn't have to work as a dental hygienist like she did. Say that's all you wanted too, to get married, and you only went to college so you could find a better class of man. Say that somewhere in there your current boyfriend, who was editor of the college paper, persuaded you to write an article. Say you found out you could write so well that eventually you became the managing editor (because they never made girls editor) and ended by majoring in journalism. What would you do then?"

"I get the point," Wallace says, placing the long, white-green leeks into one of the copper saucepans. "So how did you come to the *News*?"

Magda feels he hasn't gotten the point at all. But who ever has? What she really means to say is that her naiveté about politics, her lack of shared experience in student radical movements, in the anti-war effort, the fact that neither she nor anyone else she knew back home ever dropped out once, much less twice, and went "back to the land"—all these things left her, for years, with the feeling that she had to catch up somehow, that she had to immerse herself in the political scene and become as knowledgeable or more knowledgeable in the vernacular.

"The *News* was my Berlitz School. It taught me a whole new language."

"But now it's not enough?" Wallace inclines his head toward her empty glass and she nods. The Scotch goes down so easily that she doesn't feel at all drunk, just relaxed and stimulated at the same time. His interest gives her the chance to put all this in perspective. He doesn't seem to be judging her; what does it matter if he is?

"We go around and around with this—whether it is enough, whether it should be enough, whether it could be enough. It seems to depend on how long you've been there—new people almost always think it's wonderful; it gives them a chance to learn new skills, write things that other papers would never publish. But after you've been doing it for a while, you start feeling stuck there. You like the influence you do have, but you want more of it. When you work hard on an article, it begins to bother you that only a few thousand people, if that many, are going to read it. When the *Times* has a circulation of half a million or so. . . ."

Wallace slides the sheet of oysters under the broiler and pours wine over the pan of leeks. "Any chance of getting the paper on a more professional footing? It seems like the Northwest could use it."

"You need money to do that. One of the staff has a lot of it, and whenever the paper's been about to fold, she pumps it in. . . but never enough to make it bigger or better. I think she used to believe in the *News*, but now all she thinks about is getting out, moving on to something else. That's what happens to everybody, including me—there's nothing more to do on the *News*. I mean it's too frustrating, when you get enough experience, to find yourself arguing with newcomers who don't know what's going on. People use the *News* as a stepping-stone, is what I mean to say. And all it turns out to be then is a kind of teaching tool. . . I didn't mind being taught, but I sure as hell don't want to be a teacher all my life. I want to write."

Now Wallace begins to set the table alongside of her. He arranges the glasses and sets out the chilled bottle of wine. Magda is almost overcome by the pleasantness of all this luxury. It doesn't seem fair somehow that he can have his politics and eat them too.

"I think it's only right," she hears herself laugh (is she getting drunk after all?) "that you're giving me dinner. After all, it's your fees from this case that are buying the food."

"Oh, don't worry about the money right now," Wallace says smoothly, filling her glass with the faintly greenish wine. "It's been a coup for me to get you off. . . . I think we should drink to it, don't you?"

They raise glasses and toast, then Wallace leans over and kisses her.

At that Magda comes back to herself a little. She *cannot* and will not get carried away, however nice he is, however much he plies her with drink. Holly is waiting for her.

"What time is it?" she asks abruptly.

Wallace looks disappointed. "Nine. . . you don't have something else to do, do you?"

Immediately she is abject; she doesn't want to spoil this delicious dinner, all this delicious attention. It's not going to lead anywhere, of course, but why cut it short for Holly? Holly can just go to sleep.

"I'll just make a phone call," Magda says and wends her way unsteadily back into the living room, stopping first to put another record on the stereo. As the music streams softly into the room, she has the desire to just give in, to stay here forever, drinking wine and talking. She'd like to lie down on the thick carpet and... the heretical thought rises in her mind that they could probably have a quick one before she has to go.

"Holly?"

"Oh Magda, I'm glad you called. Where are you?"

"Well, we're about to eat... I know it's getting late and I'm sorry. I wanted to tell you not to wait up for me, if you're tired..."

"I'm not tired."

"Oh. Well, I'll see you in a couple of hours, then. How are things? How was work?"

"Okay... James came in."

"James! What did he want?"

"He said he didn't, you know, inform or anything."

"Was that all he had to say?"

"Yeah..." Holly pauses. "He did want to get together tonight, but I told him no."

"Of course you did. Christ, I hope I run into him someday. I'll tell him where he can get off."

"It's all right, Magda.... So, I'll see you in a couple of hours? You're having a good time?"

"Oh, yeah. We're just talking about the case, you know." Magda hates herself for the relief that surfaces in Holly's voice, her sincere urging to "have a good time."

Magda returns to the kitchen to find the sizzling oysters on her plate. "Had to call the woman who's staying with me," she excuses herself. "Oh, these look wonderful."

"Friend?"

"Oh, yeah, Holly, you remember her? Allison's partner? She's got some weird ex-husband who's been bugging her, so she's been staying with me and Allison...." Magda drowns her feelings of disloyalty in a long drink of the wine and begins to eat.

"Tomorrow's the day," Wallace says. He has taken his wire-rims off at some point and his brown eyes are even more melting than the oysters. Magda's thighs begin to tingle, but she ploughs on through her food. Aren't oysters aphrodisiacs? It's not fair of him to seduce her when she's trying so hard. What was pleasure earlier—at the music, the house, the liquor, and the conversation—has now become confusion and almost pain. She is strongly drawn to Wallace, alcohol or not. How ridiculous for her to have gotten involved with Holly yesterday. If only she had waited. But certainly she never felt this way about Holly. Holly pushed her into it, Holly was the one who wanted it, not Magda. I can't have a lesbian relationship, thinks Magda, and still feel this way about a man. This is so much stronger. Besides, it would never work out with Holly; they're too different, while she and Wallace have lots in common. He's her equal. Holly looks up to her too much.

But wait, is sex even on Wallace's mind? He's talking about Allison's case now, as if Magda didn't know it inside and out. How awful if he doesn't desire her as much as she desires him. She can hardly eat for the funny feeling in her stomach while he keeps swallowing oysters and talking lawyerese about contempt charges and different rulings. What has happened to her? Here they were, having an interesting conversation, and suddenly she's obsessed with having sex with him. She didn't even think him very good-looking before tonight, and now she can't stop staring at him.

"More wine?" he urges. Magda nods, unable to speak, and puts her fork down. "You're not eating!" He puts his fork down too, then smiles and places his hand on her leg.

Magda's thighs tighten convulsively; she almost groans. Her mind is racing wildly: it would only take half an hour, she could be home by ten-thirty. . .

He caresses her knee. "Have another oyster."

"I. . . I lost my appetite," she says, putting her hand on his and pressing it up above her knee.

"I'll just have one more," he says, but his hand moves up her inner thigh. He eats it slowly, looking at her as his hand strokes and presses, torturously, higher and higher up her leg.

Magda finally pushes his hand up as far as it can go and opens her legs. "Finished?" she murmurs.

"I'm just beginning."

Six o'clock, how can that be? Magda sits upright in Wallace's water-bed and stares in confusion at the red numbers on the digital clock. The liquid under her heaves, gurgling, from side to side. Her stomach follows its motions, dangerously. Her eyes are gluey and rough, her mouth feels like she ate a roll of toilet paper.

Holly. Oh crap.

"How do you get out of this thing?" she demands, futilely heaving from side to side.

"Uhnnn." Wallace is either one of those totally dead-to-the-world sleepers or else this is his way of getting rid of women in the morning.

She has used this tactic herself on occasion. Well, fuck him anyway. Clutching the side of the bed, the wooden board, Magda drags herself out of her trough and manages to fall out onto the floor. Luckily it's not far, and carpeted with the same deep pile as the living room.

She dresses in haste, though every quick movement is agony to her aching head and body. Everything is an awful reminder: the black silk blouse from the department store, the underwear dry and stiff now with last night's desire. Magda avoids looking at Wallace completely. How could I, how could I? are thoughts she wants to avoid. Much less, how can I explain this to Holly?

In her car, shooting through the black morning drizzle, Magda defends herself angrily: Big deal, so I slept with him. We're not married, Holly. It was all a mistake anyway. It's you I really care about, I just had to make sure. . . .

But that's a lie. It's not Holly she really cares about, nor is it Wallace at this point. She doesn't care about either of them, all she wants is to get into bed and forget everything.

Why am I even going home, then, if all I can look forward to is a scene? Should have stayed at Wallace's. But that would have been awful too—waking up and having to make conversation. The question is, where else can she go? The black drizzle seems to be soaking into her car, into her hastily pulled-on clothes, into her mind, with a steady and remorseful drip.

"Holly," she calls sullenly, coming into the bedroom and seeing no one there. "Holly?"

The apartment is as empty as a drained wine glass. "Holly," she mutters, throwing herself on the bed, too dazed and nauseated to care. It's better this way. It had to happen. It's better this way.

Ten: Contempt

She dreams of oysters, of course, of a man with oystery eyes sliding around on his platelike face. "The world is my oyster, sister," he says. "I'm politically correct and well-paid. . . but don't worry about the money, I just want your oyster." She puts her hand out to touch the soft folds of the oyster, now glimmering rosy pink, with a damp pearl in the middle, but the barnacle-encrusted shell keeps closing on her hand, cutting into her, making her bleed.

The doorbell blasts into her sleep. Trying to get to the door, to stop the awful ringing that rocks her head, Magda crashes into every other piece of furniture she has. Her heart is pounding with dread.

"Who is it?"

"Paul. Open up, Magda."

She considers pretending that she's had a heart attack or has been suddenly struck deaf and dumb, but after a minute she opens the door on her former lover.

Paul heaves in like a longshoreman, big, dark, morose.

"Here," he says, thrusting a big basket of spotted green apples into her arms. "A present from Ellensburg."

Magda in turn throws the basket away from her as far as she can, which isn't far, considering its weight. The hard apples roll wildly around the room, some of the soft ones burst open onto the carpet.

"I already got a present from you—your fucking letter. What do you want?"

"Temper, temper," he says, giving her a large hug. "I thought I'd better check out what was happening around here."

"Christ." Magda disengages herself and starts for the kitchen. Him on top of everything else.

"I'd like some coffee, too."

Magda slams the kettle on the burner.

"Aren't we in a foul mood this morning. What is it, morning sickness?"

"Look, if you're planning to hang around and insult me, you can leave right now. Otherwise, I don't want to hear one word out of you until I've had a shower and gotten dressed. Make the coffee, pick up your fucking wormy apples, and shut up."

Paul pretends to cower with his arms up, but he keeps quiet at least, while she stalks past him into the bathroom. Under the hot water, after a brief review of the worst events of the past few days, Magda shrugs and settles herself. Nothing is so bad that it can't be forgotten or rectified. Where would she be if she agonized over every mistake she'd ever made? Besides, is it really all so awful? Holly is a nice kid and it was a shame to hurt her, but that's the way it goes. And what is there to be ashamed of about Wallace? They slept together out of mutual desire like two consenting adults. Being with Wallace and Holly was an unfortunate juxtaposition, perhaps, but it's the kind of thing that happens when you follow your desires. And Magda places a high importance on the following of one's desires.

Magda steps out of the shower, red, tingling, light-headed, and swallows four aspirin from a bottle in the medicine cabinet. She can't really be sorry Paul is here, he brings out her most stubborn and self-preserving side these days and that can only help her to get through the day ahead. Allison's court appearance is at eleven. After that, according to Bess, today or tomorrow there will probably be a hearing before the judge to decide whether she's in contempt of court or not. And somewhere in the next day or two Magda will have to pull all her notes together and begin to write.

I wonder how much I could find out about Ted Shovik? Not that they'd give me access to the police files probably, but it's worth trying. I can raise a stink, show them they can't push me around.

Magda's mug of coffee is waiting for her on one of the tables in the living room, and Paul, after having picked up all the apples and replaced them in the basket, is straightening the rest of the room. With a start of memory, she recalls how he always used to neaten up her place of residence for her. It was something she used to love in him, his orderliness. . . it was something that used to make her want to live with him. He never wanted the same, of course.

"Feeling better?" he asks gently, perhaps overtaken by the same sense of nostalgia, that same sense of possibilities lost or neglected. But she doesn't want to feel intimate with him, she wants to feel tough and resilient.

"What's this?" she says indifferently, pointing to a slip of paper pinned to the top of the red sofa.

"Don't ask me. Looks like a note for you." He reaches over as if to give it to her, but Magda dashes past him and grabs it first. If it's from Holly, and it must be, then she doesn't want him reading it.

"Dear Magda, I have gone out for a little while. Don't worry. I'll keep calling you to see when you get home. Love, Holly."

At least she wasn't here waiting for me, Magda thinks in a kind of relief. But calling? She imagines the phone ringing over and over through the evening, with never an answer. Poor Holly. But where had she gone? And what did she mean, don't worry?

"Gotta make a phone call," she tells Paul and dials Allison's number. An older woman answers the phone, Allison's mother.

"No, Allison's not here. She left for work about an hour ago. Holly? No, she hasn't been here. No, not last night either."

Would Holly have gone home then? Magda dials her number, but there's no answer. She tries the print shop.

"Allison? Hi, how are things going? Yes, I'm coming to the courthouse. . . . Is Holly there? No. . . you haven't seen her then? No, nothing's. . . at least I don't think anything's wrong. I just wanted to know where she was. . . to tell her something. If she comes in, have her give me a call, all right? Okay, see you later, good-bye."

"What's all this about?" Paul wants to know.

Magda turns to him, hardly registering his words. She couldn't have gone out with James after all, could she? She wouldn't do something like that. Magda stares at the phone, willing it to ring now the way it must have rung in the silence last night.

Belatedly she hears Paul's question. "Nothing." Nothing to do but wait and see if Holly turns up at the courthouse in a couple of hours.

Magda reaches for her cup of coffee and remembers her headache. The remorse she so successfully repressed in the shower threatens now to overcome her. And *he* has to be here, of all people. It's as bad almost as having Toni standing over her like the Ghost of Argument Past. How Toni had screamed at her when she found that Magda had slept with Paul again. "Don't tell me it was just for old time's sake, you liar. You're still attracted to him. You're still attracted to men!"

"Well, so why don't you tell me what dragged you away from your books over in Ellensburg?" she says, crashing into the lap of a chair, as far away as she can get from him.

Paul sits too, in one of the neat spaces on the floor he has cleared for himself. His long bulky legs stick out like telephone poles. The lower part of his dark beard bristles over the top of his heavy turtleneck sweater. Magda hardens her heart against the sheer manly bulk of him.

"How can I sit and read Marx when my nearest and dearest are going around getting involved with commandos and such? Should I leave them to fight the grand jury system single-handed?"

"Setting aside that nearest-and-dearest crap—you might as well have stayed put, for all the help you can be, for all the help anyone can be. And in case you hadn't heard, I'm not being subpoenaed again."

"You're not? No, I hadn't heard that. I thought you were practically on your way to jail in defense of the First Amendment. Well, maybe you weren't so stupid, after all."

"I read your letter—before I flushed it down the toilet—you don't have to go into that stupid bit again. But I'd like you to know that I don't give a fuck what you think. I don't see where you get off criticizing me, when you've given up on political action altogether."

Paul pulls at his beard slowly, one of his more irritating habits; it makes him look the rabbi his father was. "When will you begin to understand, Magda, that you can't just jump from one cause to the next without having some understanding of what you're doing? You have a journalist's mind—one day *this* is terrible and everybody needs to know about it; the next week, it's all forgotten and something else is terrible. I'm not saying you don't have any political theories, but you apply them like frosting to the cake. You think that if you throw in an anticapitalist statement from time to time that people will know what you mean. The way you write, the way we all write or wrote on the *News*, is a case-by-case indictment of society that never adds up. Well, I wanted to get away from that, I wanted to get away and find out what I really thought independent of the day-to-day political situation here in Seattle."

"How can you find out what you think by ignoring what's happening day to day? Are you planning to sit there in Ellensburg, in exile, for twenty years, and then astound the world with your plan for revolution? While people just read the *Times* and watch the evening news? Well, I've got news for you, Paul Kravitz, the world doesn't wait for political theorists."

"Magda, what do you want?" In the past, this has been one of his favorite show-stoppers, this question. Its air of insinuation always throws Magda into turmoil—what doesn't she want? Sure, she would like to read *Das Kapital* in the original and a million other books; sure, she would like to become an expert in the field of American socialism—but there isn't time.

Today, however, she is just drained and weary enough to give a less than defensive answer. "All I want is to find out when and where things are going wrong and to tell people about them. I want to give events an interpretation they don't get in the straight media. Besides that I want to be able to eat and travel and have some nice things for myself. That's all."

"And you think the world would be overrun by fascism if you stopped writing your bimonthly articles long enough to figure out the underlying reasons for some of the things that are going wrong?"

"Yes, I do, goddamnit. One person makes a difference. Your leaving made a difference on the paper. And now Toni wants to leave and. . ." Magda is so carried away by her own sincerity that she forgets that she too wants to leave, that her letters of inquiry are even now speeding through the mails to various editorial desks.

"I wish you wouldn't keep making out that I've abandoned the paper. I feel enough guilt as it is. I worked on that paper three years, remember. I wrote articles until they were coming out my ears because we needed them, I did the distribution when nobody else would. I even had to sell ads at the end when Kathy left. I just burned myself out. If I'd left sooner I know I wouldn't feel this bitter. I never meant to be a journalist, you know. I'm not like you. Politics were my interest and I got dragged into all the rest because of the feeling that the paper would fold if I didn't give my life to it. In the end I didn't know what I thought about anything—none of you do—because you can't stop putting out the paper long enough to think about what you're doing."

"All the same," Magda mutters.

"I don't want to hear it. I didn't come here to argue with you about the *News*, we've done it often enough. I came, if you can believe it, because I was concerned."

"Your letter. . ."

"I know, and I'm sorry. It's probably all part of my guilt trip. I mean, this was the first issue I hadn't worked on, and I was looking forward to getting it, and then to read this interview. . . Who knows? Maybe I was jealous. Or just paranoid, reading it in Ellensburg, surrounded by latter-day cowboys. And then when you got subpoenaed, my first reaction was anger." He pauses and tries to smile at her. "I didn't want anything to happen to you."

"I didn't know you cared," she manages.

"Of course I care. That's why I'm here."

They sit on opposite sides of the room, hardly daring to look at each other. For some reason Magda thinks of her father, who she has never forgiven for dying on her, her father who she can hardly remember. She was only five, her sister three when the truck plowed into his car. All she remembers is his dentist's office. Shiny and white, all those glittering instruments. The dry touch of his hand on her cheek, his urging to "Open wide for Daddy."

("Sounds like incest," this asshole Paul remarked when she'd told him that. . . .)

Magda's voice catches as she tries to speak now. It is friendship he's offering her, she understands, a friendship that she was never willing to accept, because it meant the end of her best and worst fantasy—that somehow they would work through their differences and come to accept each other. But there can be no mistaking his tone now, or his eyes. There is no sexual desire, no love in them, at least not romantic love. There is only warmth and caring. I don't want anything but what we had— can't we have it again? an old, lonely voice in her wants to cry out. The friendship Paul is extending is like a hand, one of the big hands that used to caress her, stretched out across the room. Finally, with a feeling of loss and beginning, Magda decides to accept it.

"Thank you," she says, without making a move.

He, too, remains on the other side of the room, but seems closer now. Their pact won't be sealed with a kiss, that part is over forever.

"Now," Paul says, leaning forward, "for the details."

She doesn't tell him everything, and nothing at all about her ill-fated love affairs which have woven themselves so unfortunately and so inexplicably through far more important events and yet left much more of a trace. She tells him the story the way she will write it, balancing incident against incident, matching quote with quote, leaving out certain aspects and stressing others.

"I see you've made yourself quite an authority on the subject."

She bristles for a moment, but realizes his teasing is well-meant.

"I have," she says. "It's a pity I'm not more involved."

"If you were any more involved, you'd have to be the prosecutor."

"Don't laugh at him. He's got enough power to put Allison away for three months and he seems insensible to any arguments from our side."

"Deb's mother, too?"

"Doesn't that seem incredible? A fifty-year-old woman in jail for refusing to talk about her daughter?"

"So she's not talking today, either?"

"No. . . ." But even as she shakes her head, Magda feels the stirrings of a doubt. What has Mrs. Houseman got to lose by telling them that Allison dropped off Deb's child? Or by letting the jury in on what she knows of Deb's activities, which surely can't be much. She wouldn't go to jail then, and they'd let her off the hook. The cold remembrance of Mrs. Houseman walking past them without a glance sweeps over her.

The rally in front of the courthouse is even larger today, a good sign. Magda is pleased Paul is there to see how a community can unite around an issue it supports. She is glad he is with her for other reasons, too; when she sees Wallace approaching, she puts her arm around Paul for protection. Undeterred, Wallace comes over anyway, smiling, well-brushed and neat in a three-piece suit.

Magda introduces the two men, hoping that Wallace will asume that Paul is her steady lover and that he will make no comments about hangovers or oysters, either. He seems to take in her gesture the way it was meant, probably relieved to be out of the running. He is mature and discreet to the core, which, however much it made possible and enjoyable the previous night's frolics, has the effect of distancing her this morning. Better Paul, better anyone with a temper and a vision, than this affable, smiling stranger.

Magda leaves them deep in conversation about the First Amendment and goes looking for Allison and Holly.

The day is gray and sullen, but without wind. It has stopped raining briefly, but promises to start up dismally at any time. Seattle weather can be temperamental, but more often it is like someone with a terminal case of the blues, whose tears begin and end with no apparent interruption, for no apparent reason.

She sees Katey and Ben first and is struck for the first time by how much they resemble their parents: Katey, a round and energetic, curly-haired Allison in parka and jeans; Ben, a skinny, rather determined young boy who looks around him at the milling group with some disapproval. Ben's resemblance to his father is made more evident by his father's sudden appearance behind him. Together the two males look out of place and severely conscious of that fact. Allison is surrounded by a group composed of her mother, Bess, and Jill from the *News*. Magda has noticed how Allison and Jill seem to like each other; really, they are quite similar, which is probably the reason Magda has never felt close to either of them. Jill, in particular, is the robust and thoughtfully slow but stubborn kind of person who makes Magda nervous. It takes Jill a long time to make up her mind, but when she does, it's set forever, and no amount of persuasion can force her to change it. Just like Allison with her insistence on doing the right thing. Nobility of any sort makes Magda uncomfortable.

She sees Dennis and Carl out of the corner of her eye and half decides to join them instead, but remembers Holly. Maybe Allison has some idea where she is. She doesn't seem to be at the rally so far. As Magda makes her way toward them, however, she is waylaid by Toni.

"Guess who I had a phone conversation with?" Toni asks smugly. Her pale blonde hair is pulled back in a knot at the back of her well-shaped head and she has a notebook in one hand. A real reporter.

Magda shrugs without saying anything.

"Ted Shovik's father," Toni announces, not one bit put off.

"His father? I thought, I thought his parents weren't talking to reporters?"

"I convinced him that this would be a different kind of story. Not sensationalist. But that he could just talk about what his son believed. He's almost sympathetic, he used to be a big union organizer, you know. He might even ask for an investigation about the killing."

A union organizer—that's just Magda's kind of story. She knows more about labor than Toni will ever know. Christ. That's what comes of getting mixed up in love affairs. A great opportunity down the drain.

"Sounds thrilling," Magda says in a bored voice, hoping she implies that she's got a better lead in the works. "See you later. . . I've got to talk to Allison." Magda's head throbs painfully as she turns away and begins to thread her way through the crowd. Toni got to talk to the father? Shit, let her have him then, all of them, let her have these damned terrorists and their relatives shoved down her throat and welcome to them. Magda only wants to leave the city, get away from everyone. Maybe she should go back to Ellensburg with Paul for a while, recuperate, until she hears from one of the editors.

Allison, strangely enough, looks better than she has in a week. The strain around her eyes has become more a squint of determination; there is more color in her cheeks and she is attractively dressed, for once, in a corduroy skirt and wool sweater.

She pulls Magda aside after briefly introducing her to her mother, the real prototype of Allison and her daughter. How is it that they all look so much alike? Magda wonders. Round faced, curly haired, motherly. . . . If Magda looks like anyone in her family, that person hasn't been discovered.

"Did you see Tom?" Allison whispers. "I couldn't believe it when he turned up today. At first he looked pissed off to see the kids here and not in school, but he seems to be dealing with it. Bess sure had some kind of effect on him. She just laid it on the line. She told him that this was an important case with far-reaching effects, that I had a lot of support and that what happened here might set a national precedent. She even got on his Republican side and asked him if he didn't think there was too much governmental control in our lives already. And when he said yes, she asked if he believed in the Constitution and the Bill of Rights. . . . She's just great, isn't she, Magda?"

"Yeah." Magda can hear Bess now, talking to Tom about the Bill of Rights. It's disgusting—doesn't Allison see that?—that Tom would place more stock in what a lawyer says than in Allison's own tenacity and courage.

"Look at him," Allison laughs proudly. "I bet this is the first time he's ever been in a demonstration."

"He looks mostly like he's trying to avoid the photographers."

"But he's here, Magda. That says a lot. He's *supporting* me. And my mother's here, and the kids. No matter what happens, I don't feel so alone or crazy anymore."

"Where's Holly?" Magda asks abruptly.

"Holly?" Allison turns her head in several directions. "I don't know. She must be here somewhere. We just can't see her because of all the people. There are so many of them, Magda."

Magda represses the desire to answer sarcastically, Oh yeah, it's just like a Sonics game. A couple hundred lefties, big deal. "I guess I'll just try and find her then."

Allison nods abstractedly and presses Magda's shoulder. "See you inside then."

Magda wanders disconsolately through the crowd. Every few minutes someone stops her and asks questions about the case. She grows impatient and almost snaps at the television reporter who wants to film her talking about the First Amendment. "No, I don't want to be on TV," she says. "This has nothing to do with me anymore. Go ask Allison Morris what she thinks about justice. This may be your last chance before she goes to jail.

The crowd stops milling long enough to cheer a few speeches. Magda has refused to speak at this rally, leaving it to Dennis and Allison and anybody else who can grab the bullhorn to get in their favorite cause.

"I just want to tell you," she hears Allison say faintly through the distortion of the bullhorn, "what your coming here means to me. It gives me all the courage I need to continue to say 'No' to the grand jury."

Magda rejoins Paul, seeing that Wallace has moved on.

"Why aren't you up there?"

"Humph," Magda says ill-humoredly. "I don't know why I'm here at all." Her eyes twitch over the crowd continually for a glimpse of Holly. Allison's wrong, Holly's *not* here, or Magda would have seen her by now. Something must have happened to her. She wouldn't be staying away from Allison's court appearance just because she was mad at Magda, would she?

"Looks like people are going inside," Paul says. "Come on."

As they move toward the entrance, Dennis and Toni see him and rush over.

"What are you doing here?" they demand happily.

Magda feels a glow of triumph at Toni's surprise. Toni has always liked Paul, in spite of his being a man, and felt his departure probably just as much as Magda. Toni never held it against *him* that he slept with Magda, though that was the supposed end of their affair. All the same, he didn't come back to Seattle to see Toni.

Complacently, Magda takes his arm before Paul can answer. "He wanted to support old friends."

Paul looks amused as he shakes Magda off and embraces Dennis and Toni. "This is the most people I've seen gathered together, leftists I mean, in a long time."

"It's been a lot of work to organize. . ." Dennis begins while they go through the door. Toni has turned away to find Lisa, with a tight little smile. Who will be the first to stop this one-upwomanship? Magda wonders, knowing that it probably won't be her.

Outside the courtroom the marshals are keeping order by keeping everyone away from the door. The supporters who have come upstairs are congregating in small clumps near the elevators. No sign of Holly here either. Something's happened to her and nobody cares, Magda thinks, placing the blame on the people around her as an alternative to thinking, it's all my fault. And where is Mrs. Houseman? Impatiently she stomps from group to group, unable to focus on questions she is asked. Toni is circulating too, but with an air of purpose. She has her notebook out and is asking the questions rather than answering.

Of course. This whole thing is a reporter's dream come true: people questioning the system in the marble and elegant halls of the Federal Courthouse; uniformed guards and marshals providing the sinister element; the tension mounting, the drama unfolding, the crisis near. It's all very exciting—only, why doesn't Magda feel anything except her headache? If she had her choice, she would rather be any place else than here right now. She decides to go out and buy some cigarettes. Who cares if she's around or not? And what does she care if she misses something important?

Out in front of the courthouse the last vestiges of the rally are breaking up. It is beginning to rain softly, but Magda makes no attempt to cover her head with her parka. She starts off in the opposite direction from where she's sure to find a store selling cigarettes. The longer it takes her, the better.

She trudges past the municipal and county buildings without noticing where she is. Remorse and self-pity, that's all she feels; no involvement with the proceedings, no journalistic excitement, nothing. Maybe she won't even go back. No one would even miss her. . . .

As Magda turns right at the top of the hill, she sees a tall blonde woman cross the street several blocks down. Is it Holly? Magda tries to run, but her clogs slow her down. Damn these stupid shoes, anyway. Where is Holly going, if that's Holly? She's certainly not heading in the direction of the courthouse. The blonde woman vanishes behind a building, and Magda slips out of her clogs and, in her socks, begins to tear down the hill. At the bottom, puffing and anxious, she looks both ways down First Street. In one direction is Pioneer Square, in the other, pawnshops and taverns and abandoned buildings. No sign of Holly. She was probably mistaken anyway; it was too great a distance to make sure. Still, there was something about the blonde woman's slouching shoulders. . .

Magda faces Pioneer Square arbitrarily and begins to walk across the street after putting her clogs back on. She glances into a pawnshop window automatically to check her reflection and sees Holly at the back, standing at the counter. Magda opens the door to a loud tinkling and goes in as Holly spins around. A revolver with an imitation mother-of-pearl handle rests on the linoleum counter between her and a handsome older man in a canvas apron.

"Magda. . ." she says. In the overly bright light of the pawnshop

Holly looks like an elongated six-year-old, caught out at something by her mother.

Magda's first impulse is to rush up to her and push the gun away. Is she thinking of suicide? Has Magda really driven her to that? Don't do it, Magda is on the point of shouting melodramatically, but something stops her. Perhaps it's the amused expression on the pawnbroker's face. He can probably spot a scene a mile away.

"I, uh, missed you at the rally and. . . I was just going to get some cigarettes. . ."

Magda stands next to her at the counter now and they look at each other. All hope Magda had that Holly didn't understand the extent of her betrayal is gone. Holly stares coldly at her and then down at the revolver.

"How much did you say?" she asks the pawnbroker.

"I can give you twenty-five for it."

So she's selling it then? What does all this mean?

"All right," Holly says indifferently, giving the gun a slight push toward him. He writes her a receipt and slowly counts out the bills.

Without a word Holly stuffs the money in her back pocket and turns for the door. Magda, feeling more of a fool than ever, follows her out. It's not until they are out on the sidewalk and Holly is walking away that Magda can bring herself to ask why she was selling the gun. Truthfully, she feels a little frightened now of Holly. After Holly's first start of shock and guilt at being seen, she is now as collected and distant as Magda has ever seen her.

Holly doesn't answer.

"Are you going to the courthouse now?" Magda asks, hobbling to keep up with her. Her damn socks are soaking wet inside her clogs.

"Yes."

After a minute, puffing up the steep hill with Holly always a few lunges in front of her, Magda tries again, "What. . ."

"Where were you last night?" Holly turns and faces her for the first time since the pawnshop.

"Our dinner just went on later than. . ."

"Than three? I tried to call you then. You spent the night with him, didn't you?"

All the answers that Magda has prepared churn into her mouth at once, but she can't find the best way to start. She had been expecting something different: a teary, hurt Holly who would accept a lie rather than hear the awful truth; a Holly who would be mollified with a kiss and a hug; or even a Holly who could be bullied into submission by Magda's defense of non-monogamy.

Instead, Magda has to drop her eyes from Holly's terrible condemnation. Seeing that, Holly turns away again and begins to walk, a step or two in front of Magda.

"Well, I spent the night, part of it anyway, with James," she says in a low voice, so low that Magda can hardly catch her words. "James and his gun." She laughs bitterly.

"You were selling his gun?"

"Did you think I was buying it? To shoot you with?"

Magda can't bring herself to say, No, to shoot yourself. She feels worse and worse. Holly would hardly shoot herself over someone like Magda.

As if to herself, as if to convince herself of the reality of it, Holly mutters, "I almost shot *him* though."

"I'm, I'm sorry, Holly, I didn't mean to. . ."

Holly appears not to have heard her. "I almost shot him, maybe I should have. I could have kept Allison company in jail."

"Are you going to tell me what happened?" Magda pauses at the top of the hill to catch her breath. Holly, fortunately, pauses too. It's raining harder and neither of them have their hoods up. If Magda were able to use her writer's imagination now, she would see something romantic in their wild, bedraggled hair, the way they stand facing each other on the crest of a hill that overlooks the churning gray Sound. As it is, she is too conscious of her wet feet, general dampness, and misery to imagine anything dramatic about this confrontation. She can only be grateful that Holly is at last answering her.

"I guess there's no reason not to tell you," Holly says slowly, wrapping her scarf more firmly around her neck. "I waited and waited for you. I was feeling kind of crazy, I guess, when I got this sudden idea that I would go see James and tell him to get off my back. I couldn't be angry at *you* yet, so I go mad at him. I drove over to the place he was staying and found him smoking dope with some other people.

"I wanted to leave as soon as I got there. It all reminded me too much of how we used to live—the dark room with the dripping candle, the smell of cat shit, people sitting around looking spaced out. There was nothing *wrong* with it, I mean for *them*. But I hate that kind of atmosphere. . . ."

Holly stares fiercely at the sky and takes a deep breath of the rain-soaked air, missing Magda's nod of agreement.

"But I didn't go. I sat down and smoked some dope with them. Already I had sort of forgotten what I came there for. I couldn't imagine getting into a fight with James when he was just sitting there smiling at me. All the same it made me sick, the whole thing. . . . Every once in a while I would try and call you. . ."

Magda cringes, but Holly hardly looks at her. She says "you" without appearing to connect it to Magda.

"After a while people started to drift away or go to sleep. I wasn't very stoned, at least I thought I wasn't. I remember following James up to the room where he was sleeping with some idea in my head that now we would talk, now I would tell him to stop bothering me. But it seemed strange, I mean, I had come looking for *him*, this time."

Holly pauses absently as if trying to recall what happened next.

"The gun?" Magda asks.

"Oh, the gun. . . we were talking about something and I realized that he expected me to spend the night with him. He kept telling me to turn off the light. 'I have to make a phone call,' I said. 'Who is this person you've been calling all night?' 'A friend of mine,' I said. He had seemed like he was just about asleep and I didn't expect him to get so, so agitated. He started shouting about me being a whore and all of a sudden there was this gun in his hand. 'I'm not taking any more of your shit,' he said. 'I'm tired of fucking around with you.' "

Magda makes a movement toward her, but Holly steps back. "It's all right. I mean, even at the time I knew it was all right. James wouldn't ever use a gun on me—punch me, yes, but never shoot me."

"How did you know?"

"I just knew. But it was still so sudden—him lying there half asleep and then waving this revolver around—that it threw me off. I tried to get out of the room, but he threw me away from the door. Then I just grabbed it. The gun, I mean."

"Holly! It could have gone off."

"It wasn't loaded. I knew it then and I saw it wasn't afterwards. He's so pathetic. I guess I always knew *that*." Holly looks at her big hiking boots and gives a short laugh. "But he didn't seem to know that it wasn't loaded. It wasn't even his gun, for godssakes. I guess it was that—his fear—that inspired me. For the first time, *I* was the one in control, he was scared of *me*. I stood there pointing the gun at him and I said, 'You son of a bitch, if you ever come around bothering me again, I'll let you have it.' "

"You said that?"

"I said it and I meant it, at the time. This morning all I wanted to do was get rid of the thing. . . . But I don't think he'll be coming around for a while."

"Where have you been all this time, all morning? I've been trying to call you." Magda can hear the plaintiveness in her voice. She shifts from foot to foot, trying to keep warm. This is a new Holly, all right. Strong and admirable. Beside her Magda feels worse than ever. There's no chance of Holly forgiving her in the state she's in.

"I drove out of the city. I needed to think. I had breakfast in a little cafe near Hood Canal. I walked along the beach."

Magda doesn't dare to ask what she's been thinking about. She sighs and turns toward the direction of the courthouse. "I'm going on back. . . . You coming?"

"Yes, but Magda. . . why?" Her blue eyes suddenly pierce right through Magda's.

"I don't know. I don't know."

Without another word, Holly starts off, with Magda following behind, no longer trying to keep up.

Eleven: Just the Facts, Ma'am

"On the morning of Monday, October 6, I was awakened by a knocking at the door. Two FBI agents stood there demanding to know how I had gotten an interview with a member of the Cutting Edge Brigade (see *Seattle News*, October 6). I slammed the door in their faces, but I couldn't get back to sleep.

"It was a rude awakening.

"A rude awakening to much more than routine questioning. This incident marked the beginning of a series of rude awakenings: to the world of subpoenas and harassment, to the terrain of the federal grand jury.

"This knock on the door was my awakening into another world, a legal one, where the Bill of Rights has no meaning, where loyalty, freedom of press and speech, the right to keep silent, have no importance, no validity at all.

"It was also an awakening, however, to the fact that we don't have to accept this system, that we can fight against it. And win."

Magda sighs, sits back in her swivel chair, and regards the paper sticking out of her typewriter. Not a bad lead, but she has surely used those words "rude awakening" a few times too often. And that business about "fighting against it" and "winning" is pretty hackneyed. Wallace got her off all right, but is that winning or legal manipulation? And Allison isn't exactly winning if she's going to jail.

Magda takes another sip of coffee cut with creme de cacao and looks around for another pack of cigarettes. She bought a carton of them this afternoon and a bottle of her favorite liqueur to help her get going. At least she has a beginning now. . . if that's really the way she wants to begin. Is the FBI visit really the best place to start? Or should she give an account of the grand jury first? Lead into the fact that these

152

subpoenas are part of a legal conspiracy happening all around the country?

It's ten o'clock according to her old alarm clock and she has been sitting here for almost an hour in front of her typewriter. Wondering how to put it all into perspective. It doesn't help that Magda is still feeling the effects of her hangover, not to mention the emotion-packed scenes with Paul and Holly today. Allison's court appearance was pale next to those events. She went in and out the door just like before, though with more confidence. Refused to answer any questions. Was dismissed. There is going to be a hearing tomorrow. Where she will most likely be found in contempt of court and packed off to jail.

Magda suddenly rips out her sheet of paper and puts another in the machine. She types a little rapidly: "It Can't Happen Here. Or Can It?" This done, however, her enthusiasm deserts her. She stares at the almost blank page in disgust. She takes another sip from her cup and drags on a cigarette.

Who, what, when, where? The cardinal questions of journalism. Yet all the really important things that have happened to her lately have occurred outside the "terrain of the federal grand jury," as she's so grandly put it. Now if she were writing a novel or making a movie, she could put it all in—Holly glimpsed through the pawnshop window, Paul carefully picking up the apples from the corners of the room, Tom holding Katey up for a better look at her mother speaking to the crowd, Wallace letting an oyster slip down his throat. What the fuck does she care about grabbing the headlines with stories about interviews and subpoenas and juries and court sentences? None of that means anything compared to what she has been through with Holly and Paul, with Allison, Toni, and Wallace.

That's the real story. But of course she can't tell it. She's not writing a novel or making a movie, she's writing an article for the *News*.

What was it she told Paul this afternoon? "I want to give events an interpretation they don't get in the straight media." Yes, that's why she's here, that's what she's trying to do. But she doesn't give a damn.

The way Holly looked at her on the hill, rain flattening her hair to a blonde streak of limpness, her eyes full of distrust and disappointment. "Why?" she had asked.

"I don't know why," Magda says aloud. "It's just the way I am." This defense doesn't help her now any more than it did then. Hopeless to try and get out of it now. Holly will probably never speak to her again. She didn't say another word today; after they got to the courthouse, she slipped to Allison and Bess' side and never left it. Magda had

153

to make do with Paul and his well-meant but abrasive questions. They quarreled again, just before he left for Ellensburg, their moment of reconciliation stamped out, voided, unable to bear up under the weight of argument.

It was his fault; why couldn't he keep his mouth shut? He had to keep asking her why she hadn't been harder on Deb in the interview. He was just like Toni. "Why didn't you ask her if she saw a contradiction in her theory of the vanguard and her belief that revolution had to come from the so-called masses?"

Christ. As if people wanted to read sectarian stuff like that. And just where did he get off criticizing Magda's questions when he would never, never have the guts to do what she'd done?

Magda lights another cigarette from her butt. If this keeps up, she'll become a chain smoker again. But why is everyone so hard on her? Can't she do anything without the whole world coming down on her?

And it hurts, it hurts with redoubled force, to have parted with Paul on bad terms. At least before, she was able to write him off as a worker who had abandoned the *News* as well as a lover who had abandoned her. But after this afternoon. . . and he had said he cared about her. Now she probably won't see him for months.

She stares at the page in her typewriter, fiddles with the cartridge, drums the keys. Come *on*, she encourages herself. Since when has writing ever been a problem for you? Just get an idea and go with it.

"I can write about anything. I can write it faster and better than anyone," was the sales pitch she gave one editor. She meant it; it was true. Whatever her personal circumstances, whichever lover she was leaving or was leaving her, she had always turned in her copy on time.

"I don't know how you do it," Dennis said to her once. "I sit down at my desk and I can't think of a thing." How patronizing she had been then. "That's how I sit down, too, but I don't get up until I have something."

Willpower, Magda thinks, pouring more crème de cacao into her cup. I've got willpower coming out my ears. So what's the problem now? She's never had a story this big before, has never been so involved.

Or is that the problem? Maybe she's too much in the limelight, too much an active participant to see the facts clearly enough to write about them. She has to use the first person in this story, and somehow the first person keeps leading her into other areas.

The matter of her own complicity, for instance. Her ambivalence about Deb and the whole CEB. It's fine to get up on her high horse and talk about the horrors of the grand jury, but she can't be so self-right-eous about her own motivation for interviewing Deb.

Her ambivalence about that has given another cast to the story. "I wouldn't give a flying fuck if they were all arrested," she says aloud. "They deserve it." In her heart of hearts she has to acknowledge that she doesn't see anything strange about the government wanting to know who's blowing up power stations and Safeways. " 'Course they want to know what I know," she mutters.

But she can't put those sentiments into a story for the *News*. She has to act the role of outraged victim; she has to write from that per-spective. Besides, there's Ted Shovik. It might not just be a question of Deb's getting arrested.

"Damn Allison," she says, finding some comfort in uttering her feelings out loud. "Why'd she do a thing like that?" If Allison hadn't been such a pushover, none of this would have happened. Magda wouldn't be in the hot seat having to justify herself. "Damn Allison," she says again. "She should have to write this article."

Magda can feel herself getting drunk, but she doesn't care. She can often write better when she's had a few drinks; alcohol has certainly gotten her through some boring enough articles. "Come on," she urges herself, "write something. Anything."

She looks again at her title and snorts. Didn't Sinclair Lewis write a book called *It Can't Happen Here?* She really should write a novel. Put it all in. Journalism can't begin to do justice to the personalities, the nuances of the past two weeks. "Could write a thriller," she says aloud. "A feminist thriller." For a moment, excited, she fantasizes a plot. An underground heroine. James as the villain. Holly with a gun. She could make Toni a character and take her apart. There would be vengeance and only Toni would know. You can't do stuff like that in an article. No fun.

But just as quickly the plot deserts her. She has never been able to write fiction. She took creative writing once and did badly at it. Mag-da remembers one story she wrote and was proud of; the teacher ripped it to shreds. He called her language clichéd and unimaginative, found her characters unconvincing. "You get tangled up whenever you try and write a sentence more than six words long," he said. "And you don't have to give every separate idea a new paragraph." Well, that was the end of that. She went back to the praise of her journalism teachers pretty quickly.

Besides, who ever made any money writing literature? She doesn't want to be like Carl, does she, sorting books at the library and writing poetry about sunsets and ferries on the Sound? Hell, she doesn't even *like* most fiction. All it is is verbal masturbation, getting off on the sound of your own words, talking about things nobody gives a damn about. The public doesn't want to read that kind of thing anymore, won't buy it, won't even look at it. It's not like when Dickens or somebody was alive and they hung on every word. Nowadays people want facts, they want to understand this crazy world they're living in.

This line of reasoning leads Magda back to the page in her typewriter. With a flourish she goes back and "x's" out the title. "You want facts, I'll give you facts," she mumbles. Where are her notes, anyway? They give her all the information she needs. All she has to do is string them together, paragraph by paragraph.

"The grand jury, some say, is one of the few resources of a democracy for gathering facts in an objective and yet confidential way. But others call it a relic of the British judicial system which has survived and flourished in a manner it was never intended to. Instead of protecting the rights of citizens it invades their privacy and robs them of their accepted legal defenses. It makes criminals of us all.

"The beginnings of the grand jury are obscure" (not that obscure, only where is that damn article that tells its history?).

Painstakingly Magda sketches in a chronology with the aid of her notes. The story of Lilburne, who refused to testify before the House of Lords in 1642 and who became a hero to the British public. The various laws and judicial precedents which established the grand jury in this country. How the grand jury was used to investigate the Mafia. How it was revived under the Nixon administration by John Mitchell to be used against student radicals and blacks and women. How First Amendment rights for reporters have steadily eroded due to the Brandenburg vs Hayes case. And so on.

Midnight comes and goes. The crème de cacao sinks past the halfway mark. But by two-thirty Magda finally has the draft of an article she can live with. Tomorrow she'll revise and type it, show it to the others on the *News*. Suddenly all her qualms are gone. She has managed to keep her own part in the story down to a minimum and to concentrate on the obvious facts and injustices of the proceedings against her and Allison. In Magda's article they have joined a galaxy of people similarly harassed and pursued. In a mood of triumph, Magda revives her phrase from the first draft, "We don't have to accept this system. . . we can fight against it. And win."

At three a.m. she goes to bed to sleep the sleep of the just. Of course, she thinks as she drifts off—have to remember to put in what happens to Allison tomorrow.

She wakes up with another hangover, the peculiarly sweet and heavy-lidded kind that comes from liqueurs. Her throat, when she tries to clear it, rasps like a broom being dragged across the floor. After drinking half a pitcher of grapefruit juice Magda plods into the bathroom and considers herself in the mirror. Does an alcoholic still feel remorse in the morning? She wonders. She feels as much remorse as she is capable of feeling; it drowns out every other thought and emotion in a cacophony of accusing voices. How many days this week has she woken up with a hangover?

It's bad, it's very bad, Magda, she tells herself in the mirror, beginning to brush her teeth. Broad-faced, glum, she stares back and forth at herself, mirror to reality. How she used to hate that face when she was younger. In grade school they called her Injun. Maggie Ellen was the name of a pretty little girl, someone like Audrey, her sister, who had sunny yellow hair and blue eyes. But Magda's skin was brownish, her cheekbones high and slanted, her eyes slitted over them. Her mother allowed as how someone, way back, had married a Choctaw. "But you're not *Indian*, Maggie Ellen."

Later, in high school, after reading through some old issues of *National Geographic* in the dentist's office, Magda had decided she must be Russian or something. She looked just like the women peasants on the Volga. At the time the thought made her miserable. She *wanted* to look like everyone else. It wasn't until after college that she began to see her different looks as an advantage; not until she got out of Kansas and found that not everyone had blue eyes and blonde hair and turned-up noses. On the East Coast everyone thought she was Jewish.

"Maggie Ellen," they said. "What kind of a name is *that*?"

She shortened it to Maggie for a while, and then took to calling herself Margaret. But neither felt right, neither felt suitable. When she came across the name "Magda" in a newspaper somewhere, she recognized it immediately as the kind of name she should have, and when she moved to Seattle, she changed it.

Amazing how easy it was. No one ever challenged it, asked where it came from. "Magda," people said when she was introduced, and nodded. It fit her perfectly. It gave her the ethnic, even exotic quality that she craved. With a name like Magda she stood out, no one would suspect that she was from Kansas; they imagined distant steppes and broad rivers. So did she.

She doesn't hate her face now, though this morning it looks pretty awful. Swollen around the lids and sagging everywhere else. Twenty-seven. She'd better start being more careful the way she treats herself.

It's not just her face, but the rest of her body. Even in the pinkesh light of the bathroom her limbs look flabby and unused. Magda pinches the flesh of her thigh, the skin has a tough look, but underneath it the fat seems to wobble a little. Her breasts, never the springy sort, droop down toward her stomach. And her stomach. . . why does all her excess weight have to collect just there? She doesn't have a waist anymore; she looks like a log with a big burl on one side. But her hips are slim and her legs are still reasonably well-shaped. . . . . Magda splashes cold water from the tap over her face and shoulders, shivers, and begins to feel better. What she needs is a brisk walk and several strong cups of coffee.

A few hours later Magda turns up at the courthouse much invigorated. The sky is blue, the wind is slight, and she has forgotten all about alcoholic remorse. Her strong head has come out on top once again. In her shoulder bag is the article for the *News*. While consuming a three-egg omelette, four pieces of toast, and five cups of coffee with cream and sugar at her favorite cafe this morning, Magda not only rewrote it but went so far as to sketch out another article for a national paper. Where would she be, after all, if she felt bad about everything she'd ever done? The only cure for self-hatred is to work harder, to reprove herself only by re-proving herself. Nothing like coffee to make you feel confident and ambitious again. That's one vice she will never give up.

She meets Bess on the sidewalk in front of the big granite building. But even the sight of the lawyer, in her neat tweed jacket and wool skirt, can't bring Magda down this morning. Besides, Bess isn't looking so great this morning either. Some of her customary briskness is missing as she approaches Magda.

"Bad news," she tells Magda first thing. "Mrs. Houseman has decided to talk to the grand jury. Her lawyer phoned me an hour ago. When she realized that it really was a question of going to jail, she gave in."

"Oh shit." Magda stares at her. "That means she'll implicate Allison."

"I'm afraid so. I called Allison and told her to prepare for the worst. Mrs. Houseman will have already testified by the time Allison has her hearing." Bess pauses and smiles slightly. "Allison said she'd been prepared for a week."

"I suppose she's bringing her suitcase to the hearing with her."

"Her backpack. . . she said Katey asked her if she was going camping." Bess laughs and then looks depressed. "I've been preparing myself for this all along, too, but I still don't believe it's going to happen. If Deb's mother weren't talking, I think we'd still have a chance with the judge. But now it's going to be more than a question of contempt, though that's what they'll use today."

"You mean that they could legitimately arrest Allison for harboring a fugitive?"

"Yes." Bess fingers her briefcase unhappily. "It's times like these when I wonder why I ever became a lawyer."

"You mean when your clients go off to jail?" In spite of herself Magda feels a wave of sympathy. Bess really does look miserable, and because of that, more vulnerable than Magda has ever seen her.

"When I was in high school I used to do a lot of acting, and that's sometimes what being a lawyer reminds me of. I'm forced to play a role as much as the prosecutor and the judge. Not only in the courthouse, but outside it, everywhere. When you get down to it, guilt or innocence doesn't mean a thing in the courts. The academy award goes to the person who's the most convincing. I couldn't be a lawyer if I didn't play along with it, if I didn't psych myself up to believe in my own lines. Most of the time I even forget that I'm just acting a role, but sometimes I remember that it's all a play—it's a farce, even when we're making believe it's a tragedy."

"I can see that if you're representing or prosecuting a criminal, but what about this case? There are real issues at stake, aren't there?"

"Of course, but that makes it worse, that makes it more painful. I'm serious, you're serious, and Allison is most serious of all. She's prepared to go to jail to protect her right to keep silent. But that doesn't impress the law. The law has its own morality. It doesn't care how moral or immoral your intent was—if you've broken the rules and they can prove it, then they'll punish you. What does protecting a battered women's shelter mean to the law?"

"But a law *was* broken."

Bess sighs. "Of course. And our only hope—ultimately—is that if enough people break the laws, if enough people are defended strongly enough with enough publicity, if enough people go to jail for breaking those laws—then they will be forced to change the laws. That's what I believe and what I work for. But what I mean, is that the framework is somehow all wrong. It's like a badly written play where the actors attempt to change the outcome of the plot without being free to change any of the lines."

"May I quote you?"

"No, don't be ridiculous." Bess relaxes a little and smiles. "Surely

159

you must feel the same about journalism sometimes, that it's all a kind of game?''

"You mean, do I ever want to break down and tell the truth instead of the facts? Sure, I feel it's a game sometimes, but that doesn't stop me doing it. Hell, I don't even know what the truth *is* most of the time. And you've got to have some kind of framework."

"But. . ." Bess stops, automatically glances at her platinum watch. "Who does tell the truth, I wonder? Poets, writers?"

"Oh they just make stuff up."

"I like you, Magda. You're down to earth. I must seem awfully existential this morning, talking about truth and everything. It's just the way I'm feeling."

"Well, I like you better like this. Most of the time you put me off," Magda confesses. She feels dangerously close to liking Bess, too.

"I do?" Bess looks puzzled. "Why?"

I'm not going to go into that, Magda thinks. She tries to make a joke instead. "Oh, I hate everybody who makes more money than me."

"Oh." Bess doesn't see the joke. She bridles guiltily. "I'm not going to charge Allison anything, you know."

Magda stiffens, too. "Why not? Even actors have to eat."

Bess' lips tighten. If she were Toni, Toni whose therapist advised her to let her feelings out, she would make some nasty but sincere crack back. Bess, however, is too unenlightened and professional to let her anger show. She averts her eyes and looks sorry to have spoken to Magda at all.

Why do I do this kind of thing? Magda asks herself. But before she can frame any sort of apology, she sees Allison, accompanied by her mother and Holly, crossing the street toward them. Allison is indeed wearing a backpack, looking ridiculous but strangely cheerful. "Yoo-hoo," she waves.

Dennis, Carl, and Toni and Lisa appear at the same time. No one could talk Allison into a larger gathering. "I don't care if it would look more dramatic," she said. "I don't want the whole world gawking at me as I'm led off in chains." She didn't want her children to be there either. "I don't mind them seeing me fighting back. But handcuffs. No. I never would have wanted to see my mother in handcuffs."

From the looks of her mother, Magda can see why. Nothing has even happened yet and already she is teary eyed and quivery. Magda nods to her and Allison but addresses herself to the friends from the *News*. "Got an article all ready to go in this issue."

They respond in their most typical ways. "Oh great," "Let's see," "Oh," and silence from Lisa.

"I'm writing another one for *In These Times*," Magda says, and has the satisfaction of seeing Toni's thin nostrils quiver. Lisa puts her arm around Toni's waist but Toni moves away. Doesn't say anything.

"Where is everybody?" Carl asks.

"Allison didn't want a rally today."

"I still expected some people to show up." Even as he speaks, some down-jacketed, muffler-wrapped acquaintances begin to drift toward them. Allison notices them too, but doesn't seem very bothered. By now she looks almost beyond everything, detached and resigned.

"Did you tell them?" she asks, coming over to their group.

"Tell us what?" Toni, Miss Nose-for-News, says eagerly.

"About Mrs. Houseman. She's going to talk."

"Oh no!" Toni says. That's right, Magda remembers. She told Toni that Allison dropped Deb's kid off with her mother. So Toni understands that it's more than a matter of Mrs. Houseman deserting the cause; it means the end of the road for Allison.

The others don't understand that yet and express their disappointment and sympathy loudly. They tell the news to others as they are joined and soon a small crowd is gathered discussing all the aspects of the grand jury system. Magda is bored and begins to wish it were all over. She can't help glancing at Holly from time to time, and wondering if she should go over to her. She would hate for Holly to pointedly ignore her with so many people looking on, and she's almost sure Holly would.

She won't go over to her; still, it makes her defensive and miserable. She saw something in Holly yesterday that attracted her more than the persona of sweet shyness and sympathy. Strength and determination without bitchiness. Unlike Magda with the petty rancours that blight her personality. But now to make Holly see that Magda isn't really so bad, that she would like to be a better person, that she could change.

I have never asked anyone for forgiveness, Magda realizes. She's apologized a lot. She practically got down on her hands and knees and begged one or two people not to leave her. But through it all she knew that she was lying. She knew that she wouldn't die if they left her or stayed angry. She despised herself and she despised them if they were taken in by her begging.

She certainly won't beg Holly's pardon. Only. . . Holly does look nice today, why had Magda never realized what a beautiful woman she was? With ready nostalgia Magda recalls the details of their lovemaking. Holly's strong and lanky body, her fresh iris eyes, her passion.

Oh, fuck it. Magda goes over to her.

"Hi, Holly."

"Hi." Holly looks down at her briefly and then shifts her eyes to the wet manicured lawn of the courthouse.

"Have you thought about what you're going to do after today? With the business, I mean?" Magda tries.

"No."

"Are you going to get someone else to work there?"

"I don't know."

"Are you going to stay mad at me forever?"

Holly stares harder at the courthouse lawn and then at some of the others. "Looks like they're going in now."

"So don't answer me," Magda snaps. If Holly is just going to ignore her, ignore the whole thing, then fine. Forget it. She hates that kind of attitude, that refusal to deal with problems and hurts. It makes everything worse.

The little band falls in behind Allison and Bess like pallbearers, talking in subdued voices. Magda feels like the corpse in the coffin. Is she doomed to alienate everyone then? Won't they see that she means well, it's just her damned pride that gets in the way, that makes her lash out?

Into the courthouse, through the marble foyer, up in the elevators. The routine is beginning to seem like a repetitious nightmare. The same hall, though on a different floor; the same benches. A new dark painting in a gold-leafed frame that looks just like the one on the other floor— a heavyset judge in a black suit, jowls sinking down over his immaculate collar. Power incarnate.

Magda fishes for a cigarette, lights it, and stares irritably around her. Toni is hedging up on Bess' and Allison's last-minute conversation with a reporterly ease. Let her. Magda would like to say something cheerful and encouraging to Allison, but it doesn't look as if she even needs it. She listens seriously and intently to what Bess is saying about the manner of appeal, but her eyes are far away. Probably looking forward to this martyrdom by now, Magda thinks. How pure can you get, going to jail for your beliefs? When she gets out, she won't be the same.

The marshal opens the courthouse door and ushers Allison and Bess in, leaving the rest of them to wait—endlessly, it seems. There is nothing to do except talk, and Magda is too restless to talk in the hall. She captures Carl and together they leave in search of a cup of coffee.

Over the scarred linoleum table of a nearby coffee shop Magda lets him read her article for the *News*. While she knows his praise comes too easily, she still basks in it.

"One of these days," he says, "you're going to be famous."

"Oh, I don't know about that," she smiles.

"No, I mean it—I'll be able to say I knew you when." His brown-gold eyes are like two lamps of worship in his pudgy face.

"How about you? Don't you want to be famous? How's that poetry going—or are you working on your novel yet?"

"Oh." Carl's eyes quench slightly. "All right, the poetry, I mean. I get published here and there. I don't think I'll be famous though. And the novel, well, it's still in my head."

"Am I still in it?"

"You're the main character."

"So I'm the main character now, well! Do I have a name yet?"

"Sonya," he says promptly. "You're going to be very mysterious. You'll come and go and throw everybody into confusion. And everybody will be in love with you. I'm going to set it in Paris, did I tell you that? I lived there for a year, you know. Probably if I'm going to write my novel, I should go back there."

"Paris, huh? I've never been there. . . I've never been anywhere."

"Oh, you'd love it, Magda. You'd feel right at home there, I can tell."

He babbles on about cafes and bridges and cathedrals while Magda falls into revery. Of course he's a jerk—as if there weren't enough mysterious women floating around in men's literature already. Still, it must be pleasant to live so completely in a dream world. She can see that the life of cafes and organ concerts, little bookstores and not much to do would suit him. He doesn't have the drive to do much else. What would she do in Paris? She could never learn to speak the language, for one thing, and she'd lose touch with the American political scene for another. That doesn't seem to bother him. His politics are ethereal, if anything. Always suggesting that art can change consciousness, provide models. She accepts his presence on the *News*, mainly because of his ready support, even as she's continually surprised by his vagueness and lethargy. He said when he first began to work with them that he wanted to write some in-depth articles on art and politics, but these have never materialized. Occasionally he writes a torturous review of some obscure book or movie, but for the most part he simply sits around in the office, reading and answering the telephone. No one, least of all Magda, ever really questions him, in part because he's so sincere and pleasant, but mostly because they need someone to answer the telephone.

Now she lets him drone on and drinks her coffee. This is one person she could never quarrel with; when she's in the right mood, he doesn't even make her impatient. He's harmless really, and so grateful when she gives him space in her life.

But finally she has to interrupt. "Maybe we'd better be getting back?"

He quickly puts his hand over the check as if Magda, the ardent feminist, were going to fight him for it, and offers to pay. Another one of his gallant gestures. You should be in Paris, dear, she thinks pityingly. You're wasted on me.

Back in the courthouse they find the same group of people huddled wearily in the hall. Allison and Bess have been in there for over an hour now, and there is much debate about whether this is a hopeful sign or not.

Magda can hear Toni telling someone that she's going to try and talk to Mrs. Houseman. Magda wonders if she's speaking loud enough for her benefit. Go ahead, she thinks, and good luck. All the same she feels pissed. The sooner I get out of this city, the better, she tells herself. I wonder when I'll hear something.

Holly is, as usual, reading in a far corner, seemingly oblivious to everyone around her. Magda sits down beside her, but Holly doesn't look up from her book. We are the two people closest to Allison here, Magda thinks defensively; we should be able to talk about that, at least. But she can't think of anything to say. She suddenly notices Allison's well-stuffed backpack leaning against the wall across from them, looking forlornly sturdy. The futility and sadness of the whole thing strikes her all at once. A game, Bess said, and yes, it was a game, a fucking stupid and depressing game. Allison is in there right now, only a wall away, not able to give her real reasons for doing what she did, only able to keep asserting her rights as a citizen of this patriarchal and oppressive system, while she and Bess and the judge all know that she's broken a law.

Immediately Magda regrets having written her article for the *News* so objectively. She hadn't wanted to use the first person, hadn't wanted to expose herself—but that's what it's all about, isn't it? Real fucking people caught up in this game, and not just anyone, but Allison Morris, mother of Katey and Ben, someone who only wanted to help another woman.

It is a shitty game when Magda can't even mention Deb, arrogant Deb who got them into this mess and is now probably hundreds of miles away. I hope they catch you, I hope they do, goddamn bitch. Then she thinks of Ted Shovik, murdered, and shudders. Get away then, Deb, get away and stay away and remember what people like Allison have done for you the next time you start talking about revolution.

Tom appears in the corridor at the moment the doors open so that he is the first person Allison sees as she steps out. Neither says anything, but he goes to her and puts his arms around her. Allison is crying and no one else makes a move. They can see from Bess' set and concerned face that Allison has been found in contempt. That she is going to jail. It's not even ironic that Allison should be finding comfort in the arms of her former husband, not when he looks like a grown-up Ben.

Magda is aware then of Holly weeping next to her. She puts out her hand and Holly takes it, clutches it rather, so that it's almost painful. Slowly everyone moves toward Allison and begins to talk. They touch her, they try and hold on to her, as if by some gesture of affection they could keep her there with them a little longer. Allison's mother suddenly lets out a strangled noise and pushes everyone away.

"It's all right, mom, it's all right." Allison is no longer crying. She even smiles as she strokes and hugs her mother. "Take good care of them, won't you?"

She turns to Holly and Magda, the only ones holding back. "That business better be there when I get out, you hear?"

Holly nods, silent tears coursing down her pale face.

Allison gives her a pat and a hug which includes Magda. "Glad you're together," she whispers. She doesn't know, Magda realizes with a start, almost of renewed hope.

Two marshals appear, as if on cue in this strange melodrama. One of them has a pair of handcuffs.

"Sorry," he says, as he fastens them on. He looks as if he feels a little ridiculous. Allison isn't going to run away at this point. "Regulations," he says.

Allison looks at her backpack. "You'll have to carry it for me, then. I'm not Houdini, unfortunately."

The last glimpse they have of Allison is just before the elevator doors close on her. Her hands are bound together, but her face is oddly peaceful. There are no last words, no last quote for Magda's article. Allison has nothing more to say.

PART THREE:
HOLLY'S AMBITION

I like to think of Harriet Tubman
Harriet Tubman who carried a revolver,
who had a scar on her head from a brick thrown
by a slave master (because she
talked back) and who
had a ransom on her head
of thousands of dollars and who
was never caught, and who
had no use for the law
when the law was wrong. . .

        Susan Griffin, "I Like to Think of Harriet Tubman"

November 10

Since Magda left for New York I've been happier, I think. Just knowing I won't run into her on the street—and have to make some kind of conversation, see her embarrassment or distaste for me and what I remind her of. I'm glad she's out of the city, on the other side of the country. I've always been this way—if love or friendship ends, I don't want to see that person again. I'd like them blown off the face of the earth. I'd like them to disappear. Completely. I'm not good at starting over with lowered expectations.

Why is this? With James it was the same way. Once something is over, it's over. It's more than over, worse than over. Because those people are still walking around, wanting to talk to you, to talk about *it*. Strangers again, but strangers that you've known intimately.

When I went to a meeting with Magda, half the people she waved at or hugged had been lovers of hers. "Hi, how *are* you?" she'd call, and when I'd ask, "Who's that?" she'd say, "Oh him?" "Oh, her?" "He was a lover of mine." "She and I were lovers once." I'm not kidding, there were five or six of them. And they seemed on the best of terms. . . at least they all greeted each other.

With me it's all or nothing. Magda tried to be friendly after that night, tried to talk to me about what was happening. But I wasn't interested, couldn't deal with it. We both knew that it was finished after she slept with that lawyer. Why pretend that we could go on as before, or even that we were friends.

For a while it was sticky, avoiding her. We were the core of the Committee Against Grand Jury Abuse, after all. But after Allison went away I had more work than I could handle at the shop, and that was as good an excuse as any I could have invented for refusing Magda's invitations to dinner, i.e., "to talk about it."

I avoided her because I knew I couldn't make her understand that what had happened was irrevocable. . . that once I turn against somebody, I turn against them. It's as if a door in my heart closes; I can hear it slam, why can't anybody else?

This isn't to say I don't go around forever trying to figure out what went wrong.

Allison said, "Magda's so casual, I'm used to it, though I don't like it much. Maybe you shouldn't take it so seriously."

But I stopped her, "It's all over, Allison, please."

Magda tried to apologize once, on the telephone. When I asked her to leave me alone, she said, "It wasn't as if we had an agreement or anything. . ."

"I didn't know people signed contracts these days."

"You give it more importance than it deserves," she said. "Because it was your first lesbian relationship."

"Don't tell me how much importance I gave it!" I hung up. And cried and cried.

My one night with Magda meant more to me than my three years with James. But it hurts me more, too. I never thought a woman could hurt me as much as he did. It's different though. I was afraid of him. I couldn't be afraid of Magda. But I could hate her just the same.

Toni heard about it (from Allison? from Magda? along with how many others?) and took it politically. She stopped me in the street one day and, after a few minutes' chat about the grand jury, expressed her sympathy for me. "In my opinion you can't trust bisexuals—they don't love women out of a real political commitment to feminism but just with some kind of passing eroticism, you know, just titillation. I've seen her do this before. She's immoral, you know. She'll pick up some inexperienced woman and then drop her just like that when some guy comes along. I'm only telling you this because I wouldn't want you to think that all lesbians are like her."

"I don't," I assured her, only wanting to get away. Afterwards I was mad at myself for letting her talk to me that way, well-meaning as she was. I didn't feel that Magda had hooked me, not really. When I thought about it, in fact, I could have seen something like this coming for a long time. I may have been inexperienced, as Toni so patronizingly put it (and how did she know, anyway?), but it didn't follow that I wasn't responsible for my acts.

For the first time I began to see what happened with Magda as inevitable, necessary, and continuing. I'd liked sex with a woman, liked it better than I had with James or with the two other men in my life. It may not be much of a comparison, but it was enough of a comparison for me.

Magda laughed at me when I told her how much I liked it with her, how much better it was. She wasn't about to take sides.

"Different, yes, and good. I don't know about better," she said.

I tried to argue, strengthened by the conviction that I was giving her pleasure. "But a man can't know how this feels," I said, touching her. "I know."

She was, I see now, sophisticated enough to have had this conversation before. She didn't argue back, but laughed and said, lazily putting her hand over mine to increase the pressure, "That's just it—a man doesn't know—he has to use his imagination."

Later I tried to take the question up again. "I could never feel this comfortable, with my clothes off, with a man. Too self-conscious about my skinniness, my bony hips, everything."

"Hmm," said Magda, not responding to the distinction I wanted to draw. "I like your body."

And I thought she had the most beautiful body I'd ever seen. Her skin was brown, with an odd toughness, as if she had a patina of varnish

168

over even her least exposed parts. Though on the fat side, she wasn't spongy—her fat wasn't even in the usual places for a woman; for instance, her legs were thin and longish, and her hips and buttocks only lightly padded. Her extra weight was all in her torso, in her protruding stomach and huge breasts. When she unfastened her bra, her breasts spilled down her rib cage; her almost black nipples rested on her heavy, many-folded stomach. Seen from the back she looked thin; from the side, pregnant; from the front like a goddess of fertility. I looked at her from every angle with terrible greediness; once I took handfuls of her brown stomach fat and kneaded it. "Oh, gross," she said, but she laughed.

There were so many things I wanted to ask her: about herself, about her other love affairs with women. There wasn't time. What did it last, two days? Should I be glad I didn't expose myself more or sorry I didn't find out what I wanted to know?

Allison was the one who told me Magda was leaving. Over the phone on her weekly call to me. "She got a job with *Challenge* in New York City. She wrote me a letter."

"She's leaving you in the lurch like this?" I was furious and depressed. Allison had been in the women's prison over two weeks, while Magda, who had just as much to do with what had happened, was preparing to lead the glamorous life of a journalist. In New York City. So far away.

"Well," said Allison reasonably. "What could she do here, now? It should be obvious that I'm going to be here for as long as the grand jury's sitting and maybe longer."

"There's plenty she could do. . . you don't think we're going to let you rot in there, do you?"

"I'm not rotting. If it weren't for thinking about the shop and Katey and Ben, I'd be perfectly comfortable. It's not like I'm in a dungeon or anything. . . . I have a lot of freedom, really. I've read more books in the past week than I've read in the past ten years and I. . ."

"Yes, but you do have the shop and the kids!"

"Holly, come on, don't remind me. Anyway, it's Magda you're upset about, not me. So let's talk about that."

"I don't want to talk about her, I don't even know her anymore, I have to hear she's leaving from you."

"Well, she hasn't treated you very well, that's for sure, but some of it is your fault. Yes, it is. You were the one who broke it off, not her. Yes, you did. I know all about it. I tried to explain to Magda that you took things more seriously than most people, and it *was* your first relationship with a woman."

"Why is everybody harping on that? I feel like a goldfish in a bowl, something being studied. 'Her first lesbian relationship.' Why is everybody so interested?"

"I guess we should leave you alone. . ." Allison sounded apologetic.

"If you don't mind." Not that I didn't need to talk about it, but I didn't know how, or to whom. I didn't want to be thought as stupid as I felt, as naive. And another thing, why did all of them say 'first lesbian relationship,' as if there were going to be a long string of them?

Not that anybody was about to leave me alone. Toni called up soon to invite me to a party at her house. I can't stand parties and don't know why I said I'd go to this one, except that I was so surprised I didn't have time to think about it. I was pretty sure I didn't like Toni—I knew her very little but I'd heard a lot about her, from Magda, mostly.

My memory duplicates Magda's throaty voice exactly: "Antonia's pure, you can see it in her face—not wholesome, but pure-itan, and too good for the rest of us. It's not something she puts on, it's just there, fuck her. More than anything it's a class difference between us. . .she called me promiscuous, can you believe? As if that word has any meaning now. She said I was acting out male fantasies of the Sixties, that that was my idea of liberation. Having lots of lovers. Implying that I was some kind of slut. I told her that she didn't have to act out male fantasies, because she was practically a man herself, dominating, controlling, trying to set standards that *she* felt comfortable with. Have you seen her and Lisa together? It's disgusting, the way Toni pushes that woman around. That's Toni's idea of a good relationship—monogamous, man and wife, dominant and submissive, everybody playing their roles, and meanwhile trying to impose that kind of thing on everyone else."

"Why do you say it's class?" I asked. "It just sounds like. . ."

"The upper classes always think the lower classes are being promiscuous. Christ, what do you think birth control and sterilization are all about? 'The lower classes don't have anything to do but fuck, they're not like us, interested in higher things, they'd fuck all day if you let them and overpopulate the world with more like them. . .' And I'll tell you what, Holly, however much I admire Toni in some ways, she's got a streak of fascism in her personality. . ."

That was all before I saw what Magda was like. I was sympathetic, I didn't see any of it applying to me. My own opinion now is that, except for the sexual thing, Magda and Toni are too much alike to be comfortable with each other, and class doesn't have that much to do with it. I never really understood Magda's obsession with class differences anyway, how she could think of herself as lower class. My family has more money than hers, but she never brought that up. It seemed like she only used it on people she didn't like for other reasons.

The party was at Toni's house and there were only women there, which worried me at first. The party had been going on for a while when I got there:; I slipped in unnoticed and put my six-pack in the refrigerator after taking one. I always drink beer at parties, probably a holdover from my days with James.

I felt self-conscious and kept to the walls, even though no one was paying me any particular attention. One or two women said hi, but I still felt awkward. All women, I thought, all lesbians probably. For some reason I kept imagining that I was going to have to pass a lie detector test or something; maybe I thought there was a room somewhere in the house where I would be tortured if I didn't give the right answers to questions like: How long have you been interested in women? Is it true you've slept with men? And married one? How do you know you're really sexually attracted to women? Does that mean you only want to be with women? You mean you've only been with one woman—Magda Jones? We know about her, she's not a lesbian, she's bisexual. Does that mean you're bisexual, too? Just experimenting?

Another thing. Most of the women had very short hair and wore baggy trousers and vests. I had long hair and was wearing jeans and a sweater. I felt out of place, lurking along the walls with a beer.

When a woman suddenly asked me to dance I must have jumped a mile. She laughed. "You must be thinking about something pretty interesting."

"Oh, no," I said. I couldn't remember what I'd been thinking about at all.

She leaned against the wall beside me and, without asking, took a swig from my beer. She had just come from dancing and her forehead was beaded with sweat; the back of her shirt was damp.

"I'm Denver," she said.

"Holly."

Denver seemed about half as tall as me and as chubby as a stuffed animal. Her smiling face was a funny combination of wrinkles and freckles, so that I had no idea whether she was old or young. I couldn't help remembering Magda's broad mobile face, her majestic shoulders just then. I felt as if I were peering down at a midget. Denver wasn't at all shy, though, and immediately began to talk about the music, how great it was, and how she'd seen this group in concert and it was terrible how they'd broken up. "We need more women's music like this, fast and funny—most of it is so drippy."

I couldn't keep up with her because I hadn't been listening to the music at all, but her quick talk did have the effect of making me relax a little. She asked me questions, but not at all the threatening ones I'd been imagining: "Do you play anything? No? Too bad, I'm always looking for women to play music with. I play the drums. I brought them tonight, and my friend Kathy brought her flute. Later we're really going to get *down*."

She laughed and I laughed too, partly at the idea of her small, many-ringed hands pounding on a set of drums, and partly because I suddenly realized that I was enjoying myself and that I had nothing to be afraid of.

"Is your name really Denver?"

"Sure," she winked. "It used to be Los Angeles, but I changed it." She took another swig of my beer and finished it. "Hey, is there any more of that?"

"In the kitchen." I turned and she started to follow me.

"Holly!" said Toni, appearing right in front of us. She nodded to Denver and hugged me. When I stepped back, Denver had disappeared. I felt as insecure as ever.

"Sit down," Toni invited, guiding me to a rattan settee piled with bright pillows. It wasn't very wide and I ended up much closer to her than I would have liked. "I'm so glad you came," she said, and looked at me expectantly. "Are you having a good time?"

"Oh yes."

"Good. You look wonderful."

"So do you." In her case it was true. Everything Magda had told me about Toni's upper class background came back. In spite of her careful dressing down, she had the appearance and air of a society hostess. She was wearing a thin white Indian blouse over a black leotard and white drawstring pants. The lines of her body, outlined in black under the white, were slim and elegant. Her long pale hair was tied back, not in its usual braid, but in a straight-falling tail. My hair is blonde, but it was positively yellow and dirty next to Toni's. She looked like a dancer and gestured like one, too, her tapering fingers forming arcs and circles.

Unlike Denver, Toni obviously expected me to keep up my side of the conversation.

"Have you been dancing? I haven't seen you before this."

172

"No. . . I like the music though. . . uh, Denver told me that there's going to be some live music later, drumming and. . ."

"I suppose so. I saw she brought her drums." Sweet condescension here. "What do you think of her? Do you like her?"

Some kind of trap here. "She's nice."

Toni leaned forward so that her white-blonde hair swung over her shoulder. "*I* didn't invite her. Lisa did. I'm afraid she's interested in Lisa. She's kind of predatory."

"Oh."

"Well, she pounced on you right away, didn't she?"

Toni's words had their effect; my paranoia came back. I had never been "pounced on" by a woman before. Is this what it would be like, being a lesbian? Getting out of the heterosexual jungle only to be sized up and propositioned by women? Learning to be wary of women as well as men? I felt a little ill and may have shown it, because Toni considerately changed the subject. Actually, she got down to what she'd no doubt invited me to the party to discuss.

"Well," she said. "So Magda's leaving for New York on Tuesday. Have you said good-bye to her yet?"

"No," I answered confusedly, thinking, Tuesday—so soon; thinking, oh, god, I won't see her again.

"Me neither. And I probably won't. I mean, I'm disgusted with her, leaving the paper like this. It's a job I could have had, you know, but I didn't want to move to New York City. No thanks. Too crazy. Besides, the *News* would fold if both of us left."

"I guess it's a good magazine. . . I haven't really ever read it."

"Oh, it's okay. It's probably what Magda deserves. Actually I think she'll find it's not as good a job as she thinks. I mean, from what I understand, there's not that much writing involved. She'll be more of a copy editor." The scorn in Toni's nasal voice was enough to wither even the sturdy rubber plant at one end of the settee; if Magda had heard Toni, she probably would have strangled her. Not that I disbelieved Toni; it might well be a low position, but I didn't doubt that Magda would make the most of it.

"They offered it to you first?" I asked cautiously.

"Well. Not exactly, but almost. You know I wrote an article for them about the grand jury stuff. . . . Magda was mad about that, you know. . . she'd been wanting to write for them for a long time, but never got it together. . . she thought she should be writing about her case when obviously she didn't have the time or the objectivity. . . . So anyway, they were very pleased with it, my article, and the managing editor

173

called me up to say they'd like to see more stuff from me. I made the mistake of telling Magda that, and you know how competitive she is, well, she apparently sent them some of her past articles and then told them she was moving to New York and asked if they had any jobs open. If I'd known that they were looking for somebody. . . not that it matters, because I came to Seattle to get away from the East Coast. . ."

It was apparent that Magda had outsmarted Toni once again, and in the most humiliating way possible. I couldn't help feeling pleased in spite of my pain.

"It makes me furious, when I think about how much I taught Magda, went over her first articles with her, helped her rewrite, discussed the political issues with her. . ."

"I thought Magda had a degree in journalism and had worked on. . ."

"She may have worked for a few newspapers, but she'd never done political writing before. She had no politics when she came to the *News*. . . in fact, she still doesn't. She's an opportunist, pure and simple. She did that interview with Deb not through any real conviction but just to piss me off." Toni's right hand clenched when she said this.

I kept quiet, unsure whether to laugh, cry or cheer. Out of the corner of my eye I saw Denver join a group of women around the stereo, obviously arguing for a wilder album than one of them was about to put on.

". . . journalism degree from the University of *Kansas*," Toni was saying. "And I bet she used it too, to get that job. While I've got a degree in art history from Radcliffe and it'll never do me a bit of good. . . I'll be writing for the *News* forever."

I wished she would stop. Every time she mentioned Magda's name my hands got dry and my heart pounded. I asked if I could get her a beer, but she had no intention of letting me escape so soon. "And when I think of what she did to you, Holly, I get so angry. . ."

I sank back into the settee and stared at my knuckles. Why wouldn't she leave me alone? It was none of her business.

"Ask anybody here about Magda," Toni said bitterly. "They share my opinion. She's been lovers with about half of us at one time or another."

Did Toni say "us?" That jolted me. Magda and Toni. "I didn't know you. . ."

"You didn't know, she didn't tell you?" Toni flicked her hair over her shoulder angrily. "That figures. I bet she told you all kinds of crap about me and never told you the real reason I stopped being friends with her."

"No, she didn't."

"Well, she did the same thing to me as she did to you. She was screwing Paul at the same time. She didn't tell either of us what was going on and when I found *out* about it, she pretended like she didn't know what I was talking about. Paul didn't care, he was through with her by then, but I was furious. I didn't become a lesbian so that I could share my lover with a *man*."

Toni spat out the last word as if it were venom. I was in a state of shock. I heard Magda saying again, "Sure I slept with Wallace, so what? It doesn't change my feeling for you."

I got up blindly and walked toward the door.

"You're not leaving?" asked Denver. She was in the middle of unpacking her drums in the hallway. "Not before the *real* music?"

I kept going.

"How about a walk instead?" She grabbed two coats, not ours, off the coatrack and slung one of them over my shoulders, reaching up high to do it. Then she took my arm and led me outside. When she touched me all the fears Toni had awakened about predatory lesbians came back, but a combination of misery and politeness kept me from drawing away.

It was an awful night, damp and windy, and before we had gone half a block it began to rain again. I couldn't hear a word of what Denver was saying to me; the top of her head came only to my shoulder and besides, the wind carried everything away. All the same, I felt better out of the house; the weather suited me, black, stormy, just plain ugly.

We must have walked for a quarter of an hour this way, when suddenly it really started to pour. Even then I might have kept on walking, but Denver tugged me into a doorway. It was the entrance to one of those old, moss-covered brick churches that look transplanted from the English countryside.

We huddled on the stone steps, finally at eye level.

"Do I look as drowned as you?" Denver wanted to know.

I looked at her for the first time since leaving the house. Her straight brown short hair was plastered to her round head, no longer covering her ears; they stuck out like a jester's with their medley of bells and gold hoops. Her clothes were soaked. She shivered as I looked at her and that made me suddenly cold, right through to the bone.

"We'll probably freeze to death," I said gloomily. The idea was almost appealing. "Whose idea was this, anyway?"

"I wanted to distract you."

"You did a good job. I would have been home by now, probably with my wrists slit."

"Don't say that. It can't be that bad. Was it Toni?"

"I guess," I muttered, not wanting to go into it, but knowing that I couldn't resist her questions if she wanted to ask them, because I did need to talk about it.

Maybe she guessed that, because she managed to get it all out of me, the whole story. Once I started, I felt as if I could talk forever, sitting on that frozen stoop with the black rain dumping out of the black sky.

"You blame yourself too much," Denver said finally. "What else could you have done?"

For all her chirpy voice, her bells and freckles, Denver has a hard core of common sense, as hard as her arm muscles from playing drums and hauling bags of dead leaves and debris, which is part of her gardener's job at the campus. She sees cause and effect more vividly than I do, and doesn't waste time pretending that things could have been different. At the time, though, I just thought that she was being obtuse.

"What *else* could I have done? I could have. . . not gotten up on my high horse. I could have given Magda a chance to explain herself. . . I could have. . ."

Denver shook her head. Her fine dark hair was drying rapidly, while mine still hung in lank wet strands along my cheeks.

"From what I know of Magda," she began. (That's right, I thought, the whole lesbian community knew of Magda, and from what they knew, they despised her.)

"Don't tell me," I burst out. "I don't care if she's bisexual, it doesn't matter to me. I mean, for all I know, I may be bisexual myself." So there.

"Let's forget the categories. It doesn't matter to me what anybody calls themselves." She laughed and then sobered, wrinkling her forehead and giving me an idea how the lines had etched themselves so firmly on her face. "The point," she said, "is loyalty to women, whether you're sleeping with them or not. And Magda's never been known for that. She's an. . ."

"Opportunist," I said, remembering Toni's condemning speech. Denver nodded. "Well, I don't care if she wants something better, wants to make something of herself. I admire that in her."

"Even when you get used?"

"I don't think she used me, what do you mean? I know she liked me." But even as I said this I felt doubtful; had she really? Could I prove it, even to myself? "I just didn't trust her enough, I wanted reassurances, I wanted. . ."

"Loyalty."

"I don't think we have a right to demand that from other people, not to demand it. If it's there, it's there. Or it comes in time, like with me and Allison, if you don't push it. I pushed it with Magda, though, and I fucked up."

"Oh, Holly," Denver said, hugging me. "You're too nice."

I misunderstood her and stiffened, thinking she was coming on to me. "You want to go back now? It's practically stopped raining." It hadn't, but it had slowed down a little.

"I guess we're not getting any warmer sitting here," she said and jumped up. "Besides, my fans are probably wondering where I am."

All the way back to the party she told me stories of her musical experiences. I think now that they *were* funny, but then I only laughed to be polite. As soon as we returned and I saw that she was busy, I got my own coat and left.

When I got home the phone was ringing. As I lifted the receiver I saw out of the corner of my eye that it was past midnight; I prepared myself for a wrong number or an obscene suggestion, but it was neither. It was Magda.

"Holly, where have you been? I've been trying to call you forever."

I closed my eyes and transported her into the room next to me. Her rich body pressing up against me on the sofa.

"A party," I managed.

"Oh, whose?"

"Just a party."

"I heard Toni was giving a party tonight. She didn't invite me, though." Her rough, flat laugh.

No way out of it. "Yes."

Now she was pissed at me, the warmth gone from her voice. I settled myself on the floor and began to remove my wet socks.

"Well, I just called to tell you that I got a job in New York City on *Challenge* and I'm leaving on Tuesday." She made it sound like a threat.

"I know. That's. . . great."

"Who told you? Toni?"

"Allison told me. Toni gave me her version tonight."

"I'll bet. Jesus Christ," Magda's voice swelled, "for some reason, she considers it a personal insult that I got the job."

As I had defended Magda to Toni, now I defended Toni to Magda, more out of perversity than anything else. "It sounds like you really pulled the rug out from under her again."

I didn't listen closely to what followed. It was really the same story Toni had told me earlier from a different perspective. What did it matter, anyway, their petty revenges on each other? Loyalty, Denver had said. Sisterhood. She must be joking. Women were no different from men when it came to getting ahead. Ambition corrupted both sexes alike.

I thought of saying, Look, I don't want to hear anymore, Magda, but instead began to strip off all my wet clothes and kick them into a corner. Too bad if they mildewed. The fact was that I could have listened to Magda's voice all night, no matter what she was saying. Naked, I lay on my back on the carpet, the red Persian carpet that my mother loved so and that I had salvaged out of my parents' garage when I moved here.

"Toni expects things to be handed to her on a silver platter. She talks about moving up, doing something more ambitious, but she doesn't realize that it's not as easy as all that—you have to be single-minded and go after what you want."

Magda sounded drunk. It was one of her bad habits, I knew, to drink late at night, by herself. She had told me, "I do it to get to sleep, but sometimes it gets me more wound up. I'll start cleaning my apartment, or calling people." I pictured her in her blue and red kimono, dark and disheveled, with a bottle of crème de cacao and a glass, the Simone Signoret of Seattle. I still wanted her.

But she was asking me something. . . . don't you think, Holly?"

"I'm sorry?"

"Don't you think I'm a better writer?"

Didn't Magda realize how painful this was for me? Here she was, going away in three days, and nothing was clear or even friendly between us—yet all she seemed to want was my reassurance that she was a better writer than Toni. I wanted to tell her, no, or even, I don't know, just to spite her—and I really didn't know, I don't know how to measure these things, measure people against each other—but instead I mumbled, "Yes, I guess so."

"I think I'm snappier, more concise." (This was slurred to "con-size.") "Don't you think so?"

"Are you all packed?"

"Oh, no. No." I could feel Magda looking around, could imagine the shape the room was in. "It's all pretty sudden, you know, they want me to come right away. . . I still haven't figured out what to do with my furniture. . . I can't afford to have it shipped back there. . . maybe I should just store it. Hey, would you like to keep it for me, Holly? I mean, your apartment's totally bare."

"I like it like this."

"I don't know, I was never much for the pillows-on-the-floor bit."

"I know." Another example of the difference between us. For a brief wild moment I thought of taking Magda's offer up, it would mean another tie. . . . Going, she was really going. I couldn't stand it.

"Allison might want to keep it. Do you think she might, Holly?"

"You could ask her."

"Yes. . . you know, that's the main thing I feel bad about. . . leaving Allison locked up while I just go off to New York, but I really can't do anything more here, can I? And there I can write articles, I'll write articles about her and what happened. National coverage is really the ticket. They won't subpoena her or anybody else again if I have anything to do with it."

"I think Allison understands." So that was the main thing she felt bad about? Not me, not anything to do with me?

But even the thought of Allison didn't seem to bother her too much, because I had barely answered when she was off on another tack: Did I know New York at all? Or had I heard of the best neighborhoods to live in?

It was then that I hung up. It was a kind of reflex action. I just didn't want to hear anymore.

The phone rang. I thought how easy it would be to pick it up and pretend that we had been cut off. I even thought with a crazy hope— she's so drunk she would probably let me come over. I could make love to her again.

I never felt so much in love with Magda as I did right then.

The phone rang six times while I sat there debating, my hand poised above the receiver but unable to pick it up.

That's how we said good-bye.

I know it's stupid, but that's how I am.

November 15

I'm not going to sell the shop. I write this holding my breath, but for the first time without the admission hiding in the back of my throat that I really want to.

No, I write it knowing actually what it will mean. Horror upon horror. Slavery and not enough sleep at night. Exactly the same kind of life, in fact, as the last few weeks have meant.

Can I stand it? I thought not, was ready to sign it all away at eleven o'clock this morning, and too bad Allison. Thinking, you got me into this but I'm not you. Then I had lunch with Tom.

He first called me up a week after Allison had gone to jail. "Give it up before you go under," he said. "Sell it all," he said. I couldn't have agreed with him more. After only one week alone in the shop I was convinced that I couldn't do it without Allison. She always handled the business end of things. I couldn't be bothered to learn, was sure I couldn't understand how it all worked. So I went along with Tom at first. He promised to take care of the whole thing, he didn't even want Allison to know, can you believe it? Can you believe I agreed with him? "No sense upsetting her now," he said, and I said, "No." I even put an ad for the xerox machine in the paper, as he suggested. All the second week after she left.

It wasn't that business was slow. In fact, before Allison got subpoenaed, we had almost more than we could handle. From my end of it, considering the number of times the door rang open and the amount of printing I had to do, I'd imagined that we were doing well and better. When Allison asked me about the second bank loan, I said, sure, it's a good idea. And then forgot it. When she expressed worry over losing a customer now and then, I felt sorry only because I thought I hadn't done a good job on their business cards or something. What did I know about credit, bad debts, collection agencies? When Allison wondered whether we should take "steps" against people who hadn't paid us, I always said, "Oh, wait a while. I'm sure they'll pay us."

Often enough she'd tried to show me the books, but I'd always laughed or groaned. I hate thinking about money. My thriftiness comes, more than anything, from an unwillingness to transact. The biggest thing on my conscience was the debt to my father for my share of the business. More than once I'd secretly thought of working a graveyard shift somewhere to pay him back faster. The first frightening thing about the possibility of closing down the shop was the thought that I would no longer be able to send him his fifty dollars a month. That was until I realized I could send him four times as much with another job.

I never had the feeling for the shop that Allison had. I never thought of it as *mine*. I know she didn't understand that, and my indifference hurt her. She wanted to succeed more than anything; I knew that and loved her for it. That's why I went in with her in the first place.

I remember how I liked her right from the first day of class. Her eagerness to do everything right. Her enthusiasm. The way she asked questions and wrote everything down in a new notebook. I was thinking about dropping out. I was only there because the auto mechanics class I wanted to take was filled. At least they told me it was filled. A man I met once in the cafeteria told me that there were no women in his auto mechanics class. But it wasn't filled. It used to be that way with printing too—when it was all unionized and paid well. But now that the quick-print offset shops were opening up all over the place, non-union and paying little, they wanted women in the field. The idea of being a printer didn't interest me that much. I only took the class because I had to do something, and I knew I wanted to do something with my hands. That's the only thing I'd ever been much good at. Comes of having brothers, I guess.

But Allison was crazy with enthusiasm. She asked me if I would go to lunch with her the first day, and while she ate her rice and vegetables, she talked on and on about how she'd been a waitress for years and hated it and wanted to do something else, something with her *hands*. I remember looking at her hands and smiling, they were so small and plump next to mine on the table. I liked her though and was grateful she had asked me to lunch. She was one of the first people I met in Seattle after I left James.

Maybe my liking her was even the reason I stayed in the class. She was so nice to me, asking me to her house to dinner, bringing me bread she'd baked, things like that. I told her right away that I didn't go in for that health food stuff she was always eating, tofu and such, but I liked the bread. We became a kind of team. Right away I saw that she wasn't very good at printing, though she tried so hard. I thought at first that it was because she was older than most of us. I didn't know how old she was, but I imagined that because she had kids and a house, and because she was dumpy and had some gray hair, that she was in her forties. When I found out she was twenty-eight, I still thought of her as much, much older.

She tried so *hard*. Long after it was time to go home, she'd be struggling to finish one of her projects. Once I found her crying in the darkroom; she'd poured the wrong chemicals into the plastic tubs and couldn't understand why her film wasn't developing. I remember once how one of the teachers yelled at her in front of everybody, saying, how could anyone be so stupid? If it had been me, I would have quit right then. Allison didn't say anything, though, she just took it. I knew she hated him, because she told me afterwards. She felt he had it in for her because she was a woman. She said she'd show him, though.

Up to then, I'd just been watching her to see how she did. I'd answer a question if she'd ask me, but I didn't go out of my way to make sure she was doing it right. That would have been like helping someone cheat on a test. But when Mr. Moot yelled at her that day, something changed; I took responsibility for her, I guess. It was more important for her to learn to print than for me. I respected that, I had to help her.

So I'd rush through my assignments to make sure I had enough time to be with her. Sometimes it was hard; I would have liked to spend more time fooling around with a layout, making it perfect instead of good enough. But I didn't really care; I was being useful and I liked that. I hadn't often been very useful in my life.

It wasn't that Allison was stupid. She usually had good ideas, and a solid kind of practicality about how to go about things. Once she learned something, she knew it. It just took her a long time. Her problem, basically, was hand-eye coordination or whatever they call it, and she never really got that down, even though she gradually learned how to run the press. I remember the first time she set up and ran off a business card. She was so happy she could hardly believe it; everything had gone the way it was supposed to, nothing had broken down.

And it was only the tiniest bit crooked. But only I saw that—and I didn't say a word.

I thought it might bother her that I helped her so much. I think, in fact, it did at first. She had the air of "well, only this once," and sometimes she said, "No, I can do it." But gradually we both got used to it.

We worked side by side and it was nothing for her to say, "Holly, why do you think this is happening?"

We were in the program two years together and all that time I think I was half expecting her to give it up, to realize one day that she had no aptitude for printing. As intelligent as she was, she could have gone back to school and done anything. I asked her once why she didn't.

"And be a secretary?" she said. "That's what you do with a college degree these days if you're a woman. No thanks. I have other plans."

That was when she told me that she wanted to have her own business. I couldn't believe it.

"Printing?" I said. "You mean a print shop?"

"What else? You don't think I'm taking this program for my health, do you?"

I had wondered, but all I'd come up with was that she wanted to do something different from waitressing. I assumed that she would get the same kind of job I would when she graduated, and work for somebody. If anything, I'd worried about her getting a job at all.

That was the night we got drunk and she told me about her marriage and divorce and everything. She said she was going to get a loan to start the business with, her ex-husband who knew a bank officer was going to help her.

"How come you never told me this before, that you wanted to go into business?" I asked her.

"I thought you'd laugh at me. I wanted to wait until I got better at it."

So she actually thought she could print well enough to charge people. . . I was amazed.

It turned out she'd done a lot of research about the printing business. She had talked to the Small Business Administration and had attended seminars called "Women in Business" and "Starting a Small Business," things like that. She had talked to a lawyer and an accountant, and to people who already had printing businesses. She had a big manila envelope that she showed me, full of information, brochures, estimates. . . . Finally I began to believe she was serious.

"Well," I said cautiously, "you'd probably have to have somebody working for you, don't you think?"

"That's something I wanted to talk to you about, Holly."

"Work for you?" I laughed. "That's an idea."

"Not work *for* me. Be my partner."

"Oh no. That's impossible. I don't have any money, I couldn't. . ."

How eager she looked that night, in spite of her drunkenness. She looked years younger, not like a mother or a waitress or the tired, anxious student, but like somebody with the world opening up in front of them, a believer. How could I say to her, "No, forget it."

"Think about it, Holly. Say you'll think about it?"

"Okay."

So the next two months I thought and she persuaded, and finally I said I would write to my father and ask him for a loan. I knew he would never go for it—after all, hadn't he as much as paid me off when I said I was leaving James and wanted to go back to school? I hadn't even seen him for over two years, had only talked to him a couple of times on the telephone at Christmas. So I was amazed when he wrote back agreeing to lend me the money. It made me nervous. Why was he doing this? Did he want me to be in debt to him? Probably. Now that he was getting old, he had to forge his ties where he could. He'd probably been waiting for an opportunity like this to bind me to him.

I almost backed out a couple of times. Out of the middle of nowhere it would hit me what I was getting into—no picking up and leaving if I got tired of it, no calling in sick if I wanted to lie around and finish a novel. No vacations, no nothing but work and worry. But every time I thought of calling it quits there was Allison with her big manila envelope full of information and her terrible, pitiful determination.

Finally I just decided that if we folded, we folded, so much the better and no use worrying about it. Or maybe I hoped that she'd get sick of me eventually and find someone else. But I couldn't back out. No way.

Of course I liked it—more and more. I got to do everything, much more than I would have been able to do in an ordinary shop. Printing and layout, all the best parts, it was great, like a dream. I realized how much of a dream it had been when Allison was no longer there to keep the rest of it going.

I don't know what I thought—maybe that Allison would still be able to do the books from prison or something. That I could call her up and say, "They want our taxes. . . what do all these forms *mean*?" Right up until the minute they took her off, she was doing the books. Still available. I know she was worried about the shop, but she didn't let on. She took the time to make up a list of things that had to be done every day, and how to do them. She left the numbers of people who could probably explain things. Neither of us talked about getting anybody else to help; that would have made it seem like she wasn't going to get out for a long time, and we weren't ready to think about that.

It wasn't until after she was actually gone, when I walked into the shop the next day, that I knew it would be impossible. I spent most of the day answering the phone and making copies. I didn't have time to print until after the shop had closed. It was the same the next day and the day after and the day after that. Every night I had to stay up later and later in order to try and finish the work. I didn't mind that, it was the business stuff during the day that threw me. By the end of the week, not only was I exhausted but I just couldn't seem to understand any longer what people wanted or what I was doing wrong. That was the day I closed at one o'clock and hid behind the press bawling, while the phone rang and the door rattled.

I wanted so much to ask somebody for help, but I found I didn't know where to start. Didn't even know what kind of questions to ask.

That weekend Tom called and suggested I bag everything, and I was only too ready to go along with him.

I guess I should explain our relationship. He treats me like my older brothers treated me when I was about eleven. When I was very young, a baby, Bob and Gary used to cuddle me and pick me up (so I've heard); then came a period, a long one, of teasing. When I was an adolescent, they teased me again, not with brutality, but with self-consciousness. When I was older, too, they often condescended to teach me things, displaying their knowledge—how to change tires, rewire lamps, things like that. But when I was eleven and around that age, they completely ignored me. I somehow was no longer there for them; when they wanted to make something known to me, they addressed me through my mother, as in: Mom, the next time you see Holly would you tell her not to go in our room to borrow anything? This was when I'd be standing a couple of feet away from them.

Tom had a similar attitude. When the three of us were together, Tom talked only to Allison. At first it seemed natural; after all, they'd been married. But then I began to realize that certain things he said were directed toward me: warnings, rumors, even jokes. Allison seemed unaware of this, or pretended to be. She preferred to treat him as if he were a kindly old bear. Occasionally her attitude broke down, but it was useful for getting what she wanted.

"He's not a bad person," Allison often said, "He just wants to be treated like he's the center of the universe."

But I wasn't sure that there wasn't something bad in him, something greedy for our failure, though he acted so pleasant and assured.

Allison told me that I was crazy and not all men were like James. I said I knew that, and that wasn't what bothered me. But then I couldn't explain exactly *what* bothered me. Maybe it was even Allison who bothered me. When she was around him she acted a little stupider than I knew her to be. She played up to him, and then, suddenly, when he'd gone too far, she turned sarcastic. To me she acted as though it were all a big joke, this dominance/submission thing, her acceptance and rejection of it. I guess she had to treat it as a joke; otherwise she couldn't have gone on meeting with him about financial deals. I know that before she called him up wanting his help to buy a house, they hadn't seen each other more than once or twice a year.

It was different with me, I didn't have to be nice to him. It wasn't *my* business, what did I care if it went under? Better than kowtowing to Mr. Morris. Then suddenly the business was left in my hands and it was my turn to deal with him.

When he called that night I was in the bathtub drinking coffee. In spite of all my weeping and wailing, I hadn't been able to come to any decision, other than to just keep on, somehow.

"Holly," he said, coming right to the point, "have you considered giving the business up?"

"No," I said. Then, "I don't know."

"Allison isn't going to be in very good financial shape when she gets out—she'll be house payments and car payments behind. It would be too bad if she had a business backruptcy on her hands, too."

He was heavy-handed about it, but he was right. It would be too bad. I had forgotten about Allison's other, extra-business commitments—house payments, car payments—had forgotten that it was her salary from the shop that paid the bills.

"I don't know," I repeated, but he sensed that I was wavering toward his side and pressed on.

"Most likely you'll be money ahead, once you sell everything. At the very least you'll break even. And even if you don't, I think I could see my way to making up the difference."

"You would?" It was so tempting, to be done with it forever, to work some place else, for somebody. Why, with a better job, I could even help Allison out financially, the way I couldn't by keeping the shop open. Still, I made a last stab at independence. "I know Allison would be disappointed, it means so much to her, she's worked so hard. . ."

"One more reason you should consider giving it up, before you go under."

"I'll have to talk to Allison."

"No sense upsetting her now."

"No. . . I'll think about it then, I'll call you." His calm, businesslike voice filled me with guilt, anger, fear. I was afraid of him somehow, angry at Allison. How could I not tell her, but how could I persuade her, either? I had never been able to persuade her of anything, had never even tried, had only gone along with her. Just then I almost hated her, as I lay in the bathtub with the water going cold on me. I'd let her push me around, like my brothers, like James, like my father, like Magda, like everyone else in my life. Why should I be in business because she wanted to be in business? She might need the shop, but I didn't.

I've been lonely most of my life, lonely and without friends. It was an advantage to learn not to make attachments when we moved so often. The first couple of times I left a best friend behind I cried and cried. You'll make new friends, my mother always said, but after a while I didn't want to. I knew I'd have to leave them eventually. I learned to shut off advances, invitations, to play by myself, to be self-sufficient in a world of books. The girls in the books were my friends and I could take them anywhere, be with them any time. I think Jo March may have been my best friend for years.

I was jealous of my brothers. Only a year and a half apart in age, they did everything together. Wore the same clothes, played the same games. They slept in the same room in bunk beds and sometimes at night I could hear them whispering and laughing.

When I was six, Gary, my oldest brother, told me that I'd had a little sister once. She was born when I was only one, but right after Gary mentioned it, I began to remember her—a bassinet, a tiny hand. My mother never wanted to talk about her, she was angry that Gary told me. I know now that Susan, that was her name, was sick for a long time before she died; she was born with a hole in her heart that even my father, the surgeon, couldn't fix. But this I only learned later. When I was six and asking questions, all I got was an averted face and a "please don't bother me now."

I used to dream about Susan after that. My little sister. The one who could have been for me what Bob was for Gary. The smaller one, the one who could be teased, cajoled, beaten up if necessary. The one who would grow into my shoes, into my dresses. The one who would want to borrow my lipstick, my tampons, my boyfriends. The one who would tell Dad I'd been smoking, I'd been drinking, I'd been necking. The one who would carry some secrets to the grave. My bridesmaid, my confidante, my supporting actress. Born with a hole in her heart, vanishing from my life before I even knew she was there.

All my life I have carried around this sense of loss for Susan. If I could have had girl friends, I might have gotten over it. But I never had any friends, unless it was the girl I used to kiss sometimes in junior high, and I hardly remember her name. She moved away about a month after I arrived.

Allison was my first woman friend. Not a girl friend, not a younger sister, not the person I could giggle with and confide in, but a serious friend. More than that, a business partner. A partner.

But a partnership implies equality, and we never really had that. She might have been capable of it, but I wasn't. I was only in business to please her. If I did what she wanted and then later cursed myself, I had only myself to blame.

The idea of liquidating the business was maybe the first independent idea I ever had about it. And if I had really had the idea first, who knows but that I might have gone through with it, just because I needed to do *something*. If Tom hadn't gotten himself involved, I might have chucked it all. But everything got more complicated once I began to deal with him. I wasn't only fighting my old feelings of being dominated by Allison but my feelings of being his pawn, too.

I met with Tom before I had a chance to talk with Allison or write her a letter about what was going on. That's not true. Two more terrible weeks had passed since Tom's first phone call. I had gone so far as to advertise the xerox machine for sale. I had had plenty of chances in my conversations with Allison to bring up the subject. . .

He picked me up at the shop for lunch when I called to say I had almost come to a decision. He was buying, of course, but he was careful not to take me to a fancy restaurant. We were going to talk about the demise of a poor women's business, after all, and his role was to be the serious and staid advisor. He took me to a little Greek restaurant near the university. He said he remembered it from his college days. I wondered if Allison had ever been there.

Tom. Early thirties. Tall and very broad-shouldered, indistinguishable in his handsomeness from any other executive. Indistinguishable in his three-piece suit and in his attitudes, the attitudes that have molded the expression on his face.

He's the kind of person you could stare at forever, looking for some flaw—and be forever disappointed. I can't imagine that he has always looked like this—so rigidly good-looking—it must have come as part of his corporate training. I try always when I see him to think of him young, the high school basketball star who married his high school sweetheart. Even then, though, his jaw must have been set in the lines of authority. His eyes must have always had their cold expression. Even his thickish lips have a set rather than sensual look.

I tried to give him the benefit of the doubt. After all, he had come through for Allison. I remembered the way he held her before they put the handcuffs on at the courthouse. He did care about her. He wasn't trying to take her children away. He was only trying to help, in the only way he knew how.

He ordered retsina and asked if I'd talked to Allison yet.

I told him no, explained that I had felt I needed to think about it more. That wasn't quite true, the fact was that I was tired of thinking about it and was ready to hand over the keys before we sat down. It was just that something about him made me react stubbornly.

He nodded, sipping his retsina and urging me to taste mine. Obviously he wasn't going to push hard, at first.

"Kinsey's quite a model place, I've heard," he said. "I'm going out to visit her on Sunday."

I, too, had heard it was a model for women's prisons everywhere. I had been there only once so far. It looked like a girl's college with its well-kept grounds and neat buildings. There were no bars or anything I associated with penitentiaries. Inside, the walls were painted with bright colors and there were notices posted regarding social activities and sports. Allison said it was quiet and no one bothered her; the food wasn't bad and they had a fairly good library. At first I was relieved to see how pleasant it was there. The first place they'd taken her had been the county jail, where she'd had to share a cell with five other women. At Kinsey she just had one roommate, a young black woman in for robbery. I was glad that Allison was safe in this nice place, and we walked around the grounds and looked at everything. But after a while the strange lassitude of Kinsey began to overtake me. The notices on the walls were written as if for children; the guards strolled around like teachers on lunch duty; and everyone seemed unnaturally dim and subdued. It was like being in Sleeping Beauty's castle. Underneath the saccharine veneer of niceness and gentility was some angry, fearful tension. However much it was like a college campus, it was still a prison. These weren't coeds walking around, but prisoners of the state. Locked up. They couldn't leave.

I went out the gate with my heart pounding, thinking that after all I could have better stood a real dungeonlike fortress than this pretense of an institution. Correctional institution. The word took on new meaning after I'd been to Kinsey. No more punishment; they would take women and turn them into ladies, like it or not.

But Tom would probably approve, wouldn't sense the futility and listlessness that had seemed so apparent to me.

All of a sudden I was overwhelmed by guilt. Allison and I had spent most of our time talking about the shop. "When I get out. . ." she'd said over and over. Across from Tom I felt like a conspirator. I choked on my restsina.

"Okay?" he asked patronizingly. "Retsina can be hard to get used to." The waitress appeared again and he ordered salads and Greek omelettes without consulting me. I gulped water, thinking, forget about Kinsey, be sensible, you can't manage the shop alone, it was unfair of Allison to imagine that you could. You'll drive yourself crazy if you go on like this and you'll lose the business anyway. Tom is right, damn him. Sell now before you go bankrupt.

We began to talk about the shop. To my surprise I found myself contradicting him on a number of points. By the time we had finished our salads, I was beginning to realize that he didn't know as much about the business as I did. Without knowing it, I had absorbed more of Allison's terminology and outlook than I'd realized. I had a day-to-day feeling for the shop, a factual perspective that Tom lacked, with all his business experience.

He said, for instance, something about our lack of credit with the paper companies, the fact that the companies' payment-on-delivery policy meant that our own billing was screwed up, since we gave our customers thirty days to pay.

"But Washington Paper, our main supplier, still gives us thirty days," I interrupted in surprise.

Tom looked disconcerted for a moment and then said smoothly, "Well, it's not important."

I tried to puzzle that out while Tom breezed ahead. I made several more objections to his assumptions about our rates, our credit, our methods of payment. And I made them in an increasingly obstinate tone.

Finally he smiled and said, "I may have some details wrong, but that's not really the point, is it?"

I stared at my omelette.

"I'm not underestimating you. . ." he started to say.

"But you *are*. It's my shop, too, you know. You talk as if Allison were the only one who worked there."

"But you've said that you did the printing and left the bookkeeping to Allison." He smiled ingratiatingly, but with some impatience.

Coffee arrived, while I wondered what had come into me. I felt not only stubborn but strangely sure of myself. I hadn't come here to argue with him, but if he didn't even know how our credit worked, then how could I trust him to tell me what to do?

Sensing that he was losing ground, Tom turned from the business scenario back to the specter of poor Allison going bankrupt. But even that couldn't touch me now. I had had a revelation of sorts: Tom, who knew everything didn't know how our credit worked, that we still had a month to pay the paper company. It was a small point, but an important one to me. I had been believing that I knew nothing about how the shop operated, but I knew *that*. And I knew lots more. Not all the details, but the essentials. I knew how it *worked*.

Allison, I thought, see, I'm not so stupid. You were right to trust me. I won't disappoint you. I can understand it. I will. I'll do that for you. And for me.

I could have almost laughed then at Tom, wasting his money and his eloquence on me. Not a chance, I thought. It's my shop, too. I'm keeping it open for me as much as for Allison.

". . . bank payments. . ." he was saying, draining his cup of coffee and looking grim. I watched him with as much fascination as if he were the Devil. I had been tempted, but I wasn't going to give in. I would be loyal to Allison, to the shop, to my new awareness of understanding.

Loyalty, Denver had said, speaking of Magda. But it could mean much, much more.

I tested the word out on Tom, guessing that he wouldn't see the overwhelming meaning it suddenly had for me. "Giving up the shop doesn't seem loyal to Allison."

"Loyal!" he said, astounded. "What does loyalty have to do with it? It's purely a business matter. It's the only sensible thing to do. Right now anyway. Now, if Allison wants to try again when she gets out. . ."

"No," I said. "But thank you for helping me to decide."

He started to get angry and for a moment I saw how he had kept his power over Allison all these years. James had kept me down the same way. I couldn't help feeling sorry for Tom, though. He never even knew what it was he said.

I took the bus back to the shop, refusing his ride, thinking of the word "loyalty" in a spirit of triumph. I felt as if I had found the one word that expressed it all, that gave a meaning to the most disparate things: Allison going to jail to protect the shelter; Magda's betrayal; the shop and all it stood for. It was the loyalty of friends, it was women's loyalty, maybe all we have. The fact that Tom couldn't understand what I meant (it must have come out of the blue to him) only made it clearer.

Most of it is rhetoric, like the articles in the *News* that talk about solidarity. Magda could write stuff like that and then turn around and sleep with someone else. And all the words about support and sticking together that the grand jury defense committee put out came to nothing when the government closed in on Allison. But there is a core of truth to it. Loyalty is the only thing we can do for each other. The only thing women can do for each other. "Whither thou goest I will go," said Ruth. If Dante had been a woman he might have said, "Do not abandon your sister, all ye who enter here."

Anybody reading this would laugh; I'd laugh, too, but I'd start crying.

I went back to the shop; everything was a mess, but for the first time it seemed manageable.

The retsina probably helped a little.

November 22

I looked up from the counter today and there was Denver standing at the door, round and compact as a little drum, gnomish almost in a tight-fitting bright cap with ear flaps. Nothing to beat her face for sheer friendliness.

"How ya doin?" she said. "I heard you might need some help here."

I just stared at her while she began to walk around the shop. "Hmm, hmm," she said, darting from the light table to the press. "Used to run one of these things. It was a few years back, but I think I remember how."

"But you have a job, you told me. At the university, raking up leaves."

"Temporary, my dear Watson," she said, continuing her investigations, poking her nose into some of the boxes of paper. "All my jobs are temporary, especially ones involving leaves. I mean, fall can only go on so long, right?" She came back to where I was standing and gestured to the window full of cold purplish sky. "I'm looking for some place to hibernate for the winter."

Still I was suspicious. "I didn't tell anyone that I needed help."

"Don't be coy. Of course you need help, it's obvious you need help very badly. So what do you want, my resumé? That's easy enough. Thirty-five, single, though divorced once and separated many times. No children, no dogs, no parrots, no rabbits, one cat. Jack-of-all-trades, master of some. I really have worked as a printer, you know, though right now I would like to consider myself a musician. . . a starving musician. . . what's the matter, don't you support the arts? Seriously, Holly. . ."

"All right," I said laughing. "You're hired. But I can't pay you much and I don't know how long it will last. When Allison gets out. . ."

"Didn't I say all my jobs were temporary?"

The miracle of miracles was that she really did know how to run a press, she wasn't kidding. She listened politely with her freckled face all screwed up into wrinkles while I explained the job that had to run off, and then, while I answered the phone and did some xeroxing, she started the press. Within an hour she was finished and it was perfect.

"How long did you say it's been since you worked as a printer?" I asked, amazed, hardly able to believe my luck.

"Oh, couple of years," she shrugged. "But it's like riding a bike, as they say—once you learn, you never forget. Now, I might have trouble if you gave me some two-color jobs." She pulled her cap more closely down over her ears and looked hopeful. "Got anything like that?"

"I was planning to do a two-color job tonight, after the shop closed. . ."

"Hand it over, lady."

Riding a bike, yes, that's how it was for me too. I couldn't imagine ever forgetting how a machine worked once I understood it. But after working with Allison so long I had almost begun to believe that I was the only person in the world who thought like that. Around Allison I'd been almost ashamed of my facility with mechanical things, was always having to downplay it, to argue that running a press was nothing compared to running a business. The press was something we never discussed except when Allison was trying to print. Then I was the teacher, patiently going over the same steps with her until she did it right, all the while assuring her that yes, it was difficult to get it right, but no, it wasn't important.

"You're so *good*, Holly," Allison would say. "It frustrates me."

"I had brothers," I would say consolingly. "And a father who said, What do you think is wrong? when the car stalled. I mean, he made me get out in the middle of the thunderstorm and crawl under the hood. . ."

"You're lucky," Allison would sigh. "My father called the AAA if he got a flat tire. I still don't even know what's inside my car. I keep thinking it's important for women to know these things and I keep trying, but it's like I have a built-in block."

"Your parents gave you other things, some kind of determination. . . but I was never good enough, never pretty enough, never smart enough. One of my brothers went to Yale, you know. The other to Stanford. While I could barely get into the community college in Monterey. One of my brothers married Miss New Jersey and the other married a biochemist, while I got stuck with a woman-hating Vietnam vet on downers. . ."

No, I never said all that to Allison. I just helped her adjust the press and told her that she had it all over me in brains and business sense.

She used to talk sometimes about our "unequal roles," but I never paid much attention to that. I like doing this part of it, I told her. And you like your end. So what's the difference? How can it be unequal? Today I began to understand a lot of things. How it might be to work with somebody who got a thrill out of a clean two-color registration, for instance.

It's funny, today I felt more like Allison than Holly. There I was, making phone calls, ordering papers, making mistakes, sure, and having to call them back; figuring accounts, writing letters, talking to customers; in general, keeping things going—while in the back of the shop Denver worked on, churning out the orders. Boss and worker. I had never thought of my relationship with Allison like that. Now I could see that it would make me uncomfortable, too. At least Allison had tried to print, while I had given up on understanding the business end without a struggle.

I took Denver out to lunch at Mrs. Silver's down the street and was glad to see that she liked cheeseburgers and pie with lots of coffee.

Over the third cup I said to her, "You know, if you're going to keep working here, I'd kind of like to explain some of the business side of things to you. . . I mean, I'd like it if we could trade off once in a while, I mean, you handle the counter and ordering, and me run the press. . ."

I was all ready for her to say, as I would have said to Allison, "Me? Oh, no, I couldn't. . . it's better if you do it."

But instead Denver's eyes lit up. "That would be fun. I used to do some ordering at my other place. Not too much, but I liked it. Sure, that would be fun."

Fun, she thought it would be fun. For a moment I felt a cold fear—what if she was much better than me at everything? What if she could run the press and run the business just as easily? I would lose the little self-confidence I'd gained in the last few weeks and be back where I'd started. But Denver said, fun. She didn't seem threatened by the idea. Why should I be? Fun. I'd never thought that working at the shop might be fun, though I had enjoyed my work. Allison took everything so seriously. Would we make it? Would the customers come back? Would I quit? Would we get the orders out on time? It was only by paying strict attention to the work I was doing and not bothering about deadlines and credit and financial worries that I had been able to get anything done at all.

Right then I wanted to know a lot more about Denver, who she was, why she took things as a challenge and not as a threat.

"Where are you from?" I began.

"Oh, round and about. Say, how about another piece of pie? I'll pay. No? Well, I'm going to. Printing's hard work, you know. Almost as strenuous as raking leaves." She opted for blackberry this time and dug into it with relish.

"My life history would take too long," she said, winking at me. "Let's just say I've settled down. And now you can tell me about yourself."

So I ended, as I had the night of Toni's party, talking about myself. By that time, I felt as if I'd known her for years. I told her about Allison and the shop and how Tom had tried to talk me into selling out. I told her how I'd suddenly gotten the idea of loyalty, "from something you said," I told her, not at all shy.

"It's important," she agreed, wrinkling up like a prune and then relaxing. I no longer thought she looked gnomish. She had taken off her bright cap, but her fine dark hair fit her head like a soft helmet. The lobes of her ears were punctured four times each; today I paid attention to the variety of earrings she had on. No two were alike—stars, moons, bells, lightning, hoops. Anybody else would have looked ridiculous with all that stuff jangling around, but not her. The earrings suited her, the way her cap suited her, the way her wrinkled forehead and freckles suited her. She didn't seem self-conscious about anything, not even about being fat. If Allison had been sitting there in Mrs. Silver's shoveling down another piece of pie, I would have had to listen to a whole litany about how she knew she shouldn't, and she would be sorry the next time she weighed herself. I didn't mind—it always did seem unfair that I was able to pig out without gaining an ounce, while everything Allison ate turned to fat. Still, it was nice to see another woman eat without complaining. Enjoying herself. Denver's fat was nice, too, solid and round and muscled, not flabby.

These were the kinds of thoughts that crossed my mind today as I drank as much coffee as I wanted and talked and felt that I had finally found a friend.

December 1

I've been so happy that I knew it couldn't last. In the back of my mind has been guilt about Allison. There she is, still at Kinsey, going slowly crazy after weeks of being treated like a bad girl, with the prosecutor still holding firm, still threatening to leave her in there until the grand jury's term is up, and worse, the prospect of a felony charge for harboring Deb. Bess says not to worry—all Mrs. Houseman had told them was that someone who looked like Allison dropped off Deb's child early one morning. Bess says they can't prove it was Allison, or that if it was Allison, that she even knew who Deb was. She says this knowing that about a million FBI agents are lurking around, getting more and more pissed off because they can't pick up any trace of Deb or any of the others. The newspapers have dropped the subject and no one talks about it anymore, not even about Ted Shovik. It's like it never happened. No more bombings, no more shoot-outs, no more nothing. There were some people calling for an investigation of Ted's death, but there wasn't enough support. It seems like most people think a terrorist deserves to die. And meanwhile Allison sits in Kinsey, reading a book a day, putting on weight from lack of exercise and too much starch, worrying about her kids and writing me long letters.

And meanwhile I'm working my head off, laughing every other minute and falling in love. I knew it couldn't last, knew something had to happen to convince me that nothing had changed, that life was really terrible.

But why did it have to be James again, and today of all days?

Last night I stayed with Denver for the first time. I had seen it coming for a while, at least I had hoped it was coming. She's turned working into a game, which isn't to say we don't work hard. We get twice as much done as Allison and I ever did. But it's a much different atmosphere with Denver always cracking jokes, bringing in beer and coffeecake, dancing around to the radio. The first time she touched me, even though she only grabbed me in fun, I drew back. The thought in my mind. She's a lesbian. I was afraid, remembering how I had felt with Magda, the power of it, and the hurt. But then I thought, She's not just a lesbian, she's friend. So the next time she came around, I grabbed her. We wrestled over a piece of paper until we tore it apart. It was a letterhead design someone had given us, but what the hell, we kept laughing. We began to hug each other regularly before saying good-bye at night, and then last night, she said, "Want to go hear some good music?"

We went to a women's bar, drank a lot, and danced. It seemed the most natural thing in the world to go home with her. It didn't feel strange and upsetting and wonderful as it had with Magda. It just felt nice and comfortable. She made jokes the whole time, but she also acted as if it were important to know how I felt, what felt good, and important for me to know what she liked. She didn't tell me that a man would make me feel the same way.

"Oh sure, I've been to bed with a few men," she said when I asked. "It was no big deal. Hank in the back seat and Bill in his mother's garage. Right in the middle of an oil slick, as it turned out. Don't believe I didn't have a hard time explaining *that* to my mother."

"How did you know, I mean, that you were a lesbian?"

"What do you mean, how did I know? How do *you* know?" She punched me in the ribs and then took pity. "I knew because I fell in love. With a traveling saleswoman. . . No, it's true."

"What happened?"

"She moved on and I went with her. I was eighteen and I've never stopped traveling."

"I thought you said you'd settled down."

"Well, relatively. What would life be like if you'd completely settled down?"

"I hate traveling," I told her. "I hope I never see another airport again."

"I don't wonder. You should get the Purple Heart as a casualty of the Army."

"It's not funny, Denver."

"I know it's not," she said, pulling a grim face. "It's damn serious and don't you ever forget it!"

"You idiot."

The whole night went like that. She punctured all my traumas with her good humor. She only looked sober when I mentioned James. I hadn't told her much about him, only that I'd been married and divorced. I told her that I'd turned his gun on him.

"Whew," she said. "And he hasn't been around since? I guess that's what it takes with some of them. But it must have been pretty scary for you."

She hugged me close and I hugged her back, feeling safe, protected. It was true, he hadn't been around since. And it had been almost a month. Lying in Denver's warm grip, I could almost believe that I would never see him again.

Then this morning the phone rang and it was someone at a hospital asking if I were Mrs. James Killien.

"I'm Holly Killien," I said. "But I'm not married anymore."

That didn't seem to register. "Your husband was admitted yesterday with infectious hepatitis. He's on Four South in room 411, bed 2, and he's asking for you."

"But I'm not married," I tried to tell her even as she was ringing off, her duty accomplished.

No, I said to myself. I won't. I can't. But my entire day was ruined. I had come back from Denver's in an energetic mood, determined, on this Sunday, my one free day, to do everything that needed to be done, laundry, dishes, letter to Allison to tell her about Denver, visit to Katey and Ben. I had been sorting my socks with the radio turned up full-blast when the phone rang. I turned the radio off and stuffed my socks into the hamper, then I lay face down on the floor, immobilized.

So what if he had hepatitis? I tried to tell myself that it was nothing to me. He could die for all I cared. Besides, I'd been through this all before. Only then it had been pneumonia. He got it in Monterey just as I was on the point of leaving the first time. Two weeks in the hospital and then a long recovery. I didn't leave him; instead we moved up to Seattle to make a new start.

Hepatitis. Dirty needles. Dirty life. My stomach rose in disgust. He had dragged me down, down, and would continue to do it if I let him.

"He's asking for you," the nurse had said. And what if he really were dying?

I put on my hat and coat and drove to the hospital. The sky was dead white with premonitions of snow. It seemed such a long time ago that this all began.

I met James in Monterey when I was twenty. He picked me up hitchhiking home from the community college one afternoon. G.I.'s always picked me up. I could tell them coming a mile away. They bore down on me in their shiny new Volkswagens, hair clipped, beads around their necks, a joint between their teeth. This one was handsome, but to me he still looked as military and dumb as the rest of them. He drove too fast. We made some converstation. He said he was getting out in a few months and I said that's nice. Then he dropped me off.

A few months later, during my last quarter at Monterey Peninsula, he saw me walking across campus and hurried to catch up. I almost didn't recognize him. His hair was longer, golden in the sun; he was tan, had his shirt open to the waist to show it off. Barefoot, beads, a beard starting. I was bowled over by him right away, though I kept telling him and myself that I'd had enough of the military.

"Baby, all that's past," he said. He was going to study law, he said. From the first day he kept telling me that he and I were made for each other. Who had ever said that to me before? Never pretty, always too tall and too awkward, I wasn't even smart. I read a lot, sure, kept a journal even then, but I was too shy to keep up well in class. The idea that the teacher might call on me always had a paralyzing effect. And I'd always been bad at tests. Besides that, I'd never had a boyfriend, had only been out once or twice on what could be termed a date. I still lived with my parents. My mother had had cancer for a year by then, and both my parents depended a lot on me. I didn't have time for boys, I thought.

But when James came into my life, I found I suddenly had lots of time. Time to cut class and drive down the coast, time to spend afternoons in his beat-up little house in Seaside, making his dinners, rolling his joints, changing his records. I stayed away from home for longer and longer periods until I stopped coming home at all. It was easier to stay away than to face my father yelling about no-good bums and my mother's sad eyes. I drowned myself in James' life, in his dope, in his bed, in his dreams.

Right after I turned twenty-one we were married and left Monterey without completing spring quarter. I have thought and thought about it, with anger and remorse and everything else, but I still can't give a good reason for why I did what I did. As the saying goes, "You had to have been there." Well, I *was* there, I was *there*, in love, so much so that I can't even remember what it was really like when it was good. I only remember when it began to change.

His drugs, for one thing. "Baby, that's all past," he'd said, talking about the Army. But what the Army had given him and a whole lot of others was a need and a greed for drugs that he never got over. Later he told me that he was stoned the whole time he was in Vietnam. And when he came back he continued to require huge quantities of hash and speed and downers to keep him satisfied. When I first knew him I thought he just smoked marijuana, a lot of it all right, but nothing to be worried about. After all, it was 1970. Even hash was all right, too strong for me, but he could handle it. After all, wasn't he a man?

Whatever else he took he kept hidden from me until we started our cross-country honeymoon. He drove all night on speed then, even when I suggested we stop in motels. Along the way he sold hash to make money, sometimes trading it for pills. By the time we got to Florida, we were broke, but we had half a pharmacy. We sold the car there and took a bus back to California.

The ride back on the Greyhound is when it all began to hit me. James slept most of the way, with his head on my shoulder, while I counted license plates beginning with the letter "A" and tried to imagine what life would be like from now on.

We were supposed to go back to school and finish, but James didn't even bother to enroll, and I had to drop out after a few weeks to get a job as a motel maid. My father wasn't speaking to me, wouldn't let me come to the house. I only saw my mother when she came into town for her doctor's visits.

I remember the day she died. We were living in a little coffin-shaped house on the hill, near enough to Fort Ord to see the mortars going off every night from our front porch. When he was in the mood, James used to cheer them on, but their sound and bright light reminded me of *Gone With the Wind*—how it must have felt in Atlanta with Sherman's army approaching.

Our house had three rooms and no halls; you had to go through each room to get to the next. We had no way of avoiding each other. I felt like a spider sometimes crawling along the walls so as not to have to face James when he hadn't had a good day.

The day my mother died had not been a good one for him. He was pissed that his G.I. benefits had stopped. "Shouldn't make any differ-ence if you're going to school or not," he shouted. "We fucking fought and died for this country and I want to see a little thanks."

My salary wasn't enough to buy the right kind of drugs, just second-rate hash and a few downers now and then. A deal he'd been working on fell through at the last minute; one of James' former bud-dies had undercut his sale.

So he was pissed and in the middle of trying to show me who was boss around this house, even if he weren't boss anywhere else, when the phone rang. It was my father and all he said was, "Can you come to the hospital? Your mother's going."

If I had my choice I'd remember that day because of my mother, her face seeking me out from the crowd of doctors and nurses before she turned away forever. I'd remember only, if I could, that my father and I stood there holding hands over her, the first time that we had touched in years. I wouldn't remember that that was the day James first hit me. But I don't have any choice and it's all bound up together.

He didn't want me to go to the hospital. "She'll be dead by the time you get there," he said. "I need you more." When I got up to go anyway, he pushed me down on the couch. Then when I struggled up and toward the door, he said, "Holly, if you think you're leaving you'd better think twice." He raised his fist, but I didn't think he'd do it until I felt my head jerk back and then the hot heavy pain along my jaw. Neither of us said a word, we just stared at each other. Then he got his coat and drove me to the hospital, waited for me in the car.

How could I hate him? I understood that his need to hold on to me, to make sure that I belonged to him and only him, came from his fears that I could leave him. He knew that I was planning to long before I did, would accuse me of thinking I was too good for him, would blame me for his failures. He would sink into self-pity. "Of course you'll leave me. What have I ever done for you but make you miserable? I can't do anything right."

"I'll never leave you," I told him. I let him beat me to prove it. In the back of my mind I believed that it was my not loving him enough that made him turn to drugs. If he knew how important he was to me and how much I cared, then he could do anything, go to school, become a lawyer, do whatever he wanted. How could I leave him? Hadn't he been the first person to really pay attention to me, to see me as a woman, to need me? He had problems, yes, but it wasn't his fault. It was the war, it was the Army. He had learned to be violent and fatalistic, like a whole generation of men. I was a woman, I hadn't known what it was like to kill and sit for hours in a hideout waiting to be killed. The least I could do was let him take out some of his anger on me.

Driving to the hospital, I still wondered: Why did I ever leave him? What made me change? Or did I ever change? Wasn't it the same feeling of being somehow to blame that sent me rushing to his bedside this afternoon?

His room had a sign on it that said you had to put on a mask and gown. A nurse helped me with the gown and said, "Don't tire him too much. He's very sick."

"Is he going to be all right?"

"Are you his wife?"

"I. . .no."

"I'm sorry, then, that I can't discuss his case with you."

A slip of paper that I had replaced with another one would have made it possible for me to know how things stood with him. I was no longer married but when do you stop being related to someone?

"I knew you'd come," James said weakly. He tried to raise his head off the pillow to look at me, but fell back again with the effort. I went over and stood by his bed. He had two I.V. bottles going into his arm; his skin was as yellow and splotched as an old banana peel. He said again, "I knew you'd come."

How did you know? I wanted to say. What right did you have to expect that I'd come? I just nodded.

He was quiet for a moment, seemed to drift off, then roused himself. It was pitiful to see his efforts to talk, to move his unwilling body. Except when on downers, he had always been so active, loving danger, movement. He drove his car at breakneck speed, had at various times taken up motorcycle racing, surfing, parachuting. Even his conversation had been energetic—how else could he have gone on persuading me that he loved me, that he was going to do great things, or even that it was my fault that he didn't?

"They say my liver's pretty bad," he said. "Can't take out a liver like an appendix."

I reached for his hand, which seemed so much thinner than I remembered it. "You'll pull through. You always do. Remember your pneumonia? One night they thought you were a goner and the next day you were sitting up in your chair when I came in."

"Yeah, that's right." Confidence flushed into his face for a moment and then drained out. He closed his eyes, but pressed my hand slightly.

He wasn't going to die, was he? I didn't know how to act if he was. I recalled our big deathbed scene in Monterey; James asking forgiveness, me sobbing, "It's all my fault." When he recovered he held it against me that he'd said he was sorry; all he wanted to remember was that it had been all my fault. I wouldn't do that this time—only, what if he really were dying? I had gotten to my mother too late to tell her what I wanted to tell her, that I loved her and would miss her. So many people around and then she looked at me and turned away. I thought there had been love in her eyes, but had she even seen me, did she know who I was, that I had come? But if I told James that I loved him, and he didn't die, then I'd be stuck with him again. He'd arrive on my doorstep, healthy as a horse, and remind me of my words.

I wondered how long he had been sick. Here I'd thought that I really scared him with my gun trick into leaving me alone, when in fact he had probably been too ill to care. While all the rest of it was going on, the grand jury, Allison, Magda, Denver, my life changing, James had been turning yellower and yellower, fading away.

"James, James," I said. He hadn't opened his eyes again, his breathing seemed too shallow to support a life. I pressed frantically on the nurse's call button, and the nurse came right away. A different nurse from the one who had refused to give me any information.

She took his pulse, whispered, "He's fine, just tired. Perhaps you'd better leave now." Outside the room she said, "Don't worry. He'll make it."

Did I want him to make it? Didn't I just want him to die so that I could be free of him forever? By the time I got down to the lobby my knees were shaking so badly that I knew I couldn't drive home by myself. I called Denver from the pay phone. "I'll be right there," she said.

A hospital lobby is the one public place where nobody minds if you cry, but I held back until I saw Denver come through the door, striding toward me on short muscular legs, her bright cap framing her wise funny face. Then I just broke down and let her hold me.

She was not self-conscious, did not tell me, "Now, now," or even "Tell me about it." She just let me cry and when I was all cried out, she took me back to her apartment.

We had tea, and when I felt as though I could talk again, I told her everything. I said, "I wanted so badly to be rid of him, but not like this."

"Why do you feel responsible for him?" she asked, but not with any accusation in her voice. When I shook my head, unable to answer, she said, "Seems like you're about even-steven—he ruined your life and you ruined his. You just think you ruined his more because he's sick."

That was it, of course. "But what can I do?"

"Wait and hope he gets better. Look forward to the day when you can tell him you've got a girl friend."

"Oh great." I would have laughed but the prospect scared me too much.

"We can both enroll in a karate class tomorrow," Denver elaborated. "And start taking shooting lessons and. . ."

"You're crazy." But I did feel better. Only, "Do you think *I'm* crazy, Denver, being so afraid of him?"

She sighed and wrinkled her forehead. "Honey, you're normal," she said. "Ain't you a woman?"

December 8

Snow was falling by the time we all arrived at Kinsey today, lightly, but steadily enough to cover the ground and make snowballs, as Katey and Ben insisted on proving. I wasn't really looking forward to this visit with Allison and felt glad that I had the protection of the children and Allison's mother.

Allison had sounded so distant on the phone when I told her about Denver. It was my fault, of course, I didn't know how to regulate my praise. What I wanted was to reassure Allison that everything was all right, that Tom's worries were unfounded and that business was better than ever. What I'm sure I ended up implying was that Denver was a kind of wonderwoman at the shop, one who could print, do layout, charm the customers, and do the bookkeeping better than Allison and I put together. It wasn't surprising then that Allison had responded so lukewarmly to my suggestion of bringing Denver today.

"Another time," she said. "Today I just want to spend some time with the kids."

She began to cry as soon as she saw them running toward her in the main visiting hall. "Look at you, snow all over your clothes," she said, vainly trying to brush the wet flakes away as she hugged them both to her.

This was the second time I'd brought the kids to see her and again it just about broke my heart. God, but I hate that sterile set of buildings and the people who put Allison there. She says she's used to it, now, that it's worse for the people who come to visit her. That must be true, because I no sooner get inside that place than I start to feel claustrophobic. Not to be able to leave, ever. Not to see your friends and go to a movie or out for a beer when you want one. Not to go to work every day and feel the tired satisfaction that comes from finishing a job. Since I've come to know how important the shop is to me, I can't imagine what it would be like not to go there every day, not to see the old familiar things day after day, talk to the same people.

But Allison is a stronger person than I am. She doesn't complain. If I were at Kinsey I probably wouldn't get out of bed, but Allison is working at the library. She's reading history and the Russian novelists, is all excited about some woman named Mandelstam, the wife of a poet who died in a concentration camp in Stalinist Russia. "People like that make you realize what it would be like, to really suffer because of what you believe. This isn't exactly Siberia, you know."

She has friends here now, too, her roommate and a few others. Has gotten involved in some of their classes, their lives. Every time I see her she has some new atrocity of the court system to tell me about. "We have a daycare center here," she told me last time. "But it's not for the children of the prisoners. They have to take care of other women's children during the day, but can only see their own on weekends and that's only if they can get somebody to bring them. A lot of women don't have anybody they can count on. The women who are pregnant have to give up their babies as soon as they're born. Hospitals and then foster homes. They aren't even allowed to nurse them—their own babies."

With that in mind, it's easy to see why Katey and Ben are such a big hit. No sooner had Allison hugged them and kissed them and dusted the snow off and made them presentable, than she introduced them to everyone around. Katey loves the attention and gets all worked up and silly, Ben is more formal. I have often wondered what he thinks of all this. He's not a talkative boy, but he thinks a lot. In his TV shows the bad people always go to jail. You never see them there but you know they deserve to be put away for their crimes. How does he reconcile the idea of his mother, his very own mother, having to stay away from home indefinitely because someone said she was "bad"?

I asked Ben once, in a roundabout way, if anybody at school ever bothered him about what happened to Allison and what he said surprised me.

"One guy," he muttered in embarrassment. His blonde hair hung in his face and he scuffed his shoes.

"What did you say to him?"

"I punched him. And don't tell mom"

I had to laugh, even as I worried. I didn't want for him to have to fight over his mother's honor without understanding the reasons why she'd acted the way she had.

"What your mother did was a very courageous thing," I said slowly. "Not many people would have kept quiet to help somebody else.

She didn't deserve to go to prison for it, but now that she's there, we have to show her that we understand. . ."

"I know," Ben blurted out. "But this guy, he called her a con. I had to hit him, Holly, I *had* to."

I thought at first that Allison was going to have an uphill battle teaching her son about the dangers of male violence, then it occurred to me that there were a number of people in my life I wished I'd punched rather than tried to explain something important to. But I wasn't going to tell Ben that.

"Next time," I said, "see if you can make this guy understand that people sometimes look bad even when they do things for the right reasons, okay?"

He sighed and looked as if being an adult were far more complicated and distasteful than he'd imagined. "Okay," he said and then added again, "Don't tell mom."

Allison's mother brought a pan of fudge and enough cookies to feed a regiment, and set them in the center of the room. The first part of the visit was always chaotic, taken up with questions for Katey and Ben about their school and friends.

After that Allison's mother had to give her version: Ben had broken a window by throwing a shoe at Katey; Katey had *not* wanted to help with the dishes; but Ben had also done *very well* on his English test and Katey was going to be an angel in the Christmas pageant. She had bought them both new shoes.

"Oh, mom, you shouldn't have." It was things like this, rather than windows broken or dishes unwashed, that upset Allison. Little things, like a new pair of shoes, that made her feel that she was no longer a real mother.

"Holly gave me the money."

"Oh Holly." She turned to me anxiously.

"Big job," I excused myself. "We're rolling in wealth. Besides, it's your salary."

"You can't pay me a salary when I'm not doing anything. Aren't you paying this, this woman?"

"Denver? Sure I'm paying her. I told her it wouldn't be much, but. . ."

The look in Allison's eyes said that this was something we would have to discuss later. But the opportunity didn't come up until visiting hours were almost up and it was time for us to leave.

"This. . . Denver, she knows, doesn't she, that this isn't a permanent thing? I mean, we couldn't afford to keep her on after I get out."

We were hanging back while Allison's mother helped Katey and Ben wrap themselves up for the cold ride home. I looked at Allison for a minute, so overweight and so much older looking, the worried lines on her face so different from Denver's funny mock-prune grimace. What I had been wanting to say to Allison, my hope that somehow Denver could keep working with us, seemed an impossibility now. Allison had given her life to the business and I couldn't let her down by allowing her to believe that I'd found someone else I worked with better. Much less that I was in love with this person and wanted to spend my whole life with her.

"She knows it's just temporary," I said. "It'll be like old times as soon as you get out." This lie gave me the relief of seeing Allison's eyes clear. She smiled and hugged me. "It won't be long," she whispered. "Even if I have to stay here until the grand jury's term is over, it will only be a couple more months."

I don't think I ever admired her more than at that moment.

It was only as we were driving back to Seattle, Ben in the back reading comic books, Katey keeping up a running commentary of "Oh, look-it," and Allison's mother knitting and looking, that I realized I had told Allison nothing at all about James. He's better, I excused myself. He's not going to die and I don't have to feel guilty for having killed him. I had been to the hospital every day to see him improve while Denver waited for me in the lobby and continued to make jokes about karate classes. With her help, I was beginning to think that when the time came, I would be able to stand up to him.

With her help, with Denver's help. But hadn't Allison tried to help me? She had taken me home with her that awful day, had helped me move, had volunteered to call the police, Legal Services. Why hadn't I taken her seriously, why had I tried to hide what was happening from her for so long? I guess I was afraid of her thinking me stupider than I was. I didn't want her to connect me with those poor women at her shelter. I didn't want her to think of me as battered, didn't want her sympathy to come between us. Even when she knew, I always tried to pretend that it was nothing, that I could handle it. Stupid. When had she ever tried to keep anything from me? She hadn't been afraid to tell me how Tom had screwed her over. I was the one who held everything back.

Now I was doing it again. Not telling her that I wanted Denver to continue working with us. Thinking that it was disloyal of me to imagine anything other than what had been. But how loyal was it to lie about my feelings? Loyalty was only a dead word, like marriage, if there was no honesty to it.

All the way home I kept hearing Denver asking me, "Why do you feel responsible for him?" Why did I feel responsible for James, for Allison, for anyone? Why should I lie and hide what I thought and what I felt? I thought of Allison and the way she took responsibility for the shelter, for Deb's safety. . . and felt guilty all over again.

The snow turned into sleet and pelted the windshield so hard I could hardly see to drive. Ben hit Katey with his comic book when she tried to "borrow" it, and Allison's mother threatened them both with no TV that night, which made Katey start bawling. "I want my *mother*," she screamed. "Shut up, shut up, shut up!" Ben punched her.

You little bastard, I wanted to throttle him. You goddamn little *man*. Why don't you show your feelings? You miss your mother just as much. I felt like screaming myself.

By the time I pulled up in front of their house we were a gloomy and silent bunch. Allison's mother herded them out of the car before I could get my customary hug from Katey.

"Too much excitement," she threw back at me disapprovingly as she closed the car door.

I drove back home thinking, how can you be loyal and truthful at the same time?

December 15

Tom took the kids and Allison's mother out to Kinsey today and I took Denver. We got there only an hour before visiting hours were over. The rest of them had departed long before. Tom wanted to get back in time for the football game. I was sure there wouldn't be any ruckus on the way home this time. Katey and Ben were too awed by their father to make any trouble in the back of *his* car.

"Well, this is one person I'm sure interested in meeting," Denver said on the way down between songs and outrageous stories of her life.

I was pretty sure the feeling wasn't mutual. I had tried to prepare Denver for Allison's understandable antagonism. "It's not that she's not *glad* you're helping us. . . it's just that. . . that she *worries* a lot about the business. I mean, she was the one who really started it, and. . ."

"Any woman who'd do what she did is a friend of mine," Denver said.

Yes, but will you be a friend of hers? I wondered.

"I didn't think you were going to make it," was the first thing Allison said. "The weather's been so bad and you're so late. . ."

"We wanted to do some work at the shop this morning and got a late start," I apologized self-consciously, remembering how we had lain in bed drinking coffee and eating bear claws with all Denver's records on the stereo. It worried me that Allison would guess how happy I was before I had a chance to tell her in the right way.

I introduced them. Denver was totally at ease, Allison anxiously distant.

"Shall we go for a walk?" I suggested, eager to get out of that stuffy room. After a day of visitors the big room always smelled to me like a cigarette factory on fire.

We went back to Allison's room to get her coat. Conversation languished. Denver, more curious than shy, regarded everything with interest, but didn't ask any questions. That's just like her; she never pushes, never tries to make talk where there isn't any. At the time it almost irritated me, though, and I wished she would do something, say something to make Allison like her. I was severely aware of her presence beside me. I had thought Denver funny-looking when I first met her; it bothered me now that Allison might see her short plump body, her ridiculous cap, her eight different earrings with anything less than total love and affection.

"Shop going all right?" Allison asked, her indifference masking a desire to know everything.

"Oh fine." I told her about some of the orders we'd had, including a full-color brochure for a small trade school.

"Ten thousand of them," she repeated. "Holly, that's great." But she looked wistful as we went into her small room.

While she got into her coat, which I noticed was so tight that she could hardly button it, Denver sat on the narrow institutional bed and started looking through some of the book titles on the shelf.

"Nadezhda Mandelstam," she pronounced slowly. "What's this about, *Hope Against Hope*?"

"It's about Stalinist Russia and a woman whose husband goes to a concentration camp," I jumped in, cutting off whatever Allison's reply may have been. I felt stupid. "I've been meaning to read it," I said by way of apology to Allison.

"You should," she answered shortly. "Ready?"

We trooped back out into the hall, went out through one of the heavy doors into a courtyard. All the snow from last week had melted, but it was cold and wet and miserable. There was nowhere to go, nothing to see. After about fifteen minutes we gave up and went back to Allison's room. Even Denver looked soggy and miserable, her usual good temper depressed by the damp chill of the weather and the place.

Allison took off her coat carefully and hung it back up, while I resolved to buy her a new one as an early Christmas present just as soon as the stores opened on Monday. She lay down on her bed as if she were thoroughly exhausted.

"I feel like I get so much more tired here with nothing to do," she explained to no one in particular.

"Guess I'll hit the john," Denver said and vanished.

Neither Allison or I said anything for a minute and then Allison announced in that same colorless voice, "You might as well go when she comes back. We don't seem to have anything to say and visiting hours will be over in a few minutes anyway."

I knew it was all my fault—sleeping late with Denver, bringing her with me, hoping that they would like each other. All week long I had planned what I would say to Allison. I had a little speech about loyalty and responsibility and honesty all rehearsed. "With business the way it is, and the holidays coming," was how I planned to start out, and to end with, "I would be so happy, Allison, if you just gave her a chance. . ." Now I couldn't say anything. It would be futile.

Allison suddenly sat up restlessly. "I'm tired all day and then I can't sleep at night. As soon as I lie down, I feel like the walls are closing in on me."

I stared at her helplessly. I could never, never stand one night in this room, in this place.

"Where is she, anyway, isn't she coming back?" Allison demanded, looking at the clock. The bathroom is practically next door."

"I think she wanted to leave us alone for a minute to. . . to talk."

"Talk about what?" Allison stared at me. "You're lovers with her, aren't you?" she demanded bitterly.

I nodded. What could I say? That I was sorry I was happy and she wasn't? At the moment I had never felt unhappier. It was all so unfair. I stuffed my hands in my pockets and touched paper. I had almost forgotten what I was going to give Allison.

"Here," I said, thrusting the clipping at her. "It's Magda's first article. It's about you."

"It is?" She grabbed at it eagerly, all bitterness fallen away. The more she read, the more she looked like her old self, strong, confident. "This is great. Oh, I could kiss her."

She looked up at me, beaming, and then recollected just who Magda was. "Do you. . . I mean, does it hurt you to read something she's written?"

"No. Not anymore, not now."

"Then that's good." Allison jumped up and hugged me enthusiastically, waving the clipping behind my back. "Oh, Holly, you don't know how much better I feel. This may not do any good, but it's something. It's a hell of a lot after weeks of nothing, feeling that I could stay here forever and nobody would give a shit." She began to dance me around the room in the narrow space between the two beds.

"You're not alone," I said, but I don't know if she even heard me.

Denver laughed when she opened the door. "Recreation activities are confined strictly to the recreation room, ladies! And none of this cheek-to-cheek business. This is a nice house."

To my relief Allison laughed, too. "Have you read this?" She waved the clipping.

"I certainly have. And I hear Toni is writhing with jealousy."

"Oh, Toni," said Allison. "Her article wasn't half as good."

I did feel a slight tug then, Magda asking, "Don't you think I'm a better writer?" But it was only a tug. I hoped Magda was happy; she had gotten what she wanted.

All the way back to the visitor's room Allison couldn't stop talking. To me, to Denver, to anybody who seemed or didn't seem interested. I had known she would be pleased, but I hadn't counted on such utter joy. In the back of her mind she knew, as I did, that it was only an article in a leftist magazine, but in her loneliness and fear she took it as a sign. She wasn't going to be here forever. People would know what she had done and why she had done it.

The parting I had been dreading so much went off instead with laughter and hugs. She even urged Denver to come with me next week.

"Is she always like that?" Denver asked as we got back to the car. "Depressed one minute, happy the next? I leave for the bathroom with her on the bed in a coma and I come back five minutes later and she's waltzing you around the room."

"It was the article," I defended Allison. "She's usually the most stable person in the world, but she's started believing that nobody cares about her. . ." To my surprise I felt tears start down my cheeks. Denver made a move toward me but I shook her off, embarrassed and almost angry. "Don't you ever cry, Denver?"

"Plenty of time for that when you break my heart." She heaved a mock sigh. "Here, give me the keys. You women are too emotional to be driving along one of our great national highways."

"I'm driving or we're not going anywhere." I clutched the keys knowing she was joking but still a little defensive. Damn her anyway. I'd gone years without crying and now that's all I did.

"Don't leave me here. I didn't do it, Your Honor. I swear I didn't rape him."

"You idiot. I wouldn't leave anyone here if I could help it." And if I could help you, Allison, I would.

On the way back I asked Denver if she'd ever been political.

"Now what does that mean?" she asked. "Is that like when you asked me if I'd always been a lesbian?"

"You know what I mean."

"I'm assuming, then, that you wish to know whether I have ever engaged in any altercations with the government of the United States. I'm assuming that by asking me whether I've ever been political, you are not asking me whether I have ever voted in a national, state, county, or special election or whether I have ever run for political office, been elected, ejected, or taken bribes?"

"Yes," I said, confused. "No, I mean, oh, Denver, you *know* what I mean."

"Well, then, no."

"Just—no?"

"Unless loving women is a political action. Some say it is, others, primarily of the male species, disagree strongly. Myself, I don't know. I just think you're cute."

"Would you please be serious."

"You first. Please tell the grand jury every political meeting you have been to in the last twenty years, who was there, what they said, what they wore, who they went to bed with. Describe every demonstration you've ever marched in and tell the grand jury who was there, what slogans were chanted (that should be easy, most of them began with "stop——") what they wore. . ."

"I'd never been to a demonstration before Allison and Magda were subpoenaed. Or any kind of political meeting," I interrupted.

"Really?" Denver's earrings tinkled as she turned to look at me, her forehead wrinkled, a sure sign that she was serious for a moment. "I thought you were joking. No, well, I guess not."

"Why would I joke about a thing like that?"

"It's quite fashionable these days. Radical burn-out and all that. The famous passivity of the Seventies which followed hot on the heels of the impassioned Sixties. But I guess you wouldn't know about that. I keep forgetting you're almost ten years younger than me."

"Only nine," I corrected her. "So you were political? What did you do?"

"You name it, I was there. Birmingham, Washington, D.C.; Chicago in '68. I didn't have anything better to do than shout 'End discrimination now,' and 'Stop the war.'"

"I remember there was a demonstration in Monterey once against the war. Jane Fonda came and spoke. But I didn't go." James said it was useless to protest. It never made any difference. "Why did you stop? Why did everybody stop caring?"

"Maybe we got tired of shouting. Maybe I wanted to save my voice for singing. I don't know, Holly. Maybe I got tired of male politics after

I realized that that's all they were—male politics. The Revolution could come and go, but I began to see that it wasn't in the plan for women to enjoy the fruits of equality and freedom from oppression. Maybe I just saw it sooner and clearer than a lot of women because I was just a poor old dyke without some Neo-Che for a lover."

She sounded more bitter than I'd ever heard her. "I feel so ignorant sometimes."

"Don't worry about it," she said. "You know what's what. You know that women have to take care of each other, that it sometimes takes a gun to stop a man, and that if the economy doesn't screw you over, the government will. What else do you need to know?"

"But people can fight back, women can," I said. "Don't you ever feel like fighting back?"

"What do you want to do, bust Allison out of Kinsey?" She smiled at me. "Sure, I feel like fighting back sometimes. Sometimes I do. But mostly I just beat on my drums. I'm not like Allison."

"But Allison never *decided* to do what she did. It just happened. It could have happened to you. You wouldn't have talked to the grand jury, would you?"

"No," Denver said slowly. "Maybe it's not dead, after all, my old revolutionary spirit, maybe there's still a slogan in the old girl yet, maybe. . ."

"Oh shut up," I said affectionately. "You're a bag of hot air."

"You're so right."

"And you don't act your age."

"Right again."

"And you're never serious—except sometimes."

"So young and yet so perceptive."

"I don't know why I even bother to talk to you."

"You'd be talking to yourself if I weren't here. And everyone knows that's not a good sign. It's a sign of incipient insanity, Holly. You should be glad I'm here, preventing you from going crazy."

"I am glad. Very glad."

We stayed quiet most of the way home. I don't know what she was thinking about, maybe her past political activity, more likely the prospect of her rehearsal when we got back. It didn't matter. It didn't matter that she had laughed at me, either. I had said something important, I had said, people can fight back, women can. I had read those words, and I had heard them. But for the first time, I had *said* them, understanding what they meant.

December 17

I went out and saw Allison by myself this evening, the first time I'd been on a Wednesday night. There weren't half as many people in the visitors' room and only a couple of kids, and everything seemed a little sadder and lonelier, in spite of the Christmas decorations that had made their appearance—a scrawny tree, some diseased-looking wreaths, and a whole slew of handmade ugly Santa Clauses and snowmen in felt and glitter tacked up on the walls.

Allison was surprised and almost desperately pleased to see me.

"They're having carols tonight," she complained. "Again. One of those godawful church groups, the Mormons, I think this time. I was just going to hide in my room and read."

"Oh Allison," I said guiltily. "I'd forgotten about Christmas." It's true that I'd managed to put Christmas, never one of my favorite seasons, pretty much out of my mind. I knew for Allison it must be different. Last year and the year before she'd invited me home with her for dinner. It had been a big deal, turkey and oyster dressing and champagne and friends over with their kids. A huge tree and eggnog and games. Laughter and even some drunken caroling at the end. Not my style, but I'd still enjoyed it. What must Allison be feeling over the prospect of spending that day in this place?

"We'll come and see you," was all I could promise. "We'll have Christmas here."

Allison nodded, cleared her throat, and then said with forced cheerfulness, "Well, there are a lot of others in the same boat. And some of them won't have any visitors at all. Besides, didn't I tell you, all week I've been getting cards and packages like you wouldn't believe."

That reminded me. "Here," I said, handing her an envelope. "This came for you at the shop."

There was no return address. The postmark was Tampa, Florida.

"Florida, who do I know in Florida?" Allison wondered, opening it up. The card said "Don't Celebrate, Organize." Cranberry red on garish green. "Who. . .?" Allison read the note quickly and then laughed strangely and handed it to me.

Dear Tubman,

Believe it or not I often think of you. I heard what happened and I'm sorry. But maybe now you'll see what we're up against. I see Magda is writing for *Challenge*. I read about you. She hasn't changed her line a bit, has she?

I am fine, together with all my friends except one. We miss him a lot. His leaving made us re-examine our priorities, though, and we should come out of this time stronger than ever. The people will prevail!

Thanks again,
Love, Mary.

"Mary?" I asked. "That's not. . .?"

Allison nodded and I had the sudden urge to crumple up the card like contraband and hide it. Allison looked amused at my obvious horror.

"Arrogant little thing, isn't she?"

"Arrogant! She's crazy, saying she's sorry but maybe now you'll realize what they're up against. While she's in Florida and you're here at Kinsey." I stared around again at the depressing room and noticed that a group of young women, missionary zeal vying with natural curiosity on their faces, were filing in, song sheets in hand. "What good does her being sorry do you?"

Allison took the card back and stared at it again. "I guess I'm glad she's safe more than anything. I've wondered about her all this time, what happened, where she went. . . It was nice of her to write."

"Nice!" I raged. "It's the least she could do." Although I'd never met Deb, I had developed a strong antipathy toward her, something like what I felt for Toni, but much, much stronger.

"I think they're going to start," whispered Allison, leading me to a corner of the room, away from the rest of the residents and their visitors who were grouped in chairs facing the choir. An older woman in a neat black dress, lace-trimmed, was introducing "my girls," and announcing their repertoire. She managed to get in a few words at the same time about church services and outreach, and how "We have literature with us and would be very glad to discuss it with you later."

The choir bounced into a nervous, off-key "Jingle Bells," but soon recovered themselves and were politely, if not enthusiastically, applauded. Allison clapped too, but I had other things on my mind, some sparked by Deb's card and some by my conversation with Denver about politics a few nights before.

I wanted to hear from Allison what she thought about Deb and what had happened, if she still felt the same, whether she would do it all over again.

"Silent night, Holy night
All is calm. All is bright."

"You don't want much, do you?" Allison said, looking as if she would rather listen to the carols, however depressing, than tackle political questions. "You'd think, with so much time on my hands, that I'd have thought a lot more about what happened. You'd think. But until a few weeks ago I was pretty numb. I probably was numb from the minute I realized who Deb was. I never really felt that I had a choice. I wasn't all that eager to enter into the dialectics of the question. Oh sure, I remember when I first heard about the bombings, thinking that they mirrored the kind of anger I'd often felt and done nothing about. You remember that day in the shop. . . You thought I was political, maybe I was, but not in a very conscious way. Mainly I felt guilty for not doing more, but then, just about everybody I knew felt the same way. . ."

"Round yon Virgin, filled with light. . ."

"Each person has their own way of coming to realize how the world works," Allison went on, half listening to the music. "I don't know when it started with me. My parents were church activists," she said, glancing up at the choir. "I think I always had a sense that people who were better off should help those who weren't. Canned food drives, contributions to worthy causes, things like that. . . I remember as a kid putting my favorite velvet dress in the Christmas box and thinking about the poor little girl who would get it. . . my mother was fit to be tied, of course. Charity only went so far." Allison laughed. "But I grew up with some kind of Christian conscience, all right. I was a sucker for charities, used to volunteer to collect money for the American Cancer Society. . ."

She faded off, embarrassed, while I waited, thinking of my own atheist childhood, the total emphasis on self-reliance.

"Well, anyway," said Allison, coming back abruptly when the women around us began to clap the end of "Silent Night." "Suddenly there I was with two kids and no husband and the idea of charity didn't look so all-encompassing anymore. Who was going to help me? There wasn't any governmental or church plan that I could see. I turned into a feminist then, first just for myself and then it started to extend itself to other women. I mean, I wasn't the only one getting the shaft. There were a whole hell of a lot of us out there. I looked around, I saw waitresses and secretaries, I heard stories at the restaurant about women being beaten up by their husbands and boyfriends, getting raped on the way home. I heard how nobody had enough for their rent or to buy clothes for their kids—hell, at least I had child support—and well, I saw that something had to change."

It was "Come, All Ye Faithful" now and Allison looked momentarily distracted. These carols obviously had more emotional resonance for her than for me.

"The Cutting Edge," I prompted.

"Oh yeah, bombing. . . well, I never thought of that. Even when I got angry. I never studied political theory, you know, or anything like that. My politics, whatever they were, came out of my own life, and that was what I wanted to change first. It was the reason for studying printing, the reason I wanted a business of my own. The other things I did, the co-op, the shelter, seemed important, too, but they were part of my guilt trip."

"Joyful and triumphant. . . ."

"But those are important things to do, Allison," I remonstrated, thinking how I'd never done, in a group or alone, anything to change the world. Hadn't even thought of it.

"Oh, I know. I know that now more than ever. But when I first met up with Deb? Maybe I was glad, for the first time in my life, that I was part of something really revolutionary. I mean, those people didn't do things by halves, no volunteering for them."

"But," I began, intending to argue that point.

"I've thought a lot lately about Deb and the others," interrupted Allison. "After that first shock, worrying only about my own skin, but too stubborn to give in, I've thought a lot. In spite of everything, I know I was right not to talk to the grand jury. Even though I think that the Brigade is on a doomed course. Like that guy Ted. At the time I was too numb to take it in. They've killed one of them, I thought, and that just made it more important not to say anything that might jeopardize Deb. But now I feel that that's what's going to happen to all of them eventually. There are just too few of them to effect any change. And they're too arrogant, their very beliefs make them arrogant. You can't be arrogant about who you're fighting, or arrogant toward the people who might join you." Allison shook her head sadly and looked around at the other women in the room, leaning forward now to "Deck the Halls."

"In a peculiar way I can thank Deb for giving me a chance to find out what life is like on the other side. It's hardened me and inspired me at the same time, the way conventional left politics never could have. The thing about these women here is that they don't know what comes after "A" in the political alphabet, but they do have a pretty good idea of how the system works. Even the ones from nice homes, who keep claiming they've been convicted by mistake, and are planning to write a book about it someday. . . even they don't have many illusions left about justice, or anything else for that matter. In a strange way, Holly, there's something refreshing about being around people, around women, who know they've been shafted, not just by the law, but by the entire society. It means you don't have to pretend anymore that things are okay and going to get better."

Allison stopped and sighed and I felt a moment of utter pessimism. My striking revelation of a few nights before, that people could fight against the system, seemed insipid and naive. My face must have shown my despair, because Allison suddenly laughed and said, "Oh, don't worry about me. It's not like I've given up or anything. Maybe I'm even more optimistic than before. I used to get depressed about the Fate of the Revolution, wondering when and if it would come. Now I think that the Revolution, when and if it comes, won't come with a bang or a bomb. It'll only come when people change their lives and their minds. It'll come when people bring up their kids differently and when, and only when, people work for it, every day of their lives."

I didn't know what Allison found optimistic about that. The idea of people *working* to change things seemed much more depressing to me than the idea of people *fighting* to change things. The thought of working toward an uncertain future didn't move me the way something like Magda's phrase, "We can fight against the system. And win," had moved me. I told Allison that.

"Oh, winning," she said. "If you think you're going to win someday, except for the occasional small victory, you'd better give it up right now. It's a never ending battle and I don't think anybody's going to win it in the end. But we might, we might possibly, become better people because of our struggles."

It was time to leave then. The choir had trailed off in giggles and whispers, no doubt to dream about prisoners and prisons that night, and hope dutifully that because of their charity tonight one or two confirmed lawbreakers might be moved to seek the Truth and join the Mormon church. While I drove home in the dark and fog to ponder the difference between working and fighting, wondering if there really was any difference at all.

December 19

I got Magda's number from Allison and called her up tonight.

"Holly?" she said. "Holly?"

"I wanted to thank you for the article about Allison, I. . ."

"Holly! I never thought I'd hear from you again."

The joy in her voice turned my palm all sweaty and I had to shift the receiver. I felt it too, that joy, it was like I had never stopped loving her. It almost frightened me, even though I'd been gearing myself up for the phone call all day.

"Thank you for. . ." I began again.

"How *are* you? How's Allison? How's everyone? Oh, it's so great to hear your voice!"

"How are you?" I said, confused at how the phone brought her bodily presence so near. All day I'd been thinking about her, remembering the good parts, deciding that I'd had enough of feeling stupid about what had happened between us. Besides, someone should thank her for writing that article about Allison. . . I told Denver that I was thinking about calling Magda, was nervous, almost wanted her to dissuade me.

But she was encouraging. "Sometimes it's better just to let people go—but maybe you won't be able to do that until you've talked to her again."

"Me?" Magda said, her voice filling my head. "Well, I've given up smoking again. Three days, can you believe it? And I've got an article coming out in the next issue." She started to tell me all about the magazine. Already she'd made enemies, but she sounded excited rather than surprised. I don't think Magda would be happy if she didn't see intrigue in every situation. "I don't expect to be a copy editor very long. . ." And she had a wonderful tiny apartment near Central Park, on the West Side. "I love New York, just love it."

I murmured "good" and "great" to everything. I don't know why it made me so happy to hear that she was all right. A couple of months ago I would have been pleased to hear that she'd sunk into the ground without a trace. What had changed me?

"But, Holly," she interrupted herself. "Tell me how you are. I'm so glad you called. I know Allison is still at Kinsey, she saw my article? Well, it won't be long before she's out. This magazine has more clout than the *News*, that's for sure. . . . But you, are you keeping the shop going by yourself?"

"No, I have help. A woman named Denver."

"Denver! I know her." She paused, taking it in. "Are you lovers?" Magda was never one to beat around the bush.

"Yes," I told her, thinking that someone else besides Allison knew, and that maybe some day I'd be able to tell everyone.

"So you became a lesbian," she said wonderingly. "In spite of me."

I had to laugh. "How about you?"

"Oh, it's the same old shit." She gave her rich full laugh and started to tell me about a married man at the office she was getting involved with. But then that led into more details about the magazine and what they were doing. Lovers were peripheral, after all, to the business of getting ahead.

I listened and, for the first time, didn't judge her or lose myself in admiration. Magda was Magda, would be forever, and I still loved her. In spite of her I became a lesbian. Because of her.

She didn't ask me any more about Denver, seemed to take my being lovers with her for granted. We didn't talk much about my politics either. I didn't have the urge to tell her about my revelations, my conversations with Allison and Denver. I knew how unsophisticated they would sound next to her intricate descriptions of power plays, in the office, in the city, in the world.

Only for a moment at the end did she turn nostalgic.

"Remember," she began, then she said abruptly, "I never wanted to hurt you, Holly."

"I know that," I said. "Now. . . don't worry about it." I could have told her that I still loved her and would for a while, that it was magic to hear her voice in the same room with me again, but she had already rushed on.

"You know Toni sent us an article. I had to copyedit it. I haven't enjoyed myself so much in a long time. . ."

Later tonight Denver called. ". . . Well, how did it go?"

"Oh, I'm moving to New York next week," I teased her. If I wasn't mistaken, there was a faint anxiety to Denver's silence.

"She did most of the talking, really. She always did. But it was fun to listen to her. I guess I just don't take it personally anymore."

"Did you, uh, talk about what happened?"

"No, not really. But in a way we did. Everything that needed to be said was said. You were right."

"See?" Denver's voice had regained its customary chirpiness.

"But I still care about her." I had to add that.

"Well, of course," Denver said. "Naturally."

December 21

It's official. Allison will be out for Christmas.

Bess called this morning to give me the news. She sounded as pleased with herself as I've ever known her to be.

"I thought he was weakening last week but I wasn't sure," she said. "This just proves that he has a heart after all. And a brain. He realized that if Allison hadn't given in after two months, then one more wasn't going to make a difference. The publicity has all been favorable to Allison and that wasn't making his job any easier. I heard him tell another lawyer that it was 'reprehensible' of the FBI not to have caught any of the Cutting Edge while that girl (he meant Allison) had to sit in Kinsey. You should have heard what he told me, though. 'I have children, too,' he said. The old hypocrite."

"Maybe he really felt bad."

"I'm sure he did. But I think it's more likely that he was trying to save his ass. The investigation went nowhere, and that doesn't look good on his record. Better to drop the whole thing until some real evidence turns up."

I hung up and turned to Denver. "She's getting out!"

"What? I can't hear you." She turned off the press. "Is something wrong?"

"No, for a change it's all right. The prosecutor is dropping Allison's contempt charges. She'll be out for Christmas."

"Hooray for justice." But there was something else in Denver's face besides the pure excitement that I felt. "Just in time for my winter vacation."

"What?"

"Didn't I tell you? I always go to Florida for the holidays."

"You never told me that. You told me you spent last Christmas with some friends outside Seattle."

"All the more reason why I should go to Florida this year."

"You're not going anywhere. We need you. There's plenty of work for three people."

"That's what you say. But what will Allison say? Have you asked her? Uh-huh, I thought not."

"But I will. Now that I know when she's getting out."

"Look, Holly, I don't mind. You told me this job was temporary, and I wouldn't have taken it if it had been otherwise. I don't like to be tied down."

Everything seemed to fall apart right then. She didn't like to be tied down—to anyone or anything—she was going to leave the print shop and me too. Just go away, after all that had happened. I fought back tears. I had already cried enough in front of her. I didn't want her to pity me.

"Oh, shit," she said. "Why do you have to take it personally?"

Then I did start to cry. "Personally, why shouldn't I take it personally. . . when you said you. . ." I choked. She had never said she loved me in so many words. I'd just believed she did because I loved her. But I was wrong.

"I never said anything," she said, looking at me hard, as if she was amazed that I should be taking it this way.

"I know you didn't, I just thought. . ." Here I broke down completely. "I'm so stupid, I hate myself."

She came over, took me by the shoulders, shook me. "What's the big deal, Holly, if I work here or not? We'll still see each other."

"We will?" I sobbed.

"Are you putting me on or is that what you're crying about? Never mind, I get it now. You thought my leaving the shop meant I was leaving you. Boy, you really are stupid. You're right." She began to laugh.

"I'm not that stupid. And don't laugh at me." I had immediately stopped crying as soon as I understood her. Now I was furious. "I couldn't help it, it sounded like. . ."

"If I ever leave you, it'll be because you kicked me out. And you wouldn't do that to a poor old out-to-pasture dyke like me, would you?"

"Denver, don't you ever cry about anything?"

"Only when I'm tickled. In the right spot."

I tried to find it, but all she did was laugh.

Allison called me right after work to ask if I'd heard the good news.

I told her I had and then gave her the bad news; that if Denver went, I went. I never thought I could have put it so brutally to Allison. "We've got to have somebody else. Even with Denver and me working six-and-a-half days a week, we still can't get everything done. You remember how it was before you went away? Well, it's ten times busier now. We can't make it alone, Allison. Not you and me, the kind of people we are."

She didn't say anything for a moment and then, "It's set up to be a partnership. . ."

"I don't care what we call it, a cooperative or a collective or whatever. But she's got to stay."

More silence. "Okay," Allison said.

"Okay?"

"To tell you the truth, it's something I've been thinking of, too. Making it more a collective. It just scared me, it still scares me, after so long just working with you, to have somebody else in on it. I know it's proprietary, but that's how it feels. Wasn't it weird for you to get used to somebody else in the shop?"

I thought back to the first day Denver started, to the terrible relief I'd felt when I realized that she could print. It seemed so long ago. How frightened I had been then, not of having somebody else around, but of being alone.

"I remember I was scared at first that she would be able to do everything better than me."

"Could she?"

"Some things."

"Then she'll be able to do things better than me."

"Some things. But she doesn't care like you do, Allison. Or like me. You taught me that. To care about the business. Only I never would have known it if you hadn't gone away."

Allison cleared her throat. "I guess not," she said, sounding immensely saddened. But almost immediately she turned resolute. "It will be good not to have to work such long hours," she said. "There are a lot of things I want to do when I get out. I've been reading too many books. I want some action. I'm going to spend more time at the shelter, for one thing. We need more of them, lots more. Most of the women I've talked to here never even heard of a battered women's shelter. I still want to come back here, too. I started a kind of study group. Maybe they'll let me continue it."

"You know what, Allison? I think I might want to help you, you know, with some of your political things. . ."

"You would?"

"I mean, now that we won't be working such long hours."

"Right on, Holly!" She started outlining a list of projects to keep us busy for the next ten years. I knew I didn't have a fraction of her energy and optimism, but I also knew that there was nobody who could carry me along with her like Allison.

"You're going to be as busy as ever," I finally said. "But I guess you were always ambitious."

"Ambitious, *me*?" she said. "Someone like Magda's ambitious. I just want things to change."

photo by Teri Dixon

Barbara Ellen Wilson was born and raised in Long Beach, California. After living in Europe for several years she moved to Seattle, Washinton in 1974. She is co-publisher of The Seal Press, Northwest Feminist Publishers. Her books include a children's story, *The Geography Lesson*, and two collections of fiction, *Talk & Contact* and *Thin Ice*.